A New Perspective

Fleur Elizabeth

THE CHANGE EXPERIENCE SERIES 2

First published 2025 by FE-ED Pty Ltd

Produced by Independent Ink

Copyright © FE-ED Pty Ltd 2025

The moral right of the author to be identified as the author of this work has been asserted.

All rights reserved. No part of this publication may be reproduced, stored in a retrieval system or transmitted in any form or by any means available now or in the future without the prior written permission of the author, nor be otherwise circulated in any form of binding or cover other than that in which it is published and without a similar condition being imposed on the purchaser.

Cover design by Catucci Design
Edited by Christine Egner and Daina Lindeman
Internal design by Independent Ink
Typeset in Greycliff CF by Post Pre-press Group, Brisbane

ISBN 978-1-7642293-3-3 (paperback)
ISBN 978-1-7642293-4-0 (epub)
ISBN 978-1-7642293-5-7 (kindle)

Lilian, thank you for teaching me how to take responsibility for my role in everything. It's a liberating gift. And that story you told me? It changed me. You've helped me become a better woman, and I'm forever grateful.

5 DAYS OF MY LIFE

Day 1 – I walked down a path; I fell into a hole.

Day 2 – I walked down the same path; I fell into a hole.

Day 3 – I walked down the same path; I fell into a hole.

Day 4 – I walked down the same path; I walked around the hole. Ah!

Day 5 – I walked down a different path.

Disclaimer

The content you're about to dive into reflects a coaching approach I've carefully developed. It draws upon my experiences in performance and nutritional health coaching, and blends in techniques from Acceptance and Commitment Therapy (ACT), Motivational Interviewing, and Dialectical Behaviour Therapy (DBT). It's important to understand that this is a coaching program, not clinical therapy.

Please remember, the information shared here is not a replacement for the guidance of your doctor or therapist, including psychologists, counsellors, or psychiatrists. This book isn't intended to be a substitute for any ongoing or future therapy you might be undertaking, especially trauma therapy.

This book is not a clinical treatment for mental health conditions such as mood disorders, eating disorders, body dysmorphia, or alcohol addictions, particularly those related to sexual violence, abuse, or mental abuse.

I want to be clear: The Change Experience Book Series, and I as the author, publisher, and creator of this book, cannot be held responsible or liable for any effects that actions taken, or drugs used, may have on your body or mental health as a result of engaging with this material.

If, at any point, the content brings up difficult emotions or triggers past experiences, please reach out to your doctor or therapist immediately. Your health is my priority.

Your Free Gift

As a thank you for joining me on this journey, I have a special free gift for you. You can download it, along with other helpful resources from The Change Experience book series, by signing up to the Resources page on my website.

To get your free gift, simply visit: www.fleurelizabeth.com

Contents

Preface
Introduction   3
A Recap of the Book's Structure   10

Let's Begin
1   The Search for Happiness   17
2   My Trauma Experience   32

A New Perspective Comes from Greater Understanding
3   Your Inner World   39
4   Home is the Heart of Your Story   45
5   A Child's Developmental Needs   60
6   My Trauma Experience   67
7   Reflection Time   72
8   Your Core Wounds   77
9   My Trauma Experience   90
10 Reflection Time   94
11 The Empathetic Witness   99
12 The Adult Experiences   103
13 A Life Changing Skill   107
14 Reflection Time   117

A Resilient Woman = Know-How
15 Emotion is Your Friend   125
16 Reflection Time   138

The Patterns of Trauma

17	My Trauma Experience	145
18	Repetitive Cycles	149
19	The Hooks of Your Inner Stories	153
20	Getting Yourself Unhooked	167

Triggers, Behaviours, and Consequences

21	Sticky Cycles	177
22	Those Damn Triggers	184
23	Your Trigger Playbook	198
24	Is Your Reality Being Twisted?	204
25	Taking Your Power Back	223
26	My Trauma Experience	230
27	Checking In	234

Getting On with Life Now

28	Your Liberation Toolbox	239

Your Light to Come Home

29	Your North Star	265
30	Your Beautiful Unfolding	271
31	Bye For Now	277

Appendix

Must-Have Skills for Emotional Control	283
Your Emotional Compass	298
Reflecting on Your Triggers	306
Deeper Self-Connection	312
Six Considerations When Making Change	315
References	317

Preface

THE CHANGE EXPERIENCE
Heal your past, transform your today

Project Clarity
The trauma-informed woman: Unmask hidden wounds, end automatic coping habits and embrace your authentic self.

- Why I'm here
- Is this you?
- Trauma defined
- Strategies for change
- Change is hard
- Your Future Self
- Life is automatic
- Family influences
- Values – your past and future
- Living by your values
- Your relationship with food and drink
- Stress and sleep

A New Perspective
The emotionally resilient woman: *Recognise your triggers, cultivate self-acceptance and embrace emotional health.*

- Becoming friends with your emotions
- Repetitive cycles
- Searching for happiness
- Your emotions invalidated
- Adverse Childhood Experiences
- Emotional regulation
- Triggers defined
- Trigger, behaviour, consequence
- Triggers – gaslighting
- Your liberation tool kit
- How to trust yourself, self-empathy, embrace mistakes, self-acceptance
- Grounding techniques

Liberated Connection
The energetic woman: Set healthy boundaries, honour your needs and embrace your feminine power.

- Change can be tough
- Embracing your energy
- Healing hypervigilance
- Removing chaos
- Energy Vampires
- Boundary setting
- Barriers to change
- Energetic conflict resolution
- Getting what you want in life
- S.M.A.R.T Energy focused
- Become your Future Self

I.
Introduction

A New Perspective:
The Emotionally Resilient Woman
The Next Phase of Your Journey

Welcome back, my friend! It's wonderful to continue this journey with you. This is the second book in the Change Experience Series. It offers a practical and powerful approach to developing a vital new skill: viewing yourself and your emotional world from a fresh perspective. By understanding your unique emotional blueprint – the ingrained patterns of reaction and motivation – you'll begin to see the hidden structures behind your behaviours in a completely new way.

The Quick-Fix Happiness Distraction

We'll address the elephant in the room when it comes to the topic of avoiding the pain of our past: our persistent search for "quick-fix happiness" to avoid uncomfortable thoughts and feelings. We'll explore why we pursue temporary highs and external validation, hoping to fill an internal void. These approaches are simply unsustainable. Instead, we'll reframe your definition of lasting happiness and help you find meaning and a purpose in life, thereby opening the door to a more genuine and veracious experience of joy, and ready to move forward.

The Beautiful Truth

Our emotions are not the enemy. They are powerful, dynamic forces within us, constantly whispering guidance and offering insights into the complexities of our lives. When we begin to see them not as obstacles to be avoided but as wise messengers, everything changes. This is where the real work begins – the brave and beautiful decision to stop running from your feelings and instead, lean into them. By doing so, you'll discover not just a new understanding of yourself, but a fundamental inner strength that comes from embracing every part of who you are. This brave choice is also the essence of developing true trust in yourself, as you begin to speak your own internal love language by listening to what your feelings are trying to tell you.

The Worthy Investigation

To truly get to know and befriend your emotions, we need to carefully look back and understand where you've come from. We'll start by exploring those emotionally challenging experiences you had as a child that have shaped your emotional make-up today. This includes how your emotions were validated or, indeed, invalidated back then. We'll delve into six key consequences: struggling with emotional regulation, battling self-doubt and confusion, a lack of healthy coping strategies, difficulties in forming healthy relationships, constantly questioning your own perceptions, and either suppressing or escalating your feelings. The whole point here is to help you connect what's happening with you today to your past, giving you a proper roadmap to understand your emotional make-up and empowering you to stop feeling like a victim of your own emotions.

While this might feel a bit like heavy going, it's really important, so do stick with it. I want you to truly grasp what drives your emotional turmoil – that feeling of being unable to control your emotions – and what fuels your desire for avoidance and that fleeting, temporary high.

We'll also acknowledge that a key part of our journey will be understanding the significant role of adverse childhood experiences in shaping adult behaviours and overall mental and physical health.

This is where I'm going to hold up a mirror for you and offer some reflections to help you connect with your past experiences, shining a light on those paths from your past that have become overgrown or suppressed. Together, we'll connect the dots and unpack the clear patterns of your triggers, behaviours, and consequences. The trigger is simply the specific event or starting point that sets everything in motion. I know this isn't exactly the most fun part of the process, but I promise you, it's so worth it, and it's incredibly humbling.

Knowing your patterns is a fundamental must-have life skill because, my friend, this is where you learn how to be accountable. This is where you take a massive step forward by taking ownership of your role in your repetitive cycles. When you understand why you do the things you do when you get triggered, you can make a conscious choice and stop acting blindly and automatically. This is how you take back the reins and sit firmly in the driver's seat.

Your Liberation Toolbox

The uplifting conclusion comes when I equip you with practical life skills from my Liberation Toolbox, a collection of powerful skills to help you unhook from old patterns and step into your true power.

First, we'll explore the delicate art of self-empathy, learning to treat yourself with the same kindness you'd offer a dear friend. Then, we'll shift our perspective to mistakes, understanding them not as failures but as valuable teachers. We'll also dive into the grounding power of breathwork, discovering how it can anchor you and calm the storms within. Most importantly, we'll nurture the vital journey of self-trust, learning to listen to your inner message centre and believe in your own strength.

A key part of this process is the empowering gift of acceptance. Acceptance, especially when it comes to those who have caused us pain, isn't about excusing their actions. It's about recognising that they, too, are grappling with their own demons. We can acknowledge that what they did was wrong, but their actions stemmed from their own limitations, their own lack of capacity. We don't have to carry that burden for them. Their emotional weight, their responsibility, is theirs alone. Our path to healing lies in drawing a line, in recognising the "why" behind their actions. Not to justify them, but to release ourselves from their grip. By accepting that their pain is their story, not ours, we reclaim our own narrative and grant ourselves the freedom to walk forward, lighter and more whole.

Women Standing Together

"I am not free while any woman is unfree, even when her shackles are very different from my own." – Audre Lorde

I love this quote. It beautifully captures the very heart of female empowerment and solidarity. It speaks to the deep, unshakeable connection we share as women – the understanding that our experiences are interwoven, and our liberation is collective. It's a subtle but firm reminder that true freedom for one of us is intrinsically linked to the freedom of all of us. This is why this message is so important. This quote reminds us that our journey of healing isn't just about us as individuals. It's about lifting each other up, empowering one another, and breaking free from old shackles together. By walking this path hand in hand, we create a brighter future, not just for ourselves but for every woman who comes after us.

A Final Word

In these pages, we'll walk this path together, step by step, developing a new perspective while unlocking your emotional blueprint and creating a life filled with awareness, inner peace, and joy. When you embrace your emotions, you embrace your true self. In that acceptance lies liberation, and in liberation, endless possibilities.

My role in this is to be your guide in gaining a new perspective on your life and emotions, empowering you to stop resisting and avoiding what needs to be addressed in order to heal. You'll hear me say throughout our journey: "What we avoid is what needs to be healed, and that, my friend, is the gateway to our freedom."

> **SO, THE MESSAGE HERE IS THIS:** mastering your emotions isn't about suppressing the storm within, but learning to navigate its currents with grace, transforming your raw feelings into a welcomed internal dialogue. This isn't hard; it just takes practice. Soon it will become a refined art within, and others will be looking at you, noticing how you have become a more compassionate, calm, and resilient woman.

With every page you turn, you're stepping closer to becoming that woman.

A note from me

Between us girls ...

To gain a new perspective on life is one thing, and I will certainly open the doors for you to experience that. But here is the thing: to become emotionally resilient, in how I see the true meaning of the word resilient, is where you are going to have to do the work.

True resilience, my friend, is, to me, being able to take full accountability for every single layer of who you are (even what you hide away in those scary shadows), where you have come from, and what your role has been in you arriving at this point in your life. It strengthens every day as you stand up and are true to what you value in life. It becomes even more pronounced as you keep showing up, keep doing the work, loving and accepting exactly who you are, and genuinely backing yourself. That, in my humble opinion, is the real sweetness of emotionally resilient womanhood.

You know something? You were born untouched, unburdened, with a beautiful life purpose. It's just that life, in all its complicated ways, has slapped a lot of heavy, ugly metaphorical "cement" over your light, dampening your glow so it couldn't properly shine through. By "cement," I mean all that conditioning from your past, the masks you've worn, and those narratives that have kept you feeling small.

I promise you this: the process of change becomes absolutely addictive when you start to see parts of yourself you knew were there but had, perhaps, let go of. When you watch that cement fall off, bit by bit, there's this incredible woman inside staring back at you in the mirror. She makes your heart melt and feel all warm and fuzzy inside. She's you. She is all of you, standing there and honestly asking, "Haven't you had enough of living in the shadows?"

So, get used to being nudged into a place that might feel a bit uncomfortable at first, and just trust that it will soon feel exactly as it was meant to be. Trust yourself to make the changes you absolutely have the ability to make. And please, really pay attention to the guidance I give you about having empathy for your former self, and the importance of accepting her, warts and all – because that, my friend, is where you discover the golden path where change becomes effortless, and you start to feel what it's like to be an emotionally resilient woman.

So, what do you say? Isn't it about time to give her some air and let her experience some of that wonderful light and love shining on her too?

II.
A Recap of the Book's Structure

To help you navigate your journey, remember that each topic in this book is broken down into three main sections:

Education: We'll start by exploring a new topic, giving you the information you need to understand why and how it's relevant to your life. My tone of voice may be a little more serious in these parts, so you clearly understand the principles of what I am talking about

Strategy: Next, you'll learn practical skills and tools you can use to adjust, prepare, or soothe yourself when faced with challenges or emotional storms. Here you may find me being a little more conversational and relaxed in my tone of voice.

Questions/Reflection: At the end of each section, you'll find thought-provoking questions and a reflection exercise to help you personalise your journey. This is where you use your voice to read each question out loud.

How to Approach the Questions/Reflections

As I've said to you before, the questions in this book are designed to help you connect with your unconscious mind. They aim to shed light on where your habits and behaviours originate and why things are unfolding as they are. This might not be easy, and the questions may seem simple, but I promise you there's a reason behind every single one. Please, give yourself permission to take your time.

You might read a question and feel nothing at first, or you may even wonder, "Why does she want me to answer this?" You may need to step away and let the questions sit with you for a while. That's perfectly okay.

Another way you can look at these questions and reflections is that they are your own self-coaching sessions. Just you and your inner know-how – the place where you look within and ask yourself the questions you need to hear. This helps you to connect with what has been hidden away, appreciate why you have done certain things, find the reasons and desire for change, and discover the confidence to take small steps of change to move your life forward.

Remember I said you might need a crowbar to prise some of this information out from within? This is where the work happens. You've done such a good job at surviving that when your system is in hyper-vigilant overdrive – or perhaps in a constant state of fight or flight – accessing information about yourself can be really tough. It can take work and time to connect with what you have buried deep within, but you've got to believe you can do it.

What I'm doing is condensing years of psychological investigation into your former self, your past experiences, your behaviours, your drivers, and your triggers, into three books. What you're getting here are condensed, super-tuned connection questions designed to help you navigate this journey of healing and change in a more concise and liberating way.

 **SO, THE MESSAGE HERE IS THIS:** Take your time. Allow yourself the time. Read the questions more than once. Put them down and come back to them later. Don't worry if nothing magically inspiring appears the first time you read them. The answers might not reveal themselves in question order; instead, they may unlock in layers as you delve. Allow yourself to sit with what these questions stir within you and trust that the messages will emerge in your own sweet time.

Your Journal Companion

This is your reminder to have your favourite writing journal at the ready! Your journal is your safe space – a trusted companion for your most intimate thoughts.

I'll continue to invite you to write your thoughts, feelings, and responses to thought-provoking questions and reflections. These are designed to help you deeply connect with your past, understand what changes you wish to make in your life, and keep the vision of your Future Self at the forefront of your mind.

As you write, I encourage you to read your answers aloud. Hearing your own voice say these words is a powerful way to rewire the old narratives in your brain and strengthen your inner foundations, with each word spoken bringing you closer to the life you truly desire.

Remember to date your entries and note the chapter title. This will make it easy to revisit your insights and raw and real writing later. Going back to see the energy in your words is a great way to support you in achieving your goals when you are feeling a little lost. It is a humbling reconnection to your grace.

Your Grounding Support for the Journey

Before we dive into this work together, I want to reassure you that you have a few powerful tools right by your side. You might remember the three grounding techniques we covered in Book One: *Project Clarity*? In the appendix, I've included **Name and Tame**, **Dropping Anchor**, and the **4-7-8 Breathing Technique**, with more detail than before.

I've expanded on them because I feel you're now ready to fully appreciate their power and relevance. These aren't just exercises; they are your go-to allies to soothe anxiety, navigate overwhelm, or steady yourself when things in your life get a bit loud.

I know from my own journey that this work can sometimes feel unsettling. That's why these tools are here for you, ready to help you sail safely through any emotional storms that may arise. Consider them a warm, reassuring hand to hold, especially if the content evokes uncomfortable thoughts and feelings that may have been suppressed or locked away for a while.

> Let's do this, shall we? And remember, I'm here, holding your hand, as always.

Let's Begin

1.
The Search for Happiness

What Is True Happiness?
An Honest Perspective and Journey Inward

May I ask you something? Are you happy? I mean, do you think of yourself as a happy person? Or do you find yourself with fleeting moments of happiness mixed in with a whole mess of stuff you don't know what to do with? How good are you at acting happy to please those around you? Or do you simply seek out things that make you feel good, and call that happiness? Unsure? Then let's pull this meaty topic apart, shall we?

So, first up, I want to ask you to think about what happiness truly means to you. Can you read that aloud and let yourself hear the question? Then, write down what comes to mind in your journal. I've always found it's a question that reveals so much about a person's place in life, and this will be an excellent marker to see how far you've come by the end of this book series.

For many, especially women dealing with past trauma, happiness often feels like a fleeting emotion, a high, or a relentless pursuit of pleasure, rather than a settled destination. But real happiness isn't a perpetual state of euphoria or a life free from problems. Instead, it's found in the everyday moments of cultivating inner peace and building meaningful connections. It's about accepting yourself, flaws and all, and embracing your authentic self. Ultimately, it's about coming home to yourself.

For us, women who have carried heavy burdens, true happiness often involves:

🔗 **Self-Compassion:** Treating yourself with the same kindness and understanding you'd offer a dear friend.

🔗 **Setting Boundaries:** Learning to say no, protecting your energy, and honouring your needs.

🔗 **Finding Your Voice:** Expressing your truth, even when it's uncomfortable.

🔗 **Cultivating Meaningful Connections:** Building relationships based on reciprocity and support.

🔗 **Embracing Your Emotions:** Allowing yourself to feel anger, sadness, and joy without judgement.

🔗 **Finding Your Purpose:** Engaging in activities that bring a sense of meaning and fulfilment.

🔗 **Honouring Your Body:** Moving in ways that feel good, nourishing yourself, and prioritising your precious sleep.

🔗 **Creating Space for Stillness:** Practising mindfulness, meditation, or other forms of self-reflection.

> **INTERESTING TO NOTE:** On a scale of one to eight, how many of the above do you currently do for yourself? Food for thought. Perhaps you can think about adopting the things that are missing in your life.

So, come now, this is why you are doing all this work, isn't it? Reading through these pages, learning new insights and skills to get to know yourself better. Let's be real; none of this stuff is light reading. It's hard work, at times rather unfun, and it takes real grit and honesty to make changes that will empower you to grow and evolve.

Let's agree right now that your journey to healing and finding a balance of happiness will be unique, and never a straight line. It's a process of unravelling past pain, reclaiming your power, and rediscovering your true self. But none of this will work unless you first believe you are worthy of love, acceptance, and joy. You have to believe that you possess the inner strength to create a life filled with meaning and contentment.

My friend, the good news is that by simply showing up here and doing this work, you've got the message that you're ready to walk this path with compassion, courage, and with my unwavering support. So, strap in. A wonderful ride awaits.

> You should be so proud of yourself!

The Unglamorous Truth

Carrying on with this theme of grit and honesty, I'll say that your Change Experience isn't always going to be a smooth ride. The journey to finding yourself, learning what "having purpose" means to you, and living in peace is not a constant highlight reel. It's not about endless highs or a life without challenges; it's about truly experiencing the simple things that bring you joy.

I had to be open to learning this myself, and now I can confirm without a shadow of a doubt that it's true: magic happens in ordinary, everyday moments if you allow room for it. It's often in those quiet, unglamorous moments that we discover the deepest contentment.

So, if joy isn't about chasing fleeting excitement, then what? It's about delighting in the simple things – the warmth of the sun or birdsong in the morning, the aroma of your favourite coffee or fresh peppermint tea. It's about savouring the present, appreciating the beauty around you, and being grateful for small things.

> When you make room for it, it will happen.

Embracing change often means letting go of what you thought would make you happy, such as material possessions and external validation. This is also where removing that metaphorical "cement" that has been slapped on comes in. Bit by bit, you discover that less is more. Releasing these attachments creates space for what matters: your true self, genuine connections, and inner peace. Sounds fluffy, but it is so real, my friend, so real.

A lot of women I know feel that having a purpose is a massive hill to climb. Well, I am here to tell you that finding meaningful purpose isn't always about grand gestures or external achievements. Living your true purpose, in your own skin, guided by your values, is a revolution and evolution from where you are today. Here are some things to think about:

- It's often about simple acts of kindness, looking after yourself, so you can wake up feeling good when you get out of bed in the morning.

- It's about cultivating peace in your daily life, not by escaping problems but by navigating them with grace and self-compassion, and consciously choosing to avoid chaos.

- It's about finding meaning in your work, in the process itself, not just the outcome.

- It's exploring parts of yourself left untouched. Those unseen talents. The interests that light you up, but you have been too afraid, or too busy, to try.

- It's about being brave enough to honour your gifts, embrace imperfections, as you try something new.

- It's about slowing down, appreciating the moment, and connecting with your energy. Observing yourself. Noticing what is happening in your world, and how you are responding to it.

∞ It is being committed to yourself. To your values. Backing whatever choice you make. Present, and aware. Learning from each experience as find your sweet spot.

∞ It is trusting yourself that you know you are working towards creating a life that reflects your deepest desires.

My friend, the path I am showing you here is one to find your own peace and joy. It is not complicated or elusive. This is all found in the simplicity of your choices. And ... the willingness to try.

So, start working on removing that metaphorical "cement" that I talked about earlier that is slapped over your light and dimming your glow. Healing, finding peace, and connecting to your true self is now your job to break that cement down. Spend some time in quiet reflection, in deep connection with yourself and the world and start asking your inner voice to give you a nudge about what your purpose might be. Don't you think it is now time?

I want you to realise you have all the knowledge you need to find happiness already inside of you. Pause for a minute and think about that.

I believe you have the ability within you. I do.

Moving Forward and Reclaiming Your Power

Okay, let's be real for a second. Healing? I think you'll get the picture pretty quickly in this book – it takes time, patience, and a whole lot of love for your former self, the woman you are today, and a truckload of honesty. My new mantra is, you have to be real to heal. This isn't an overnight job; it requires you to show up for yourself every day, pay attention to what's happening within you, and build new skills (which I am going to teach you here so you can practise them).

Right off the bat I am going to impress upon you, my friend, that you've got to accept that those triggered responses of yours aren't a sign of weakness. Not even close. They're proof of your strength and how much you've weathered. It's about learning to soothe your nervous system, to give your emotions the validation they deserve, and to create a life that supports your ability to feel balanced and calm.

Your strength and ability to heal will also come about with learning to say "no" without guilt weighing you down, setting boundaries with kindness, and surrounding yourself with people who lift you higher. It's about stepping into your own skin, believing in your feminine power, honouring your truth, and embracing every bit of your real and raw self. You are worthy, period. Worthy of happiness that isn't just a fleeting feeling but a deep, steady inner peace and contentment.

> Ready to dive in? Okay, my friend, let's begin.

The Illusion of Perpetual Happiness
When Chasing it Becomes a Problem

My psychologist once told me, "There are three certainties in life: pain, uncertainty, and constant work (to be done on ourselves)." She was right. I have come to believe all three should be seen as a necessary part of our evolution and growth as women.

It's a strange paradox, isn't it? The more inner hurt we carry, the more we seem to chase anything that promises to numb the ache. We build elaborate fortresses around our feelings, convinced that if we just don't look, don't feel, the pain will somehow dissolve. But emotions – especially the ones we try to bury – have a way of seeping through the cracks. They become shadows, distorting everything we see and touch, making genuine joy feel like a distant, unattainable star.

We tell ourselves we're searching for happiness, but what we're really doing is running, desperately, from the echoes of our past trauma. And so, the search intensifies. We reach for the fleeting highs, through the impulsive spending, the endless scrolling, the fleeting connections that promise validation but deliver only emptiness. We might dive headfirst into work, convinced that productivity will silence the inner turmoil, or turn to substances (food, drink, and drugs), seeking a temporary escape from the relentless barrage of memories. It's like frantically adjusting the volume on a broken radio, hoping to drown out the static but only amplifying the distortion. We become experts at distraction, masters of avoidance, yet the hollowness inside only deepens. We chase the next dopamine hit, the next fleeting moment of pleasure, believing that this time, this time, it will fill the void. But it never does, because true happiness isn't found in the absence of pain but in the courage to face pain.

The Weight of the Happy Mask

We all know that feeling, that deep yearning, trying to fit into a world that often feels ... well, like it wasn't made for us. If your story includes childhood wounds – the sting of neglect, the echoes of unmet needs, a horrific event that left you scarred, or the devastating impact of violence – then the pursuit of happiness can become a relentless, exhausting chase. Or maybe you've found yourself avoiding happiness, staying stuck in the discomfort of your fears, wading in that "misery mud", as we'll call it. Happiness seems like something that only happens in the movies, or in our fantasies of what life could have been, because what we truly desire is to belong. To belong with other people who are happy within themselves and who accept and love us for who we truly are.

The Chase

That relentless pursuit ... that feeling that if we just try harder, achieve more, look better, we'll finally arrive at that elusive state of bliss we see on TV, TikTok, or our socials. But what if I told you that the chase itself often keeps us from contentment?

We're bombarded with images of perfect lives, flawless smiles, and effortless joy. And when we carry the weight of past pain, those images become a cruel reminder of what we feel we lack. So, once again, on repeat, we reach for quick fixes, those temporary highs that promise a moment of escape: the sugar rush, the online shopping spree, the endless scrolling, that extra glass (or three) of wine. They offer a fleeting sense of relief, a brief respite from the ache, but we are just caught in a loop. Like a mirage in the desert, the relief vanishes, leaving us thirstier than before.

Why is it so hard to hold onto happiness? Because lasting contentment isn't a destination – it's a journey. It's built on a foundation of self-acceptance, inner peace, and real and raw connection. And when our foundation is riddled with the cracks of past trauma, and we're locked in a constant state of denial, those quick fixes only plaster over the damage, never repairing it.

The Avoidance of Happiness

Sometimes, after emotional storms of trauma – whether the trauma is experienced in childhood or later in life – we find ourselves clinging to the wreckage, even when the waters have calmed. It's a strange sort of safety, isn't it? We become intimately familiar with the weight of sadness, the sting of disappointment, the familiar ache of fear. On the other hand, feeling safe and happy can subconsciously feel like teetering on a dangerously exposed cliff edge because these emotions are so unfamiliar.

We've learned that vulnerability can equate to pain, and so we unconsciously build walls, brick by brick, against the experience of joy. Our subconscious narratives from the past warn us, "Don't risk it. You'll only get hurt again." This misery mud becomes a kind of perverse comfort, a known quantity. But the gentle truth we need to remember is that the danger we fear is often a lost part of ourselves, surrendered to the trauma ghost of the past. The world, right now, might be offering us sunshine, but our Inner Child, still wounded, flinches at the light. We can carefully guide that child, though. We can sit with them, listen to their stories, and offer the compassion they so desperately need. We can become the empathetic witness they never had, and rewrite the fear narrative, one tender moment at a time. And in doing so, we begin to find that happiness isn't a cliff edge after all, but a warm, safe harbour.

The "Not Enough" Wound

Remember in Book One: *Project Clarity*, when I talked about how our childhood experiences of neglect, dismissal, or lack of validation can create an imprint of "I'm not good enough"? When our needs weren't met, when our voices weren't heard, we internalised the message that we were unworthy. And as adults, we desperately seek external validation to fill that void. We chase material possessions, social status, and the approval of others, hoping that these things will finally make us feel whole.

We spend countless hours and dollars trying to measure up, to be good enough in the eyes of society. But the truth is, no amount of external validation can heal the wounds of the past. In fact, this constant striving also often leads to destructive behaviours, especially with food and alcohol, as we seek comfort and escape from the relentless pressure.

Shifting that deeply ingrained "not good enough" narrative to a loving "I am enough" takes a journey of tender self-reparenting. It's about rewriting the stories written from our past experiences and creating a new narrative of self-acceptance and love. In this book, I will teach you how to begin to activate that shift.

You are enough, more than enough!

Control Seems Impossible

Okay, you know this feeling, right? It's that sudden rush of overwhelming emotion when something triggers a deep-seated wound. It's like a wave crashing over you, leaving you feeling helpless and totally out of control. You lose yourself in that moment. It's unsettling, isn't it? Why does this happen? Well, when we experience trauma, especially in childhood, our brains develop coping mechanisms just to survive. These mechanisms often involve suppressing emotions, disconnecting from our bodies, and creating a safe persona to present to the world. We build these walls around our hearts, brick by painful brick.

> **"We are not a victim of our emotions or thoughts. We can understand our triggers and use them as tools to help us respond more objectively."**
> – Elizabeth Thornton

And when a trigger occurs, it bypasses our rational mind – that logical part of us that tries to keep things in check – and it activates those old survival responses. It's not that you can't control your emotions; it's that your body is reacting to a perceived threat, even if that threat isn't physically present. It's like your Inner Child is still trying to protect you, even when the danger passed long ago. So, you push the emotion away, plaster on a smile for friends and family, reach for the numbing comfort of scrolling on social media, food, alcohol, or indulge in online shopping to create a fleeting sense of control. These are all attempts to regulate your nervous system, to escape the overwhelming intensity of the triggered response. It feels like a desperate attempt to put a lid on a boiling pot, when what's really needed is to understand the pressure and tactfully release it. To turn down the heat, if you will, and let things simmer safely.

Automatic behaviours with food and drink are often activated by some form of trigger. To live by your values and be committed to your chosen behaviours, it's essential, as you take back control, to understand what triggers you and pushes you off balance. Because here's the thing: You are not out of control; you just need a little guidance to find the way back to what is important to you. Just you.

In the coming chapters, there is a helpful exercise, we'll look at how to identify your triggers, behaviours, and consequences. We'll shine a light on what's been hiding in your pressure cooker, and we'll do it together.

> It's okay. I'm going to hold your hand through the whole process.

The Lack of Boundaries and Chaotic Relationships

You will hear me beat this drum many times in this book series: boundaries are a must-have! Especially when you are on a journey to experience true happiness. Boundaries are not about building walls but about creating safe spaces for yourself. When you lack boundaries, you become vulnerable to the negative energy and influences of others. You allow chaotic people into your life, people who drain your energy, invalidate your feelings, and disrupt your peace. This constant exposure to negativity and drama depletes your capacity for joy and contentment. It's like trying to grow a beautiful garden in toxic soil, in the dark. Life cannot flourish in those conditions.

Without boundaries, you're constantly putting others' needs before your own, leading to resentment, exhaustion, and a deep sense of unfulfillment. You become a people-pleaser, sacrificing your own happiness to maintain peace and avoid conflict. But true happiness comes from honouring your own needs and creating a life that aligns with your values. You matter. Your needs matter. And it's okay to prioritise them! In Book Three: *Liberated Connection*, there are several pages dedicated to this topic, so make sure you stick around for that. You'll love it.

> You will hear me say rather passionately in my YouTube and online videos, "you need to hold your boundaries like a mother-fxxker" I'm not meaning to be rude, truly. I say it with a no-nonsense kind of love for this cause.

The Devastation of Gaslighting

Now, let's talk about how gaslighting impacts your happiness. When someone you trust, someone you have a connection with, manipulates your perception of reality, it's an intense violation. These days gaslighting is officially labelled as "a form of abuse involving someone deliberately causing you to doubt your sanity". On the receiving end, you may experience feelings of confusion, powerlessness, and a deep sense of unease. You might start thinking, "Am I losing my mind?" Trust me, you're not.

Being the victim of gaslighting erodes your sense of self, making you question your sanity. Gaslighting triggers past traumas because it mirrors the invalidation and dismissal you may have experienced in childhood.

It reinforces the message that your feelings don't matter, that your reality is wrong. This creates a deep sense of confusion, fear, and helplessness, amplifying the emotional turmoil and making it even harder to regulate your emotions. It reopens those old wounds of feeling unseen and unheard as a child, and it drives emotional responses and physical behaviour. It's like someone is trying to rewrite your personal history right in front of you.

Gaslighting may be a root cause for some of your triggers. In this book, you will learn to connect to this issue so you can develop skills to manage it better and regain control of your choices. You'll take back the pen and begin writing YOUR story again.

You will learn about four types of gaslighting, a set of common phrases used by gaslighters, and work through some scenarios to help you recognise your experiences. I share these with you so you can familiarise yourself with gaslighting, start to see when someone is doing this to you, and take action to protect yourself and feel safe. When you feel safe, you can heal.

> You deserve to feel grounded in your own truth, and I'm here to help you find that.

Anxiety, Depression, and the "Golden Ticket" of Happiness

Anxiety and depression can significantly impact our pursuit of happiness. When you're struggling with these conditions, happiness can feel like an unattainable "golden ticket", a distant dream that seems forever out of reach. The constant weight of anxiety and the numbness of depression can make it difficult to experience even small moments of joy. This is where those temporary highs from eating, drinking, or substance use can become particularly alluring. They offer a fleeting sense of relief, a brief escape from the pain. But these quick fixes only reinforce the cycle of seeking external validation while enduring numbing inner distress.

> And, honestly, they never really fill that void, do they?

The Silenced Fury of Anger

Now, let's talk about anger. The emotion that we, as women, are so often told to suppress. We're conditioned to smile, to be agreeable, to prioritise everyone else's comfort over our own. "Don't be dramatic," they say. "Don't be a bitch," they warn. So, we swallow our anger. We pretend to be happy even when our guts are screaming. We turn to food, alcohol, or other coping mechanisms to numb the rage threatening to erupt.

But, my friend, let me tell you something: Your anger is valid. It's a powerful emotion, a signal that something is wrong, that a boundary has been crossed. It's not "unfeminine" to be angry. On the contrary, it's fundamentally feminine. It's the fierce protectiveness of a mother, the unwavering strength of a survivor, the lioness stare that conveys, "This is wrong!" Suppressing your anger only leads to self-loathing, resentment, and the toxic cycle of keeping up appearances. It's time to reclaim your voice, to honour your anger as a vital part of your being.

Sitting with anger, without having to reach for a bottle or a bite, is a must-have life skill. I am going to walk you through a process to connect more deeply with your emotions and their function so you can become more skilled at managing all your emotions, including your anger.

> If a woman is angry, she's a "psycho", she's "aggressive", and she's "scary", as if her anger is her weakness. If a man is angry, he's "manly", he's "masculine", he's a "leader", as if his anger is his strength, and is praiseworthy.

To Wrap This Up

After reading this section, I will ask you again. Are you happy? How much of this feels like your lived experience? This is a journey of change and a new experience of happiness that requires new skills. When you slow everything down and commit to this work – because there is no magic pill, my friend, and quick fixes are a thing of the past – you will find that each moment offers an opportunity to be authentic, real, and honest with yourself.

This means no longer hiding the parts of yourself that you feel are shameful or unlovable, and instead giving your whole being the respect she deserves. It's about listening to the emotions that are trying to help you evolve as a human, and in doing so, finding what is truly important and what brings peace, joy, and meaning to your life.

> Baby steps, my friend, baby steps. Now, take a deep breath. You're going to figure this out.

Anger-Releasing Exercise

Is there anger living deep inside you, just waiting to be expressed? If so, here are a few ways to let it out. Try one or try them all.

- While you're thinking about what's making you angry, throw a mug against the back fence and watch it shatter into pieces.

- Go for a walk somewhere you can be alone, where you don't know anyone and don't see anyone, and scream out all the anger you've been holding back. (When I did this, a few F-words and C-words might have slipped out, along with other colourful language. That was how I expressed it. It might be different for you.)

- Write a letter to the person you're angry with and just let it all out. Pour every deep, honest, and colourful expression of your rage onto the page.

- Then read it aloud to yourself. Don't send this letter.

This is purely an exercise to release what's trapped inside.

WARNING: This can be surprisingly powerful! You might feel like a volcano has erupted inside. If that happens, feel free to repeat the above exercises. Whatever you do, please don't suppress it again. Once it's out, it's done. You're free. Let it all go!

And now ... dismount!

2. My Trauma Experience

Finding Comfort and Connection Through Chocolate
A Little Girl Alone in Her Pain

This is my story – a very real, very raw confession – of how I found comfort under the shade of a beautiful tree in our garden, and how, in those moments, chocolate became my way to cope with pain. It's a story I share with you from my heart, hoping it might bring a sense of connection.

After my hip replacement, in August 2020, I was incredibly proud of myself. I had health-coached myself back into the land of the living after being lost in a dark place for so long. I had endured chronic pain – bone-on-bone, nerve-pinching agony – for the last eighteen months. I had eaten and drunk my way to poor health, excess weight, and depressive behaviours.

My pride in August 2020 came from finally feeling human again, back on track. I had given up drinking, and my world felt balanced, deliciously healthy, with moderate, mainly vegetarian eating. I'd lost 10 kg, felt like a "bionic woman", and even poured my heart into writing a book about my recovery journey. I felt like I was on top of the world. But life, as we all know, has a way of throwing us curveballs, doesn't it?

The very month my book was published, I took a tumble down a flight of stairs at work, badly injuring my back. Suddenly, I was immobile. It was a devastating blow. Depression crept in like an old familiar shadow. I found myself turning to chocolate – lots of it – to soothe the ache, both physical and emotional. All the weight I'd worked so hard to lose was creeping back on. And once again, I didn't much like myself in the mirror.

Later, as I began to heal, I started to see the connections, the patterns. I realised this coping mechanism, this reliance on chocolate, went way back to my childhood trauma. And now, I want to share this with you, my friend, because I truly believe in the power of connection and understanding.

As you know, my parents ran a restaurant, which meant I was often alone and, sadly, vulnerable to more attacks from family members. Whenever things got tough at home – those horrible experiences, the "play fights" that turned violent, the humiliation, the teasing – I'd retreat. So, the tree and my chocolate stash became my companions, a safe little world where nobody could touch me or my feelings.

I had absent and dismissive parents. These complaints about my attackers annoyed them. I would be shut down and told to "belt up" and fall in line. So, when I was alone, invalidated, lacking an empathetic witness, feeling unsafe, I ate. It became a pattern, a reflex almost. After those awful times, I'd somehow manage to get some coins from a parent's drawer or wallet, slip out to the local shop, and buy chocolate or a big bag of mixed lollies. Sweet things became my escape, my solace.

With my "borrowed" coins, I'd get my scrumptious bag and head straight for the big tree in our front garden. That was my sanctuary, my haven. There, under the tree's comforting shade, I'd devour the chocolate. It wasn't just a treat; it was medicine for my soul. I particularly loved the Cadbury family bars – the peppermint and oozy caramel were my absolute favourites. I'd eat a whole block, or a large bag of lollies. It might sound a lot, but it was exactly what I needed to get through those moments. Each mouthful was a way to confront the pain, to numb it, even if just for a little while. I didn't have the words for it then, but I knew, deep down, I needed something to help.

It wasn't until much later in life that I realised this wasn't just a random thing. Every time I faced trauma or a trigger, I did the same thing. It was my not-so-wonderful coping mechanism: chocolate under the tree. It was my escape, my comfort, my place to hide and numb the pain. The "face-scoffing routine", as I call it, would last as long as it needed to, depending on the intensity of the emotions I was trying to bury.

In 2021, I had a part-time job doing up houses for holiday rentals. In a dark hallway, I fell. Hard. The accident did major damage to my L4, L5, and S1 vertebrae. I couldn't walk for more than fifteen minutes, I couldn't stand for more than twenty minutes, and I couldn't sit in a chair for more than twenty minutes without having to lie down and take medication to numb the excruciating pain. The fall brought everything to the surface. I felt completely lost. I'd just published my book about healing and weight loss and suddenly felt like a fraud. I was in so much pain, both physically and emotionally. Everything was such hard work, and I was a complete mess, blubbering in tears. I felt like I'd lost my sense of self and my freedom. One moment, I was the "bionic woman", inspiring others to be healthy, and the next, I was back under my proverbial tree, hiding and eating Easter egg chocolates to soothe the battle I was in, in my emotional storm.

Next came the added inch around my waist. I lost sight of my cheekbones, my face became round, and I grew a lovely double chin. The weight gain made me feel like such a fraud; I felt like I had no worth. (In hindsight, I can tell you that this weight also became my teacher.) Confessing to my therapist about my self-medicating was a turning point. She simply said, "Well, this is what you did as a child. This is how you soothed yourself." At forty-eight years old, it finally clicked. That's what I had been doing all those years! And I had no connection to it, no control over it; it was utterly and completely automatic.

So, I went to work on myself. I had to do my Inner Child healing meditation (I'll teach you how to do this in these pages), and I had to sit with the little girl, my former self, and tell her what she needed to hear. I have to say, there were a lot of tears for me in this process. A lot. I didn't realise just how much pain I had stored away and carried with me every day, for all these years. It showed me just how much pain she had gone through, so alone, afraid, and constantly waiting for the next attack to happen.

The immense shame I carried with me erupted out during these meditation

> **"There is no greater agony than bearing an untold story inside you."**
> – Maya Angelou

exercises. I won't lie. I had to do the meditation and literally hold my own hand many times. These scars were deep, and they were stuck there, almost like they were tattooed inside.

For me, through this healing process and Inner Child connection, I would feel a sadness for a few days afterwards, too. It felt like a type of mourning that I needed to do. What my younger self went through was horrific. And then, while carrying on with life, seeing a young girl in the street would bring me back to my former self. Her visible youth and vulnerability mirrored my own, and it always brought a wave of sadness It would also make me mad. And ... that was okay. I would tell the little girl inside me that it was okay to feel anger, hurt, and rage. That was normal. She'd been through a lot. But she was safe now.

The next big part of this process for me was acceptance. I had to accept that these things had happened. This was the play of my life, and these were the parts of the play that had already been performed and could never be changed. I couldn't change what anyone said, did, or didn't do in these scenarios. But I could change the dialogue with my little self now. I brought out a photo of her and put it on my kitchen bench. Each day, I would talk to her and remind her she was pretty damn special, and she was safe. Neither she nor I needed to dive into a bowl of melted chocolate anymore. We were safe. And we were going to be okay.

This is why I'm sharing this with you, my friend. This is exactly why I created this series: to share with many women like me the success of my personal project of change. I longed to share these "aha" moments, the hard-won know-how I've gleaned from my past challenges. I wanted to show you how I've actively faced those difficult fear stories, held the hand of my former self, and validated her. How I've become my own empathetic witness, understanding my patterns of behaviour, my triggers, and the cost of their consequences. It was hard, incredibly hard, at first. But it became easier, gentler, each day, and I am so deeply grateful that I stuck with it, that I believed in myself enough to do this. I have truly changed those patterns for the better. And now, I am back in the driver's seat of my life. I can now enjoy some chocolate, savouring it for what it is: a little sweetness, a small joy every now and again.

By sharing my story, I want to normalise the cycles of what happens behind closed doors when you get triggered and feel so alone.

A New Perspective Comes from Greater Understanding

3.
Your Inner World

Building a New Perspective
How Befriending Your Emotions Unlocks Your Best Life

If you've picked up this book, it's likely something within you is yearning to come out – a need for a deeper connection to yourself, a greater sense of peace, and perhaps, a dash more joy in your everyday life. You're not alone. Many of us travel through life feeling disconnected from our truest selves, often reacting to our emotions rather than responding to them. This is often the legacy of childhood adversity, unmet needs, or trauma, as these events can leave you vulnerable to experiencing further challenges in adulthood. We learn to protect ourselves by disconnecting from our feelings. As I said, this isn't a weakness; it's a powerful survival mechanism. However, this protective wall can also keep us from the very things we need most: understanding, managing, connecting to, and ultimately embracing our emotional world.

Avoiding your emotions often creates new, even harder problems. While it might feel like a relief in the moment, that avoidance can keep you from fully living, from experiencing genuine connection, from learning to trust yourself, and from accepting yourself for who you really are. This avoidance leaves you stuck, stagnant, emotionally rigid, and inflexible, repeating the same cycles over and over.

Can you think of moments when you've felt completely numb, simply going through the motions but detached from the life force within? Or perhaps you've experienced a sudden dip in your confidence, where tasks that once felt simple now feel overwhelming. These experiences often signal emotional dysregulation – that "daisy chain" of emotions that can sometimes derail your life and self-control, especially in your relationship with food, drink, and, most importantly, your authentic self.

The good news is, when you start to befriend and understand your emotions – your overall emotional blueprint – you can unveil an astute new perspective on yourself. As you see them laid out in front of you, with all their colours, the light and the dark, you can begin to understand what your emotions are trying to communicate. They illuminate the parts of yourself you need to get to know better, giving you the reasons behind your reactions and motivations to act in a particular way. This helps you uncover the link you didn't know was missing, but in your gut, you always knew you had to find. By connecting the dots, you can appreciate why you behave in a certain manner so much more clearly. This, my friend, is a new and very honest way of seeing who you really are and gaining a whole new perspective on your life.

> **"The cave you fear to enter holds the treasure you seek."**
> – **Joseph Campbell**

If you've experienced challenges or trauma, it makes perfect sense that your deepest instinct is to protect yourself. For a long time, perhaps your whole life, emotions have felt scary. That's ok. It's completely understandable. Please know, my friend, it's perfectly normal to have wanted to avoid painful emotions. But equally, also know, you can make friends with the parts of yourself that you have denied or felt ashamed of. You can accept your former self and what she had to do to survive those times. When you see your patterns clearly and fully accept all the things that trigger you, you can gracefully choose to sidestep them or walk down a different road altogether. (More on this later.)

You've been doing what you needed to do to survive. That's okay.

The Silent Inheritance: How Trauma's Legacy Shapes You

The landscape of womanhood is often painted with vibrant hues of resilience and strength. Yet so many of us navigate the complex terrain of unresolved childhood trauma, which can leave us vulnerable to experiencing more traumatic events in adulthood. Those early adverse experiences, like seeds sown in fertile ground, can blossom into behavioural patterns that shape our lives. We may find ourselves grappling with intimacy, struggling to trust, or repeating cycles of unhealthy relationships – all echoes of unmet needs and unresolved pain from the past.

Then there is the weight of generational trauma, that silent inheritance passed down through our families. Our parents and grandparents, in their own struggles, may have inadvertently imprinted patterns of anxiety, fear, or self-doubt upon us, creating a ripple effect that impacts our own wellbeing. It's like carrying an invisible weight. We don't appreciate how it pulls us down until we face it and give it form. In other words, we must stop denying it's there and let it out of its glass box.

This legacy of trauma often manifests in subtle yet destructive ways. We may seek solace in risky behaviours, impulsive choices, or addictions of all kinds. These might include things like: the numbing comfort of substances, the fleeting high of adrenaline, the obsessive pursuit of love, crossing your own boundaries for acceptance and validation, or engaging in sexual encounters for the wrong reasons.

Perhaps it's the quiet compulsion of overwork, the tightly held claws of perfectionism, or the inability to let go and simply be. These behaviours are often desperate attempts to regulate our emotions and fill the void left by those early wounds. Even those who appear outwardly successful may harbour deeply hidden struggles. The polished facade we present to the world masks the inner turmoil – the constant battle to manage the lingering effects of trauma.

> Does any of this sound familiar? If you are nodding yes, it's exhausting, isn't it?

It's crucial to acknowledge that these struggles are not a reflection of weakness or failure but rather a testament to the enduring power of the human spirit to survive and adapt. Recognising the impact of any trauma, be it childhood adversity, a single event, or generational trauma, is a powerful step towards healing. By understanding the roots of our behaviours, we can begin to dismantle the patterns that hold us back, cultivate self-compassion, and create a life that is truly aligned with our authentic selves. Because we deserve that.

Normalising the Unseen Wounds

As I discussed in Book One: *Project Clarity*, the insidious nature of childhood trauma isn't simply a matter of what occurred, but how it was processed and internalised. This is particularly important when considering how women may normalise or hide their trauma, even from themselves. As the very inspiring Gabor Maté once said, "Trauma is not what happens to you but what happens inside you."

The complication of hidden trauma lies in its normalisation. Within the familiar confines of our families, objectively harmful behaviours can become woven into the fabric of daily life, perceived as "just how things are." Children, especially, possess an innate loyalty to their parents, a deep-seated desire to maintain the family bond. This loyalty can create a powerful barrier to acknowledging emotional abuse or neglect. "It wasn't that bad," we might tell ourselves, or "They did their best," rationalising experiences that left lasting scars. We learn to adapt and survive, and in doing so, we unwittingly internalise the very patterns that perpetuate our pain. It's like we're stuck in a loop.

Then there is the rather common predicament of manipulation and gaslighting in the family home, which can leave us questioning our own perceptions, creating a sense of confusion and self-doubt that persists into adulthood. We may have been subtly, or overtly, led to believe that we were the problem, the cause of the family's dysfunction. Phrases like "You're too sensitive" or "You're making a big deal out of nothing" can, over time, erode our sense of self-worth and leave us bearing a heavy burden of shame. Fear of speaking out becomes a powerful silencer. We carry the weight of secrets, the unspoken truths that fester and grow in the darkness, believing that we are alone in our suffering. This internalised shame becomes a formidable obstacle to healing. But I want you to know, you're not alone.

Many women who have experienced single event or childhood trauma also find themselves living in a state of internal conflict, torn between their deeply held values and the behaviours their past has shaped. They may hold onto ideals of kindness and compassion yet struggle to embody these qualities in their own lives. The fear of not being good enough, a common by-product of trauma, can lead to self-sabotaging behaviours and unhealthy relationships. This internal discord can leave women feeling lost and trapped in a cycle of self-destructive patterns.

> If this resonates with you, I know it's hard. It's a painful place to be, isn't it? I have been there too.

The Power of Conscious Choice

While the thought of befriending your emotions may seem like a blurry mess at the moment, I am here to tell you that healing and transformation are possible. After all, this is what I'm passionately sharing in all these pages. By consciously choosing new values that align with the woman you are today and the Future Self you aspire to, you can begin to rewrite the narratives and break free from the limitations of your past.

This process, as we have stepped through in Book One: *Project Clarity*, involves a deep exploration of your core values, identifying those that resonate with your authentic self, and then consciously integrating them into your daily life. I hope this is what you have been practising.

As you embrace these new values, you begin to rewire neural pathways in your brain, replacing old, unhelpful thought patterns with new ones. These new thought patterns or 'signals' lead to new habits and behaviours that support your health and choices to foster that internal love language you're developing.

HELPFUL NOTE: Okay, you may be asking, "What does 'rewiring neural pathways' mean?" Well, think of your neural pathways as well-worn paths in a forest. For a long time, trauma and fear have carved deep, familiar trails in your mind. But now, as you embrace your new values and choose healing, you're like a gardener, planting new seeds and creating fresh, beautiful pathways. With each step you take, each act of self-love, each moment of choosing your Future Self, you're strengthening those new paths, making them brighter and more vibrant. The old, fear-filled paths start to fade as you build a new inner landscape, a place where peace, strength, and your true self can flourish.

Whoof, it sounds a lot to do, doesn't it? This is why I am breaking it all down, little by little. Peppering in these summary messages along the way. Little by little, new skill, with new skill, you will start to see how it all fits in place. But I give you permission to feel that tightness in your chest. That is normal.

This journey of change? It's not always pretty. It's a gritty, hard road of tearing down everything you thought you were to find out who you really are. But on the other side of the mess, you get to take your power back, stitch up those old wounds, and finally live a life that doesn't feel like a lie.

> Your Future Self isn't some daydream –
> she's reaching for your hand, ready to
> lead you to where all the good stuff is.

4. Home is the Heart of Your Story

The Echoes of a Language You Never Knew
The Role of Our Family in Our Emotional Makeup

Let's talk about how the unspoken emotional conditioning we learned as girls shapes the women we have become. This all forms the emotional blueprint of your life – the foundation for how you navigate your inner and outer world.

I wonder if, while you were growing up, you experienced a home where emotions were like an unspoken, possibly even foreign, language. You might have grasped a few basic phrases, but real, heartfelt conversations about feelings? They just didn't happen. Perhaps expressing emotions was seen as inconvenient, or even a bit disruptive. So, they were carefully tucked away, hidden out of sight. Maybe your parents, carrying the weight of their own unhealed pasts, navigated life with that stiff upper lip, a forced smile, or there were sudden, intense outbursts followed by an icy, isolating silence. I've seen it, and I have firsthand experience. It's heartbreaking.

As children, we absorb everything. Not just the words spoken, but the subtle, unspoken language of tension and avoidance. We begin to believe feelings are risky, unpredictable things. When we witness our parents grappling with their inner worlds, that becomes the blueprint for our own emotional lives, an imprint that shapes the women we become. We learn to mirror what we see: to hold back the tears, to swallow the anger, and to put on that brave face, pretending everything's okay, even when it's tearing us apart inside.

Those unmet needs of childhood, those deep, primal yearnings for safety, for connection, for someone to truly see and validate us – they leave lasting marks. This is where complex trauma is born. Whether it's the sting of neglect, the sharp pain of emotional abuse, the confusion and instability of a parent's mental health struggles, or the shattering experience of a family torn apart, these experiences can create a momentous sense of shame – the kind that just eats you up. As children, we learned to protect ourselves, to build walls around our hearts, because every time we showed our true selves, our vulnerability was met with pain, rejection, or indifference. Emotions became a frightening force, a chaotic storm that threatened to overwhelm us, leaving us feeling like we were drowning.

As adults, this often translates into a deep-seated fear of vulnerability. We might struggle to connect authentically, to truly express our needs, and to trust that our feelings will be met with compassion. Sometimes, just the act of feeling becomes a source of anxiety, a painful reminder of those times when our emotions were dismissed, ignored, or even used against us. Our emotional world feels less like a safe space to explore and more like a minefield where we must tread with extreme caution, leaving us feeling utterly disconnected from ourselves and others.

The Place Where Our Feelings Were First Ignored

Have you ever had those moments where you react to something and later feel your response was out of proportion? Perhaps someone has really wound you up, and you head straight to the fridge to stuff your face with something sweet or salty, or you grab a wine or a beer to take the edge off. It's more than likely you're caught in a cycle, the same patterns keep playing out, and you find yourself thinking at times, "Why on earth do I keep doing this?" I get it. I really do. These are the roots of our adult emotional experiences, often driven by triggers from our past. And you guessed it – they go all the way back to childhood.

When we talk about unmet needs, I want to shine a light on one particularly important one – invalidation. Understanding how your past still ripples through your life today means facing where your emotions were first shut down. This isn't just theory; it's a foundational experience for all of us, starting right there in our families. It's in those first interactions that we tentatively try to express ourselves, learn what relationships are supposed to feel like, and often where things go really, deeply wrong. Invalidation? Yeah, it often makes its big, whopping entrance right here. I know this from my own life, and I bet it hits home for many of you, too.

As I've said, your emotions are your inner compass, guiding you through life's messy bits. They are a delicate and essential part of being human. When you put a feeling out there, it's like sending a signal – a genuine attempt to connect, to be really seen and understood. Invalidation, especially when we're little, happens when that vital signal is brushed off, or met with silence or a harsh judgement.

Cast your mind back. Can you remember telling your parents, or whoever looked after you, that you were upset, and their response was something like, "Oh, don't be silly; you're fine"? These seemingly small moments, repeated over and over through childhood, subtly teach us to doubt our own inner world, to question if our deepest feelings are even real or valid.

 **HERE'S THE POWERFUL TRUTH OF IT:** the environment you grew up in absolutely sets the stage for how your emotions develop. If you find yourself struggling to manage your feelings today – maybe you snap when triggered, can't properly calm down when someone hurts you, or freeze up in a crisis – chances are, your emotions were dismissed or invalidated. And as a direct result, you've built your current, often deeply ingrained, ways of coping.

Your family, you see, is the very first stage where your emotional story gets written. Ideally, these spaces would be safe havens, where your heartfelt cries of "I'm scared" are met with a warm, "It's okay, darling. What's making you scared?" In a perfect world, you'd be heard, genuinely comforted, and feelings of security, love, and validation would sink deep. But for you, perhaps, like so many of us, the response was completely different.

Maybe what you got was dismissive: "There's nothing to be scared of!" Or shaming: "Stop being a baby." This constant invalidation brewed a deep confusion inside you. It's like trying to understand someone speaking a foreign language, or turning up for a netball game only to find everyone else is playing tennis. You don't consciously realise it, but you are absolutely not on the same team. Through these bewildering experiences, you learned to bury your emotions, to deeply distrust your own perceptions, and ultimately, to lose that vital trust in your own inner compass.

I recall expressing my passion and ambition to be a writer and published author to my brother. I was met with, "Ha, what a joke. No one will ever want to read your writing." Perhaps you, too, heard the dismissive "That's not a practical hobby" when you expressed your passion or saw the eye roll when you earnestly shared your heart's desire when you were young.

What I'm really trying to convey here is just how incredibly precious and sensitive our psyche is at a young age. Being invalidated bruises our delicate inner world and can create some seriously long-term effects. You see, these seemingly small moments don't just disappear; they accumulate, building a pattern where we learn to question our own reality, and to doubt the validity of our own thoughts, beliefs, and even our basic preferences. Again, this is how complex trauma is formed.

> For those of us who are naturally more sensitive, this early invalidation cuts even deeper. We feel things intensely, and when those feelings are consistently dismissed, it's a fundamental betrayal of our inner experience. It's not just the dramatic moments, but the subtle, everyday interactions.

So, here are the two sides of the coin, for you to truly appreciate these insights on a deeper level. In a **validating environment**, our feelings are acknowledged, understood, and respected, which fosters healthy emotional regulation and self-trust. But when our **environment consistently invalidates** us, we learn to distrust our own inner voice. This leads to self-doubt, confusion, and a real struggle to navigate our emotional landscape. This early invalidation teaches us that our feelings are unreliable, unimportant, or even just plain wrong, thereby setting the stage for our emotional dysregulation.

Does all of this help you to grasp this concept that the environment you grew up in absolutely laid the foundation for your emotional development? Just like we spoke about in Book One: *Project Clarity*, your parents' values imprinted on you, as did their emotional dysfunction. This is no different. In fact, this is the very soil from which it all begins to grow.

> How does that sit with you? Perhaps you felt brushed off when you were younger too?

The Consequence of Invalidation
Building Awareness and Strategies for Change

Okay, my friend, this next part might not feel warm and fuzzy, but it's a necessary step in your evolution. I'm offering you a mixed bag here: I'll help you appreciate more of your emotional vulnerabilities, give you some thought-provoking questions to connect with your former self, and share some healing strategies to help you build yourself back up again in times of need.

I want to explore further with you how the invalidation of our feelings in childhood can deeply impact our emotional health and resilience as women. We'll look at six integral consequences – from emotional dysregulation to challenges in relationships – so you can connect to what's happening with you today on a more significant level. The purpose of this is to uncover another part of the roadmap of your emotional make-up, empowering you to move on from feeling like a victim of your emotions.

> **IMPORTANT NOTE:** The healing techniques that follow each section aren't quick fixes or temporary solutions. Think of them as new, additional tools for your Change Experience, helping you navigate your emotional landscape. My goal is to help you build the skills that will give you the means to move forward and create the life you truly want.

Here's a closer look at the consequences of invalidation and how they manifest:

1. Emotional Dysregulation

When your feelings were consistently dismissed as a child, you were essentially taught a very painful lesson: your inner world isn't safe or acceptable. This meant you never learned the fundamental skills needed to manage your emotions, because you weren't given a chance to.

The consequence? As an adult, your emotional system is on shaky ground. You may find yourself with a low tolerance for discomfort, meaning you can't cope with difficult feelings or situations. Small things might trigger intense, overwhelming reactions, like anger, anxiety, or sadness. It's as if you're stuck on an emotional rollercoaster, you can't get off.

Since you were taught to suppress your feelings rather than understand them, you may also have trouble knowing what you're actually feeling, which can lead to impulsive behaviour. For example, when you feel overwhelmed, you might turn to things like spending sprees, binge eating, or alcohol to soothe yourself, because you haven't learned healthier ways to cope. This is the very definition of emotional dysregulation: a chronic inability to manage your emotions in a healthy, controlled way.

Questions to Explore Your Inner World

Can you recall a specific time when you've had a strong emotional reaction that felt out of proportion to the situation?

? How has that feeling of being on an "emotional rollercoaster" impacted your relationships or your sense of self-worth?

? What happens inside you when you feel a strong emotion that you think you aren't "allowed" to have?

Healing Strategies

Learn Self-Compassion: Practice acknowledging your emotions without judgement. When a strong feeling arises, pause and simply label it internally. For example: "I'm feeling anger" or "This is sadness". Instead of trying to suppress it, place a hand on your heart and say something kind to yourself, like, "This is a moment of suffering, and it's okay to feel this way."

The "Emotional Thermometer" Technique: This strategy really helps you to better understand the intensity of your emotions. Imagine a scale from 1 to 10. When you feel a strong emotion, take a moment to rate its intensity. This simple act creates a little bit of space between you and the feeling, allowing you to respond rather than just react.

2. Self-Doubt and Confusion

When your feelings and thoughts were consistently dismissed as a child, you were taught a very painful lesson: your inner voice can't be trusted. You were told you were "wrong," "dramatic," or "too sensitive," and this slowly chipped away at your ability to trust yourself. It's like having a faulty internal compass for finding your way in your emotional world.

The consequence? As an adult, you may be left with a deep sense of self-doubt and confusion. You might find it incredibly difficult to make even simple decisions because you're always questioning your own judgement. You may constantly seek external validation, looking to others for approval and reassurance, because your own inner voice has been silenced.

In some women, this can manifest as imposter syndrome, where you feel like a fraud despite your accomplishments. You might also find yourself being easily influenced by others, and you may struggle with a weighty feeling of not truly knowing who you are. This is because your perceptions were consistently invalidated, leaving you with a shaky sense of self and an overwhelming confusion about your own identity and reality.

Questions to Explore Your Inner World

When you've had to make a decision, have you ever felt that deep sense of confusion, or perhaps a constant need for others to tell you what to do?

Thinking back to your childhood, did you ever feel like your opinions were just consistently brushed aside, or that your feelings seemed to frustrate others?

If your inner voice were to speak without interruption, what do you imagine it would say? And how do you feel it's been silenced?

Healing Strategies

Voice-to-Paper Journalling: Use this technique to really reclaim your inner voice. Set aside just ten minutes to write freely about a feeling or a decision without stopping. Please don't worry about spelling, grammar, or making perfect sense; the main goal here is simply to get your thoughts out of your head and onto the paper. This practice is brilliant for helping you build confidence in your very own perceptions.

The "Inner Expert" Exercise: For those smaller decisions, try to stop seeking external advice. Instead, quietly ask yourself, "What would my inner expert (or my Future Self) say about this?" Take a nice deep breath and just wait for the answer. This is such a lovely, subtle way to start rebuilding trust in your own inner messenger – that precious intuition.

3. Lack of Healthy Coping Strategies

When you were a child, your feelings were a lot to deal with, and you needed guidance on how to manage them. But when you were told to "just calm down" or "stop being silly," you were left to manage your powerful emotions on your own. This taught you that your needs were a burden and that you had to deal with your distress in isolation.

The consequence? As an adult, you may lack the effective coping strategies needed to manage your pain. Instead of dealing with your emotions directly, you might turn to unhealthy coping mechanisms to temporarily numb or escape your distress. This can manifest in various ways, such as emotional eating, substance abuse, or other addictive behaviours. These actions provide a quick, temporary sense of relief, but they don't address the root cause of the emotional turmoil.

This is a vicious cycle. The more you rely on these unhealthy strategies, the less you learn how to process your feelings in a healthy way, which only reinforces the pattern. You're trying to put out a fire with gasoline, and it can feel like you're constantly fighting an inner battle. And all because you were never given the tools to soothe yourself.

Questions to Explore Your Inner World

How have you learned to soothe yourself when you feel overwhelmed or distressed?

Can you recall a time when you felt incredibly lonely or scared and had to manage those feelings all by yourself?

What's the temporary relief you get from an unhealthy coping mechanism, and what's the long-term cost?

Healing Strategies

Soothe, Ground, Distract: This simple technique really helps you to break the cycle of unhealthy coping. First, soothe yourself with something gentle (a warm cup of tea, a soft blanket). Second, ground yourself by focusing on your senses. For example: notice five things you can see, four things you can feel, three things you can hear. Finally, distract yourself with a healthy activity like reading, art, gardening, singing, dancing, calling a friend, or going for a walk.

Values-Driven Coping: Connect to the core values you chose in Book One: *Project Clarity*. When you feel that urge to use an unhealthy coping mechanism, simply ask yourself, "What's a healthy way to move towards my values right now?" This subtly shifts your focus from avoiding pain to living in alignment with what really matters to you.

4. Challenges in Forming Healthy Relationships

When your emotions weren't truly seen or accepted as a child, you learned a very painful lesson: that seeking connection and validation is a source of disappointment and pain. Your emotional needs were unmet, and as a result, you never developed a strong foundation for understanding and expressing your feelings within a relationship.

The consequence? As an adult, you may find it incredibly difficult to form and maintain healthy relationships. You might become a people-pleaser to avoid conflict, or you may suppress your emotions, fearing that vulnerability will only lead to more invalidation. You might even find yourself over-dramatising your emotions, desperately trying to get the attention and validation you crave.

This can lead to two extremes: either you become overly dependent on others for emotional support, which can be exhausting for them, or you become emotionally distant, pushing people away before they can get too close. The unresolved pain from your childhood makes you fear true intimacy, trust, and setting healthy boundaries, as you unconsciously protect yourself from the hurt of being unseen all over again.

Questions to Explore Your Inner World

? Have you ever felt an intense need to be truly seen or heard by a partner, so much so that it led to conflict or drama?

? When a disagreement or difficult moment arises in a relationship, what's your first instinct? Do you tend to withdraw, or do you amplify your emotions?

? How has a history of feeling "unseen" impacted your ability to trust others or set healthy boundaries?

Healing Strategies

Express and Release Technique: This is for when you feel that powerful urge to suppress or amplify your emotions. Try writing a letter that you won't send to someone about how you truly feel. Allow yourself to be completely honest and expressive. This practice gives your emotions a safe outlet and really helps you process them before you try to communicate with others.

Boundary-Setting Practice: Start small. Identify just one area where you can practise a healthy boundary, such as a phone call with a family member or a simple request from a friend. Rehearse saying no or making a request in a firm but kind way. Begin with a boundary that feels easy to set and build from there.

5. Doubting Your Own Perceptions

When you were a child, the people you looked to for safety and reassurance told you that your feelings were wrong. You were dismissed with phrases like, "You're making a mountain out of a molehill" or "You're overreacting." This constant invalidation taught you a very painful lesson: you can't trust what you feel and know to be true.

The consequence? As an adult, you may find yourself constantly second-guessing your own perceptions. It's as if your inner compass has been broken, leaving you deeply uncertain of your own feelings, instincts, and judgement. You might dismiss your gut feelings as irrational, and you may find yourself struggling with a visceral sense of confusion about who you are.

This can manifest as an overwhelming need for external validation, where you prioritise others' needs and opinions over your own. It can also lead to a deep-seated perfectionism, driven by an underlying fear of not being good enough. Your perceptive sensitivity to rejection, and the feeling that something fundamental is missing, all stems from that early message that your emotions and perceptions were not only wrong but a burden to others.

Questions to Explore Your Inner World

? Have you ever found yourself dismissing your gut feelings, only to later realise they were right all along?

? How has a fear of being "too much" or "overreacting" influenced your decisions or your communication with others?

? When someone criticises you, what is the loudest voice in your head telling you?

Healing Strategies

Evidence Journal for Know-How: Start a journal dedicated to your intuition. Whenever you have a gut feeling about something, big or small, write it down. Later, if your feeling proves to be correct, make a note of it. This simple practice provides concrete evidence that your inner compass is reliable, helping you to trust yourself over time.

You Are Right to Feel Affirmation: When you find yourself second-guessing your feelings, pause and say to yourself, "I am right to feel this way." This statement directly counters the invalidating messages you received in the past and affirms the validity of your emotional experience.

6. Suppression or Escalation of Emotions

When your emotions were consistently invalidated as a child, you were taught that your feelings weren't acceptable. To cope with this, you had to make a heartbreaking choice: either silence your feelings completely or amplify them to be heard. It's a lose-lose situation, and both paths can lead to a lot of pain.

Emotional Suppression
If you chose to suppress your emotions, you may have learned to bottle them up to avoid being dismissed or criticised. This can manifest in adulthood as a penetrating disconnection from your feelings. The unspoken pain doesn't just disapear. It often shows up in other ways. Such as unexplained physical symptoms, chronic fatigue, or sudden, seemingly out-of-the-blue explosive outbursts of anger or sadness. You may be carrying the weight of all the feelings you were never allowed to have.

Emotional Escalation
Alternatively, if your quiet expressions of need were always ignored, you may have learned that only loud, dramatic emotional displays get a reaction. In adulthood, this can lead to a pattern of emotional escalation, where you feel a constant need to create a crisis to get attention and be heard. You might explode in anger or engage in dramatic, attention-seeking behaviour, all because your younger self learned that to be seen, you had to shout.

Both of these coping mechanisms – suppression and escalation – are driven by the same core wound: the belief that your emotions don't matter unless you either hide them entirely or express them in a way that can't be ignored.

Questions to Explore Your Inner World

❓ Have you ever "bottled up" your emotions, only for them to absolutely erupt unexpectedly later on?

❓ Is there a part of you that feels like you have to create a crisis or a dramatic situation to finally get the attention you desperately need?

❓ What is the loudest message your body sends you when you are actively suppressing your emotions?

Healing Strategies

🔗 **The Glass Jar Exercise:** When you feel that urge to suppress an emotion, try visualising placing it in a glass jar. You're not getting rid of the feeling, mind you, but simply acknowledging it and giving it a safe, temporary space to exist. This creates a helpful bit of distance between you and the emotion and gives you a real sense of control. You can always revisit the container later when you're in a safe place.

 **NOTE:** When I have a heavy thought, I focus on it and visualise putting it in a jar, and then I pop that jar in the freezer to emphasise that I'm freezing that thought out of my life. That is very powerful! Do try it if you have a bit of room in yours!

🔗 **Action Technique:** When you feel that powerful urge to escalate an emotion, try taking the complete opposite action. For instance, if you really want to yell, try speaking in a quiet, calm voice instead. This does wonders to break that old pattern and create a new, healthier response. And when you feel the urge to suppress an emotion, try sharing a small part of it with a trusted friend or partner. This delicately helps you build trust, both in yourself and in others.

After the Questions and Healing Homework

So, I really want you to sit with this and create a bit of space for it in your mind. By recognising yourself in these scenarios, or perhaps even opening the door to a deeper understanding of your past, you will begin to reclaim your emotional truth.

It's about giving yourself permission to feel, to acknowledge the pain of those early experiences, to start building a life where your feelings are honoured and valued. That is how, my dear friend, you can be more in control of your emotions. Do you see that now?

As you start to feel more comfortable with the idea of befriending your emotions, things will start to shift. Tune in, listen. Observe yourself. You may be shocked to finally hear and connect with those signals that were once silenced.

> My friend, your journey towards emotional regulation is such a deeply personal one, it's like finding your own unique path through a beautiful, sometimes tangled garden.

5. A Child's Developmental Needs

The Ten Core Needs of Your Inner Child
Revisited For Your Benefit

My friend, we are going over this again because it is relevant to this discussion. This is a recap of the foundational emotional and psychological needs we all have as children. It's so easy to dismiss our past and not see how it shaped us. But understanding what we may have missed is a compassionate way to make sense of the adult we are today, and a starting point to unlock that unspoken conditioning you may have taken on.

    I wonder, do you consciously know if your needs were not met as a kid? Many of us have felt a knot in our tummies that we couldn't name, in relation to what was really out of sorts in our upbringing. Perhaps some parts of what you missed out on are as clear as day from the list I am about to share. Or maybe it wasn't a big, obvious story of lacking, but a quiet, niggling sense that something was absent. Or it could still be fresh in your mind after reading Book One: *Project Clarity*, so you are more aware and connected to what happened to you. Either way, I wanted to share this with you again, as a tool for you to find that missing link and see how the environment in which you grew up might just be the issue that is still impacting you.

As you read through this list, allow yourself some time to deeply connect with it. Remember, as I said before, you may need a crowbar to prise some things out so you might need to sit with this for a while. There's a chance you'll connect to a feeling inside you that has been there for a long time, a feeling you didn't know how to deal with. Here they are:

 Safety: A Sanctuary to Grow

A child requires a profound sense of safety. Not just physical safety, which is obviously paramount, but also emotional security – knowing they are protected from harm and that their wellbeing is a top priority. A child who feels safe can relax, explore, and learn without the constant fear of being hurt or abandoned. When safety is absent, a child is often in a state of hypervigilance, always on guard, which can severely hinder development.

 Basic Needs: The Emotional and Physical Building Blocks

Basic survival needs, such as a roof over their head, nutritious food, and adequate clothing, are absolutely essential. They provide the physical foundation for healthy growth. A child who is hungry, cold, or lacks basic necessities cannot focus on learning or playing.

These basic needs include **Secure Attachment and Connection**: having a dependable safe place with a primary caregiver who was consistently there for you, so you know you were seen, heard, and cared for.

 Respect and Value: Recognising Their Worth

Beyond the physical, a child's emotional health is deeply intertwined with their sense of self-worth. They need to feel respected and valued as individuals, with their thoughts and feelings acknowledged and considered. This includes a sense of **Significance** – the feeling that you mattered and that your presence made a difference to the people around you.

 Validation: Understanding Their Inner World

Validation of emotions is crucial for a child to understand and regulate their feelings. When their emotions are validated, they learn that their inner world matters. This helps them build emotional intelligence and healthy coping mechanisms. This also includes **Support and Encouragement** – feeling that someone has your back, and **Autonomy** – the freedom to explore and make age-appropriate choices, knowing you were supported.

 ### Acceptance and Belonging: Unconditional Love
This is the fundamental need to be accepted for who they are, without conditions or judgement. Children need to know they are loved for their unique selves, not for what they do or achieve. Conditional love can create anxiety and a constant need for external validation. This is closely connected to **Nurturing** – the need for physical and emotional warmth, comfort, and care.

 ### Belonging: Connection and Community
A sense of belonging and feeling part of a "tribe" provides a crucial support network. Children need to feel connected to others in their family or community. When they feel like they belong, they are more likely to develop healthy social skills. This need also includes **Play and Spontaneity** – having the time and space to explore the world and learn through joy.

 ### Consistent Rules: Structure and Security
A stable and predictable environment is vital. Consistent rules and fair boundaries provide a framework for understanding expectations. This sense of structure fosters a feeling of security and helps a child learn self-discipline. Inconsistent or absent boundaries can create confusion and anxiety.

 ### Honesty and Trust: Building Reliable Relationships
The ability to be honest without fear of reprisal and to trust that caregivers will act in their best interests are cornerstones of healthy relationships. Children need to feel that they can trust the adults in their lives. Dishonesty and broken promises can damage a child's ability to form healthy relationships in the future.

Clear Communication: Avoiding Mixed Messages
Clear communication, free from mixed messages, ensures a child can understand and rely on the information they receive. Mixed messages can be confusing and create distrust. Open and honest communication helps children feel secure and understood.

 A Sense of Justice: Believing in Fairness
Finally, while the world is not always fair, a child needs to have a general sense that life is just. This allows them to develop a feeling of hope and belief in their ability to shape their own future. When children feel that the world is unpredictable and unfair, it can lead to feelings of helplessness and hopelessness.

 **IMPORTANT NOTE:** This isn't about placing blame or claiming your parents "messed up" your life. Instead, it's about seeing with clarity and a new perspective what might have been missing, so you can begin to fill that piece within your heart. This is the very core of your healing: going back to give your Inner Child all the things she missed out on.

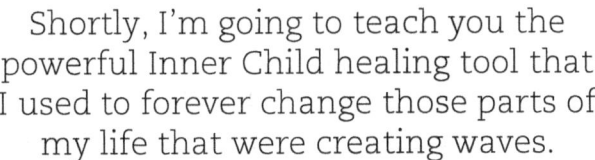

> Shortly, I'm going to teach you the powerful Inner Child healing tool that I used to forever change those parts of my life that were creating waves.

Connecting Through Storytelling

To really let this sink in, let's look at some specific examples of how these patterns play out in women's lives:

 The Silent House
In the house that Susan grew up in, her father's belief system and mantra was "we don't cry" if any issues or challenges arose. During difficult times, Susan's mother would say nothing, and she often withdrew. Susan learned

early on that sadness was weakness and that her needs were a burden. As an adult, she hides her true feelings behind a cheerful mask, avoiding deep connections. It feels easier to pretend. To cope with the emotional emptiness, Susan often binges on sweet things, like chocolate, at night. Then, when she drinks, the dam breaks, and she finds herself crying uncontrollably, releasing all the pain she's been holding in.

The Explosive Parent

Meet Michelle, living with a father whose temper could erupt at any moment. Michelle learned to suppress her own anger and walk on eggshells. As an adult, she struggles with expressing anger assertively, but when drinking, she finds herself mirroring her father's outbursts. She fears angry men, but she is attracted to them, entering relationships hoping to change the outcome. However, she will always be waiting for conflict and finds herself sabotaging the relationship, achieving that angry outburst she is so familiar with. It feels like home, yet she is still lonely in these moments. Desperately wanting to be loved.

The Absent Parent

Empathise with Emily, whose mother struggled with depression and openly expressed how much she hated her life and felt inadequate as a parent. Her mother was extremely thin and constantly worried about her weight. Emily quickly learned to be fiercely independent, often neglecting her own needs to avoid burdening her mother. She practically became the parent in the household. As an adult, Emily struggles with self-care and feels deep guilt whenever she considers asking for help. She's always the first to offer assistance to others, but never seeks it for herself. She also grapples with her weight, cycling through strict diets in an attempt to control her body image. When triggered, she experiences episodes of binge eating, followed by making herself sick. The shame surrounding her eating disorder keeps her from confiding in anyone.

The Critical Parent

Consider Diana, who had a mother who was always critical, always pushing for more. Diana learned to equate her worth with her achievements and developed a deep fear of failure. As an adult, she is a perfectionist, constantly striving for an unattainable ideal. She pushes herself hard at the gym and plays hard at night. She struggles with being able to trust in her relationship. Although she seeks validation from men, her romantic relationships are short-lived, as they seem one-dimensional, transactional, and based on superficial interests, which makes her feel lonely. So she drinks to numb this feeling of being alone, not good enough, and like no one really sees the true her.

These experiences of my clients reveal how our childhood experiences can shape the very fabric of our emotional world, leading to patterns of avoidance, suppression, and fear. That deep shame that comes from not having our emotional needs met creates a fundamental distrust – both of our own emotions and those of others. But please know, understanding these roots is a brave and crucial step towards healing and creating a new emotional landscape for yourself, one where you can feel safe, seen, and truly loved.

A question for you in the moment:

Can you relate to any of these stories? When you read them, do they spark a little pang of emotion deep within you? If so, that is telling you something. Whatever is coming up for you right now, I invite you to write in your journal. And then, read it aloud to yourself so you can hear the words. If it's too painful to read at a normal tone, whisper the words. Just allow your brain to hear what you're saying.

If this feels like a bit of a stretch right now, my friend, I get it. It may take time. I only hope you will come to understand that connecting these parts of yourself will play a significant role in the way you will learn to heal in the coming pages.

All of this is so you can shift your perspective,
get unstuck, and experience change
as something very real, very positive,
and very much within your reach.

A heads-up on the path to change

I'll be teaching you how to identify your triggers and the automatic behaviours they're connected to later in these pages. But first, let's set the scene, giving you the context you need to get a good handle on this. As I said before, to make lasting change, you need to first understand where you've come from, and then build the skills to move forward.

6.
My Trauma Experience

"Imagine What You Could Do If You Lost Weight!"
I Was Deeply Wounded by This Comment

During my adolescent years, my parents and I discovered that I was a naturally gifted athlete. I could run very fast, throw a javelin for miles, jump like I had springboards on my feet, and bring the team relay home ahead of the pack. I had this almost magical ability to get on the track, run 100 metres, and just … cream everybody else, even without training. Even as a "tubby" child, being fed restaurant food each night with no nutrition focus or portion control, happily devouring potato dauphinoise and rich flourless chocolate cake, I was an unstoppable bullet train. With long legs and a long stride, I was just super-fast.

As a young girl I competed in local and regional competitions. My father would watch most races. When I won, which I usually did, he would be standing right there at the finish line. But instead of a glowing "Well done!" or a proud hug, his first words were always, "Imagine what you could do if you lost weight, Little One!" (He called me "Little One" until the day he died in 2016.)

My father grew up with parents who believed children were trophies – they needed to look good, be the best, act the part, and yet be "seen but not heard". He spent his life trying to impress his parents, but recognition was scarce. His father would often dismiss his achievements, even when he excelled as a Victorian champion skier. "That would never be good enough for a gold medal. You're letting yourself down, son," my grandpa would say. My father played out the same attitude with his children. He projected his trauma onto us.

He wanted me to win. I know he did. But my gift – and winning itself – was always tainted by those diminishing, cold-hearted, cut-to-the-bone words, "Imagine what you could do if you lost weight." And then he'd simply walk off, leaving me shattered and humiliated. Perhaps it was his way of pushing me to improve, but did it make me better? No, of course not. It only pushed me off course for the next three decades.

After each race, I'd trail behind him like a baby gorilla, my shoulders slumped, my arms dangling, my hands dragging along the track, utterly ashamed. I didn't feel good enough for his praise – an utter failure because of my size (another gift from him, being complicit with the voluptuous eating regime in our household). Because he placed such a high value on winning and my weight, it created this horrible cycle of self-loathing and a "must try harder" narrative in my head. Winning became something I had to do, but it was never enough. It wasn't enough to gain his full acceptance. And as it would turn out, nobody else's either.

I was invited to join the experts at the Australian Institute of Sport to train and try out for the Olympic squad. I turned them down flat; it was a hard, immediate "no" from me. Deep down, I was terrified of the potential torment that lay ahead. I was petrified of being subjected to even more intense judgement and shame, convinced that I would never measure up. The thought of failing at that level, in such a public arena, was excruciatingly painful. But because we couldn't openly discuss these fears, a joke was born: "Fleur doesn't want to marry Boris the shot-putter!" It became the throw-away line and an easy dismissal, a way we as a family brushed aside the real reasons why I never pursued going for gold on the world stage.

So, to break down how this impacted me as an adult, well, it's quite a bit to unpack. "Love" being conditional, performance-based, and laced with shame left me with some pretty hefty and deep psychological scars. This conditional love made it more difficult for me to feel safe with men and to trust them on top of everything else I had been through. That also played out in my struggle to form healthy relationships. I was always fearing that others would also withhold their affection if I didn't meet their expectations. I would come to understand why intimacy felt like an unsafe place, as I subconsciously anticipated the same judgement and criticism I received from my father.

The constant refrain of "Imagine what you could do if you lost weight," coupled with the lack of genuine praise, ingrained in me a substantive sense of inadequacy. I learned that my worth was tied to my performance and appearance, not my intrinsic value. This bred a relentless inner critic, constantly whispering that I was not good enough, not thin enough, not worthy of love. This deep-seated belief that I was unworthy of love and success led to self-sabotaging behaviours. I would unconsciously undermine or downplay my achievements, reinforcing the negative narrative I had internalised.

I was a perfectionist, through and through. My dad's relentless pursuit of supremacy, stemming from his own unresolved issues, created an environment where anything less than the top spot was unacceptable. Striving to meet his expectations meant living in constant fear of failure and being unable to truly enjoy my accomplishments. The joy of winning was always overshadowed by the fear of not being good enough in the eyes of the people who I needed to encourage and support me. To validate me.

It fuelled this intense drive – this constant desire to win and be the best, no matter what. It resulted in me being chronically stuck in an unattractive cycle, always trying to be seen as someone with qualities of excellence and flawlessness.

Later in life, I wanted to know how people experienced me. That wasn't enjoyable feedback to get. I had to take it on the chin that I came across to my friends as competitive, fixated on overachieving, and a control freak. None of it was surprising with mature eyes, but you see, at the time, my disconnected mind didn't see this at all. My former self was just so desperate to be loved and accepted, never truly feeling enough or "winning" in her life at all. I was never "the best" in my sad inner world. I didn't feel accepted despite all the excruciating lengths I'd go to in an attempt to be. And all the while, I was constantly shaming my body, treating it with the disdain I felt for myself. (As you'll recall from my previous stories of suffering from bulimia, this was also going on at the time.)

The pet name "Little One", while seemingly affectionate, became a symbol of my infantilisation and lack of agency. It reinforced the power imbalance in our relationship and undermined my sense of autonomy. I was never recognised as the adult I was becoming. I was always stuck in the vivid imagery of the "Little One" – vulnerable, controllable, and weak.

I also blamed my failures on my body and my body image. Winning became a worthless endeavour because, in my mind, if I couldn't win with a "beautiful" body, there was no value in winning for its own sake. I wasn't worthy. It just didn't matter. Winning felt hollow. Athletics, which should have brought joy, tortured me with an intense self-hatred of my very beautiful gift. Later in life, this translated into beating myself up at the gym. I worked out obsessively five to seven days a week. I tried every crazy diet and took countless supplements. I pushed my body to extremes, with serious physical and mental health repercussions. This became my way of punishing my body and responding to the deep resentment I had towards it.

Walking on eggshells, constantly anticipating my father's disapproval, fostered chronic anxiety. I became hypervigilant, scanning for any sign of criticism, any indication that I had fallen short. I felt super sensitive and emotionally drained all the time. Growing up in an environment where my emotions were dismissed or invalidated, I learned to suppress my feelings and needs. This meant I struggled to connect to and express my emotions. This would present itself as a sense of numbness, followed by outbursts of anger, especially when I drank.

It's a lot to process, I know. It was hard to accept, I assure you. My father was passing on his trauma. The realisation that my father's behaviour stemmed from his own trauma doesn't excuse his actions, but it provides context. It highlights the cyclical nature of trauma and the importance of breaking these patterns. However, for the young girl I was, the damage was done. My sweet, naturally gifted former self was left to navigate the world with a fractured sense of identity, struggling to untangle her worth from her achievements.

I am proud, like I have said before, of who I am today. I protected these wounds and watched them gradually heal, which did take some time. My perfectionism can still flare up, yes, this is true, but it is a case of a quick chat with myself and prising the claws of control open again to simply ... let go.

The love that a young girl has for her father is symbiotic, and it's especially difficult to accept and make room for the thought that he inflicted these wounds on me, and still have a love for him that is timeless. He was someone who was supposed to love me unconditionally, just for who I was. Acceptance, here for me, meant agreeing with my former self that he did the best he could, with the best of his intentions at the time, within his capacity.

Today, I walk every day, twice a day, with my fur babies. My legs still have that urge to run, and the muscle memory is definitely there. My legs still have that fit, athletic look to them! I don't spend time wondering "what if" anymore; I see that as wasted energy. I can't change the past. I can only be present in this moment, and that's all there is. My weight is steady, and I move with it, and with my hormones. My diet is focused on healthy, organic food – about 70% vegetarian, and the rest of the time, I include higher iron and protein, adjusting based on where I am in my cycle. I eat balanced, non-processed foods, nothing in a packet, apart from rice and good Italian pasta, but mainly it's all pretty clean. And let me tell you, I still reckon I could win a 100-metre race without even trying!

> Loving your body is about being comfortable in your body, and only you get to set the parameters for doing that – and only you get to decide how you should feel at the finish line.

7. Reflection Time

Opening the Door
Let's Unlock Some Layers of Your Past

Okay, my friend, before we progress further into these pages, I'd love to guide you through a nice and easy "let's get to know myself again" exploration – what I always call peeling back the onion layers. I have put together ten questions to evoke some thoughts deep within.

From my own heart, I can tell you that stepping back into your past is like opening a treasure chest. Inside, you'll find precious, hidden, and insightful moments, and possibly some old, faded maps of experiences that might feel a little harder to look at. It takes such courage, I know, to embark on this journey, to softly trace the lines of your history and discover the moments that have woven together to create the beautiful, complex, and incredible person you are today, full of light and dark colours.

Think of these questions as a way to start a conversation with your younger self – a chance to truly understand her, to embrace her, and to find that deeper connection within yourself. Opening this door is like opening the channels of your

> **"Perhaps the most liberating moment in my life was when I realised that my self-loathing was not a product of my inadequacy but, rather, a product of my thoughts."**
> – Vironika Tugaleva

inner messaging centre. My deepest hope is that through this exploration, you'll find insights into some of the struggles you've carried, and that it will set you on a path to healing. By making friends with those parts of yourself that have felt hidden, suppressed, or maybe even a little too scary to get to know, you'll discover so much.

Remember, this is all for your benefit, so be curious, be honest, and have compassion. You are building a new perspective on your whole story. Trust what comes up.

Before you start, just pause for a moment. Take a deep, grounding breath, and settle into your heart space. Take out your favourite journal to write down your answers. And remember, read your answers aloud so you hear yourself speak the words and truly embrace what you're saying. Let your brain connect to what you are saying out loud.

> Remind yourself that there are absolutely no right or wrong answers here, so just take your time.

Let's Begin

1. When you close your eyes and picture your childhood home, what core needs may have felt just out of reach?

    Go beyond the surface of what happened and look at your past with a mature, adult perspective. Ask yourself what was missing, then wait and listen to what your heart tells you.

2. Is there a specific moment, a scene that plays out in your mind, where you first felt your emotions were brushed aside or told they were wrong? What happened, and how does it make your heart feel now, looking back with the clarity you have today?

3. What memories surface when you think about any difficult or challenging experiences you might have had as a child? These could include situations where you felt emotionally, physically, or even sexually unsafe, times you felt neglected, or things you witnessed that no child should ever see. As an adult, can you look at these events factually and see why they happened?

4. How do you believe those experiences have woven their way into the narratives that shape how you see the world and feel about things today? Think about how they might have shaped your beliefs about yourself, the people around you, and the way you react to situations now.

5. Part 1 – How do you usually cope when you feel triggered? Do you immediately want to suppress your feelings and distract yourself in any way possible? Be honest with yourself here, my friend.

    Part 2 – Think of a moment when you have been triggered. How does it feel in your body? Do your emotions start to swirl and escalate? What physical sensations arise? Do you have repetitive thoughts that start racing through your mind?

6. In what ways do you sense those childhood experiences are still influencing your relationships today, both with your partner and with the friends that are so dear to you?

7. How do you believe those early experiences have impacted your ability to open your heart to others, to trust them deeply, and to form the secure, loving connections we all crave?

8. Looking back with the clarity of time, what messages did you absorb about yourself and your value, based on how you were treated? What stories did you start to believe about yourself?

9. What emotions do you carry today that feel like they belong to a younger you? Can you connect these feelings to the roots of your past?

10. How would you describe your sense of self-worth and your ability to trust yourself? Do you often wrestle with self-doubt? How does that inner critic show up in your daily life, and how does it hold you back?

...

After the Reflection

After you have just completed that reflection, if you could reach back in time and offer your younger self the comfort and understanding she so desperately needed, what would you say to her?

The more you become aware of her – your former self – and what she went through, the more you can sit with her and give her what she needed back then. This is the important thing: the more you validate and accept her with loving kindness, the more barriers will quietly fall away, releasing you from what has been holding you back. This, my friend, is the "secret sauce" to truly healing those core wounds.

> **"Children don't get traumatised because of their hurt. They get traumatised because they are alone with their hurt."**
> – Dr. Gabor Maté

We'll revisit these messages to your younger self with exercises and skill-building to help you give all the love and support she needed then, in your current space. This is a huge and powerful part of healing the wild ways of emotional storms and triggers. I want you to get used to thinking like this now.

I am holding your hand.

8.
Your Core Wounds

Challenging Childhood Experiences
The Weight of Our Past Core Wounds

Good, you are still here. Good for you for bravely showing up to unpack the weight of the past. It can feel like such a heavy burden, can't it? And you are starting to see that the past truly shapes you, moulds you, and sometimes leaves wounds that, even though time passes, still linger deep within? Now we are going to take another step back, to help give context to where this dilemma of disconnecting from your emotions may also come from.

We have talked about your basic needs not being met. Well, now it is time to look at some of these challenging childhood experiences in a different way. These can be described as an "Adverse Childhood Experience", or "ACE". They're all happening in the home, within the family environment, some subtle, but most of them – like invisible scars – carried into adult life. Silent burdens that remind us of the traumas of childhood and, in ways we don't always realise, influence our relationships, our health, and our precious sense of self.

In the 1990s, pioneering doctors in the United States began to connect the dots, unveiling a truth that many of us had felt intuitively but couldn't quite articulate: our childhoods leave indelible imprints on our adult selves, shaping not just our emotional landscapes but our very physical wellbeing. Dr. Vincent Felitti and Dr. Robert Anda conducted the groundbreaking

Adverse Childhood Experiences Study (ACE Study) at Kaiser Permanente in San Diego, California. This landmark study, involving over 17,000 participants, revealed a strong correlation between childhood trauma and various health and social problems in adulthood. The ACE Study's findings have had an insightful impact on our understanding of how childhood adversity affects us on a long-term trajectory.

ACE – those three little letters, hold a thought-provoking weight, encapsulating a deep understanding of the human experience. It's like discovering a hidden map, one that finally explains so many of the winding, confusing paths we've been walking.

Think of a child's brain as a delicate garden needing nurturing to flourish. Adverse Childhood Experiences, like constant stress, fear, and uncertainty, act like a relentless storm, damaging that garden. The constant flood of stress hormones, particularly cortisol, disrupts the development of crucial brain regions like the prefrontal cortex (responsible for decision-making and emotional regulation) and the hippocampus (involved in memory and learning). This leads to difficulties with focus, impulse control, and emotional stability.

Simultaneously, this hormonal chaos throws the immune system off balance. The body is constantly primed for "fight or flight", diverting resources away from normal functions. This can lead to chronic inflammation, making a child more susceptible to illnesses. Essentially, the child's body is stuck in survival mode, prioritising immediate defence over long-term development. This early disruption leaves a lasting imprint, making the child more vulnerable to physical and mental health issues as an adult. The ACEs don't just disappear; they become embedded in the very fabric of the child's being, shaping their biology and impacting their health for a lifetime.

Here are the three pillars of how Adverse Childhood Experiences can present in the family of origin:

 **Abuse**

- Physical (being punched, pinched, hair pulled, belongings damaged)

- Emotional (constant criticism, gaslighting, humiliation)
- Sexual (the violation, stolen innocence, lack of safety)

Neglect

- Physical (lack of nutrition, adequate clothing, toys)
- Emotional (persistent failure of a parent to validate or respond)

Household Dysfunction

- Parental Mental Illness (the unpredictable moods, the fear)
- Parental Substance Abuse (the broken promises, the chaos)
- Parental Incarceration (the separation, the stigma)
- Parental Separation or Divorce (the shattering of the family unit and your safe space)
- Domestic Violence (witnessing the violence, the fear)

Here's where the hope comes in

Simply becoming aware is another step towards healing these core wounds. When we understand that our struggles – whether with addiction, anxiety, or physical ailments – might be rooted in unresolved childhood trauma, it can be incredibly freeing. Almost a sense of relief washes over you because you understand where it comes from. And now you know you can do something about it, with the right support.

Remember, this isn't about placing blame or getting lost in the past; it's about acknowledging the impact of those experiences and taking steps to rewrite our own stories.

The Ten Categories of ACEs

To unpack this on a deeper level, let's explore the detailed explanation of the ten categories of ACEs, each a unique form of trauma with its own devastating consequences. To calculate your ACE score, you simply add up how many of these exposures you have experienced.

1. **Physical Abuse:** the sting of a belt, the sharp pain of a slap, the terror of being physically overpowered. These are the wounds that leave visible marks, but also invisible scars that can linger for a lifetime.

2. **Emotional Abuse:** the constant barrage of criticism, the humiliation, the manipulation, the gaslighting. These are the wounds that erode a child's sense of self-worth, leaving them feeling unlovable and unworthy.

3. **Sexual Abuse:** the violation of innocence, the betrayal of trust, the theft of safety. These are the wounds that shatter a child's sense of security, leaving them feeling ashamed, guilty, and deeply alone.

4. **Physical Neglect:** the gnawing hunger, the shivering cold, the lack of basic care. These are the wounds that leave a child feeling abandoned and unloved, their basic needs unmet, their cries for help unheard.

5. **Emotional Neglect:** the absence of warmth, the lack of affection, the feeling of being invisible. These are the wounds that create a void in a child's heart, leaving them longing for connection, for validation, for love that never comes.

6. **Parental Mental Illness:** the unpredictable moods, the erratic behaviours, the fear of what might happen next. These are the wounds that leave a child feeling unsafe, insecure, and responsible for their parent's wellbeing.

7. **Parental Substance Abuse:** the broken promises, the neglect, the chaos, the shame. These are the wounds that leave a child feeling abandoned, betrayed, and responsible for their parent's addiction.

8. **Parental Incarceration:** the separation, the stigma, the loss of a parent, the disruption of family life. These are the wounds that leave a child feeling confused, ashamed, and abandoned by the very system that should protect them.

9. **Parental Separation or Divorce:** the shattering of the family unit, the conflict, the loss of security. These are the wounds that leave a child feeling insecure, abandoned, and responsible for their parents' unhappiness.

10. **Domestic Violence:** witnessing the violence, the fear, the helplessness. These are the wounds that shatter a child's sense of safety, leaving them feeling vulnerable and traumatised.

Each ACE, like a brick in a wall, contributes to the construction of a barrier between the child and a healthy, fulfilling life. The higher the ACE score, the greater the risk of developing physical and mental health problems, including:

- **Chronic Diseases:** heart disease, stroke, cancer, diabetes, auto-immune disorders.

- **Mental Health Challenges:** depression, anxiety, PTSD, addiction, eating disorders.

- **Relationship Difficulties:** intimacy issues, trust issues, co-dependency, domestic violence.

- **Behavioural Problems:** mood swings, inability to emotionally regulate, aggression, impulsivity, self-harm, suicidal ideation.

What was your score out of ten?

An Example of Alcohol Issues at Home

If you grew up with a parent struggling with alcoholism, you may find yourself being a chronic people-pleaser, hypervigilant, or even struggling with your own relationship with alcohol. You might try to numb the pain or find some sense of control. Or, if you don't have a problem with drinking, I'd say hands down you have a vulnerability with control. It's as if the fear of losing control, and experiencing the anxiety that lives beneath it, is terrifying to you subconsciously. But by recognising the connection between your ACE score and your behaviour, you can start to address what's really going on.

This is where you can now decide to seek the right support to specifically work through your past experiences, take committed action to form new narratives in your belief system, and learn healthier ways to cope. You can learn to manage your emotions, set healthy boundaries, and practise self-compassion. Or imagine someone who has experienced emotional neglect. They might find it hard to trust or connect with others and may struggle with intimacy. But by understanding how their early experiences affected them, they can start to heal those deep attachment wounds. They can learn to build healthy relationships, express their needs, and embrace their vulnerability.

> **Okay, I know this is a lot to process.**
> I get that. But, truly, my friend, there is hope. Awareness is another step towards healing. By understanding the impact of ACEs, you can begin to address the root causes of your struggles and create a path towards a healthier, more fulfilling life. You can learn to regulate your emotions, to heal your relationships, to cultivate self-compassion, and to build resilience in the face of adversity. You can break the cycle of trauma and create a brighter future for yourself, for your Future Self, and for generations to come.

It's about making new choices, creating new connections in your brain (new neural pathways). It's about learning to comfort that Inner Child, to offer the love and validation she didn't receive. It's about taking care of yourself with healthy habits – mindful eating, exercise, good sleep – to support your body's healing. And sometimes it's about allowing yourself to feel the pain, to acknowledge the wounds, permit yourself to grieve.

> "When you connect to the silence within you, that is when you can make sense of the disturbance going on around you."
> – Stephen Richards

I will say this over and over: this Change Experience journey is not a quick fix. There will be challenges, moments of doubt, times when old patterns try to creep back in. But with awareness, with compassion, with a willingness to heal, you can rewrite your story and reclaim your life. You can transform the pain of the past into the strength of the present, and build a future filled with hope, resilience, and doors wide open for you to experience what being happy means from within.

If you would like to know my ACE score,
I am sharing this with you, and more,
after these real life client stories.

Real-Life Stories

Sarah's Story: living through parental neglect, a child unseen

Sarah's story powerfully illustrates how our childhood's emotional landscape shapes our adult lives. Growing up in a home thick with the tension of her parents' endless arguments, they were too consumed by their own dramas to truly see what Sarah needed. Consequently, she suffered immense invalidation and emotional neglect, learning to become invisible. In that house, crying was a weakness, emotions were forbidden, and she was left to cope entirely by herself. She never felt accepted by her parents and carried a deep, painful scar of being unlovable. This imprinting left her with an overwhelming fear of being accepted and seen, and a core belief that she was fundamentally flawed – that she would never be good enough.

As an adult, this unspoken conditioning led her to replay the very patterns she had tried so desperately to escape. She found herself drawn to emotionally distant partners, like Mark, who travelled constantly, was perpetually glued to his phone when they were together and seemed to want little more than a girlfriend for sex. He was carelessly inattentive, and when she dared to address it, he was aloof, never validating her needs – an all-too-familiar reiteration of her childhood. When disagreements arose, she would back down, shouldering the blame for his emotional unavailability, her deep-seated anxiety manifesting as a familiar knot in her stomach.

These unresolved childhood wounds spiralled into a messy cycle of destructive and unhealthy coping mechanisms. In moments of crushing loneliness within the relationship, she'd find herself at the fridge, seeking the numbing comfort of processed foods – sour cream and chive crisps, chocolate biscuits, salted caramel fudge, and tubs of spearmint choc-chip ice cream. She was trapped, dependent on fleeting quick-fix relief, followed by deeply paralysing guilt, shame, and self-loathing – a grim, self-fulfilling prophecy of unworthiness. She stayed with him, miserable, feeling second-best to his iPhone, utterly unaware that the chaos she lived within was rooted in her past.

The change began when Sarah came to me, willing to look within and connect her current struggles to her childhood experiences. Gosh, she was brave. We worked on building a new perspective: that her behaviours weren't a sign of weakness but a vital link to her past – the very place where transformation and change could begin. From this point, she started to dismantle her old narratives and create new ones. None of this was easy; she had to find the courage to challenge her negative self-talk and set boundaries, which ultimately led to the end of her relationship with Mark. This was a terrifying decision – she was petrified of being alone for the rest of her life – but she persevered, proving to herself that she deserved more than the reality she was living. She began to find peace in taking walks in nature and discovered new ways to find balance when she felt triggered. Her new, meaningful connections with people who truly accepted her became her motivation to continue. She is still working on herself. She is single, yes, but a much happier lady. These days, also far choosier about who she spends her time with, and consciously committed to not inviting another unavailable man into her life again. She's taken on my mantra, happily telling herself, "Every day is a school day."

Veronica's Story: From Invisible Girl to Resilent Woman
Veronica's childhood was a brutal education in psychological manipulation. Her mother, a fiercely competitive woman, constantly measured Veronica against herself, gaslighting her with jabs like, "That dress looks better on me," or "I got a higher score than you in my day." Meanwhile, her father made Veronica the family scapegoat, blaming her for every issue between her and her sisters, instilling a deep belief that she was fundamentally a problem child. In reality, that was far from the truth. Her older sisters got away with causing havoc, giving her no privacy, playing mean tricks on her and breaking her toys, yet Veronica was left holding the blame. These experiences with her family, in their unhealed ways, left Veronica with a silent, rather grisly wound of unworthiness and a crippling need for external validation.

As an adult, this legacy of trauma manifested as an all-consuming fear of abandonment and not measuring up. Veronica completely gave away her power to her partner, Damien, a controlling and manipulative man. She had no boundaries and couldn't make a decision without his approval, even asking permission to see her friends.

Her insecurity led to an unhealthy obsession with her body. She punished herself at the gym, meticulously counted calories, and restricted food, terrified Damien would reject her if she gained weight. In fact, she was very skinny and bony, looked withdrawn, and her skin lacked any glow. She lived with immense anxiety, second-guessing every thought and action. To cope, she'd binge-drink on weekends, trying to keep up with Damien and his friends, only to wake up the next morning and sob silently in the shower while he watched football, none the wiser. Professionally, this need for acceptance fuelled extreme perfectionism, causing her to work long hours to be the best in her field – a pattern of over-giving that often left her sick and unable to work. She was trapped in a cycle of extreme highs and brutal lows.

The turning point came when Veronica hit rock bottom, a brutal hangover sparking the stark realisation: "This has to stop." Her best friend, who understood her struggles, referred her to me. Veronica bravely confronted her past, the confusion of being a victim of gaslighting and emotional abuse. She wanted to change her dependence on alcohol and the meaning she had given it in her life – a place where she didn't have to be responsible for who she had become. She came to accept all of this came from her deep-seated fear of not feeling good enough – feelings she was trying to outrun.

Veronica came to terms with a new understanding of what alcohol was doing and why it was holding her back. She was afraid and felt ashamed that she was an alcoholic, but she came to appreciate that this wasn't accurate. Yes, she had used alcohol to avoid what she needed to deal with, but soon we changed that narrative. Her problem wasn't with alcohol itself; it was a tool of distraction she used to numb a part of herself that she was struggling to heal.

The process of moving forward wasn't always easy; there were setbacks. Veronica found herself triggered and turning to the bottle a few times, feeling lost and not staying on course. She learnt to identify and challenge the negative beliefs of her Inner Child, seeing what her triggers were, and acknowledging these behaviours were in fact a message from her past. This is where the penny dropped. This newfound empowerment allowed her to put her needs first, ending her relationship with Damien – a truly liberating decision for Veronica.

She was, rather admirably, a very determined lady after this. Wanting to build skills to keep her ship steady she became committed to introducing grounding techniques, and setting daily intentions, which made a vast improvement in her world. The focus, especially, was on her new values, which brought balance through new choices. Looking for ways to experience parts of herself she had also denied, she joined an art group and found herself forming meaningful new connections. She nourished her body as an act of self-love, not punishment. Finally, Veronica was seeing the path of what it meant to be transforming into a new woman.

Veronica's still on her journey, but she's no longer defined by needing other people's acceptance or for someone to make decisions for her. That took a lot of work, but she's proud to say she knows how to set a boundary now. She's learning to love herself, embracing her resilience, and choosing her health first. She has gained some weight, is happier in her own skin, and is loving the new apartment she's just moved into.

Maya's Story: Reclaiming a Life Stolen

Maya's world imploded when she was sexually assaulted by her boyfriend's best friend. The violation was earth-shattering and extremely isolating. An even deeper cut, though, came from her parents. Seeking a safe place to support her grief, and paralysed by fear of telling her boyfriend, she experienced another level of ghastly emotional turmoil. Their chilling question, "Did you lead him on?" and their outright dismissal of her pain, was a second, nasty betrayal.

With no one to believe in her, this invalidation led to a shame narrative that went beyond the assault itself. Left alone, she festered in a belief that she could not trust her own judgement, feeling as if what happened was all her own fault. She carried this secret, almost like a punishment. In its wake, she began sabotaging her relationships with her partner and severing ties with any meaningful connection she had, especially anyone of the opposite sex. The invisible weight of trauma haunted her for decades.

This trauma and the crushing lack of validation manifested brutally. Post-traumatic stress disorder became a constant companion, ambushing her with flashbacks and night terrors, after which she would lose herself for days. Depression cast a long shadow, while a constant knot of anxiety twisted in her stomach. Physical symptoms emerged too: chronic headaches, a perpetually unsettled digestive system, and autoimmune issues – all born from relentless stress. Her ingrained belief of being flawed led to an all-consuming fear of intimacy, pushing her either to avoid relationships entirely or to gravitate towards emotionally abusive men who confirmed her deepest fears.

Food and alcohol became her desperate crutches. She cycled through destructive eating patterns, from ordering huge amounts of takeaway food to extreme restriction and calorie counting – a form of self-punishment – to wild binges and purging, a disturbing re-enactment of feeling overwhelmed and out of control. Alcohol offered a blurry escape from memories. She drank daily, feeling fleeting moments of happiness, thinking she was doing okay, only to deepen the spiral of shame and guilt the next day, hating what she saw in the mirror.

For Maya, healing was a long, emotional battle. We worked on Inner Child practices, beginning the painful process of rebuilding self-trust and finding acceptance for what had happened. She also found a lifeline in EMDR therapy (Eye Movement Desensitisation and Reprocessing), gradually lessening the power of her traumatic memories. It was a subtle and slow process: learning to set boundaries, express her needs, and employ self-compassion when she wasn't very kind to herself. Releasing the stronghold guilt and shame had on her was incredibly difficult.

It took Maya a while to fully believe in the Inner Child work and become her own empathetic witness. But going back, reframing those past struggles, and practising this at home was when things really started to shift.

Gradually, Maya released toxic relationships and began forging new, healthy connections built on trust and respect. This took time, of course, but she found the initial pain and fear of loneliness were entirely worth it for the fulfilling way she now experiences people. The journey was far from linear, with setbacks threatening to pull her back into old patterns. Yet, Maya's spirit proved resilient. She is now a woman fiercely reclaiming her power, her voice, and her body, learning to love herself and to trust again, which she does not take for granted.

She tells me it feels like her life has begun again. With a new sense of gratitude, she has come to the realisation that finding joy is her priority after all the pain she suffered a life tragically stolen, now being reclaimed.

> These are my clients stories, shared to help you appreciate how the roots of our past can unexpectedly shape our adult lives in ways we never saw coming.

9. My Trauma Experience

My ACE Score
The Big Realisation

My ACE score is a nine out of ten. That's ... a lot. I experienced the whole gamut, except for incarceration, although Mum often threatened to put Dad in jail. I had a rough upbringing, and looking back now, so much makes sense. The source of all my health problems finally started to click, and I realised I could approach them differently – I could do something about them.

From my teenage years right through to my late forties, I was constantly getting sick. I didn't know why. I genuinely thought I was reasonably healthy, but deep down, I knew I was different from everyone else. I struggled with impulse control. My anxiety was always at a much higher rate and level than most people, and I've always been acutely sensitive. I battled with depression and had suicidal thoughts on three significant occasions. Gosh, that was such a dark, lonely place to be.

Now, at this stage of my life, I have a significantly compromised immune system and deal with a lot of related health issues. To be honest with you, finding out about the ACE score was a huge relief. I could finally see why all these things were happening to me, because none of the medical professionals I went to could ever explain it. Now, I can appreciate the roots of where my vulnerabilities have come from.

In August 2020, I had a total left hip replacement, all thanks to a family argument that left me with a fractured hip and femur. In my recovery, literally out of the blue, I developed severe allergies with anaphylaxis repercussions when triggered. My tongue would swell up like a piece of meat in my mouth, and my throat would suddenly become extremely constricted, making it hard to breathe. I asked so many doctors why this was happening, but I never got any real, satisfactory answers. I often felt invalidated, like I was making it up. There were no answers that made sense, and I just had to carry my EpiPen's and antihistamine tablets everywhere and learn to cope. My world, naturally, became very small.

Friends started to tell me, "It's all in your head," suggesting I needed mental health help. How could my tongue swelling to the size of a 400-gram ribeye steak be in my head? I can assure you, when the size of your tongue and a single swallow makes it feel like two people have their hands around your throat, choking you … that's not just your mind playing tricks on you. This, my friend, is very real.

Suddenly, so many things that had never affected me before were now causing reactions, and I was in and out of the hospital every four weeks with another choking attack. It was incredibly frightening; I felt like I didn't know who I was anymore. After a battery of tests, I received another diagnosis: C1 esterase inhibitor deficiency. Essentially, I'm missing a protein in my blood that would prevent my throat and tongue from swelling uncontrollably when triggered. The triggers were many and felt like they were everywhere: nuts, sulphites, preservatives, cut grass, spider bites, shellfish, dairy, and guess what? Emotional stress.

I kept asking health professionals, "Why is this happening to me now?" None of them could tell me anything other than my immune system was severely compromised and that I'd probably had this condition since I was little. Oh, yeah, and don't forget that it's life threatening if not treated quickly and appropriately. So much fear was projected onto me, being reminded that if I didn't take this seriously, my airways could close within minutes, and I could die. "These things can spontaneously happen to people," I was told. Good grief, I lived in fear for a long time.

I was not going to just accept the "we-don't-know-syndrome" and miserable diagnosis. This answer was not enough for me – not even close.

It felt lacking and incomplete, and I knew there was more to the story. So, you can imagine that when I was finally told that my ACE score directly correlated with everything I was experiencing, it was a massive weight off my shoulders. I wasn't crazy, and none of this was in my head! It was such a validation. Knowing what and where all this came from, I could finally start to accept these conditions. Taking the mystery away and replacing it with knowledge helped me to make peace with it all.

Thinking about all the things the ACE score represents – the brain not developing properly, the immune system being compromised, the hormonal systems being out of whack – it was like a lifeline to find my new normal. "Ding, ding, ding! That's me. That's me to a tee." Okay, fine. These are the cards I've been dealt. Let's find a way to manage this effectively so I can have some freedom.

I've now set myself up to be very conscious of my health, to be acutely aware of all the things I'm at risk for. My heart rate used to start to skyrocket during an anxiety attack, but now I know how to tame that wild beast and bring it back down again with my grounding techniques. The days of constant EpiPen's, repetitive hospital trips, and all that stress have been massively reduced. In fact, I haven't had a hospital visit for an episode in nearly three years now. I can manage it so much better.

You know what? Even though I am the "compromised one," I know, deep in my heart, that I don't have a mental illness. I am not imagining things. Even though some of my old friends still treat me like I'm a weak, delicate person, I now live very peacefully with this condition. I have my injections (three of them), but because I know how to avoid situations that cause an immune stress response, I haven't had to use those injections at all. Each year, I gratefully call my doctor for a repeat prescription because the medicine has expired. I'm in control of this thing I have, and it's not in control of me.

Accepting all of this doesn't make what happened okay; there is no justification for what happened to me growing up, or how it happened. No, never. But it means I now know what I'm dealing with. I understand how to manage it. I've built a life that's gentler and more mindful, where I take all the necessary precautions to look after my health.

What about the claims of chronic health risks? I don't want to die of a heart attack. I don't want to get lung cancer. And I certainly never, ever want to feel like I want to end my life again. They say my life expectancy might be twenty years shorter than most people's. Okay, so be it. But I now question if even that is the case for me, because I have changed my life in such dramatic, peaceful, and joyful ways. Perhaps this time bomb is no longer ticking. Regardless, I intend to have a wonderful life. Even if it may be shorter than average, I know it will be filled with all the beautiful things I do have. When my time is up, it's up. But, goddammit, I'm going to be healthy. I'm going to take care of this body, this beautiful body that I have. I'm going to be on top of this, in control, rather than letting it push me around.

I give myself a hug all the time. Every night, in fact, before I go to sleep. We all need to be compassionate with ourselves when we get triggered. I wrap my arms around my chest and squeeze my shoulders. The brain doesn't know whether it's me or someone else; it just knows that my body is experiencing the warm embrace of someone who loves me. My reward is the lovely pleasure and happy hormones the brain releases because this is a feel-good, body-to-mind reaction.

As I said, some old friends have created a narrative that I must still be suffering, which I leave with them. Because for me, it is not true. I love the lane I am now living in. It works for me. I am living in my bliss, living and acting in ways that have purpose, and I know that purpose is to help others have a better human experience – and that's what I'm focused on.

I truly feel privileged to be able to share my own story with you.

> I stand here, a living testament to the power of understanding who I am, who I was, and how all of that has led me here. It's enabled me to share and create this Change Experience journey with you openly, without shame and with all my heart.

10. Reflection Time

Connecting to Your Past
Then Looking at Your Present Emotional Landscape

For this next section, please take yourself to a place you feel is your true safe haven. Imagine creating a "safe space" within yourself for your Inner Child. I want you to think about what this space looks and feels like? A space to pour out your thoughts, your feelings, and those sparks of memories that flicker within you. It's a moment just for you, a chance to reflect on the world that's passed, to digest its experiences, to process what stirred within you, and to gently acknowledge what has happened in your past.

These words you write in response to each question – they're precious, a link to your emotional freedom, a valuable gift to the woman you are today and to your Future Self! I encourage you to read your answers aloud, as always. Let your own voice resonate with you, so you truly hear and believe the inner messages that come out to see the light.

With full disclosure, some of these questions might feel a bit confronting, maybe even a little challenging. Read them through now and see how it feels. You can always come back to them later, and that's perfectly alright.

> **"The wound is the place where the Light enters you."**
> – Rumi

These are invitations, not demands, and you can explore them fully when you feel ready. Know that as you engage with these reflections, you're carefully guiding your brain to connect with the deeper layers of your subconscious, those parts of you that are always there, even if they're not always at the forefront of your mind.

SO, THE MESSAGE HERE IS THIS: my friend, please be kind to yourself. Take a pause whenever you need and take all the time you need.

This is about creating a beautifully open connection with your Inner Child and former self, so you can consciously and lovingly make choices that truly honour your Future Self.

Let's Begin

1. **Unspoken Emotional Language:** Reflecting on your childhood home, what was the unspoken language of emotions? What were the implicit or explicit rules about expressing feelings? How might these early lessons still influence how you express emotions today?

   NOTE: If you have trouble expressing your feelings here, there's a **Feelings Wheel** in the Appendix to help you articulate what might be locked away.

2. **Meeting Your Needs:** Consider your basic needs (safety, security, love, belonging, autonomy, etc.) during your childhood. Which needs felt consistently met, and which felt neglected? How has this impacted your sense of self and your ability to form healthy relationships in your present?

3. **Inconvenient Emotions:** Were there times in your childhood when expressing your feelings felt like a burden to those around you? How did this experience shape your understanding of the validity of your emotions?

4. **Parental Influences:** Imagine your parents carrying their own unhealed stories. How might their past experiences have influenced how they responded to your emotions? Can you find any compassion for their journey, and for your own, within this context?

5. **Childhood Rules About Emotions:** What were some of the "rules" in your childhood home regarding emotions? Were certain feelings deemed unacceptable or inappropriate? How might these rules still be operating in your life today?

6. **Adverse Childhood Experiences (ACEs):** Reflect on any Adverse Childhood Experiences you may have experienced. How did these experiences impact your sense of safety and security?

How do you see the echoes of these experiences in your current emotional reactions?

7. **Safe and Unsafe Figures:** Think about the adults in your life during your childhood. Who were the safe figures, and who triggered feelings of insecurity or fear? How have these relationships shaped your trust in others and yourself?

8. **Emotional Neglect:** Were there times when your emotions were simply ignored or dismissed? How did this impact your ability to recognise and trust your own feelings?

9. **Messages About Your Worth:** Reflect on the messages you received about your worth and value as a young girl. Were these messages consistent and affirming, or were they conditional? How do these messages influence your self-esteem today?

10. **Coping Mechanisms:** Think about the ways you learned to cope with difficult emotions as a child. Did you develop healthy coping mechanisms, or did you resort to avoidance, suppression, or other patterns? How do these patterns manifest in your life now?

...

After the Reflection

You know, life is a series of chapters in itself, really, isn't it? We've all experienced cycles of change, times of loss and times of gain, and those moments when we realise things weren't quite as we once thought. These are the seasons that have shaped us into who we are today.

So, as *you* journey deeper into self-awareness, it becomes so important to embrace every part of your story, including your upbringing and family of origin. I know this isn't always easy. Believe me, I truly understand that. It can bring up a lot.

In this process, you might find yourself wanting to push away certain truths or signals from your past. And that's okay; it's natural. But I warmly encourage you to sit with those feelings for a while. When we deny our true emotions, it can lead to automatic reactions and a sense of disharmony within ourselves, both in our minds and bodies. It can hold us back, suppress our needs, and dim our desires.

I am still here ... holding your hand.

11.
The Empathetic Witness

The Person Who Validates Your Pain
Becoming Your Own Source of Affirmation and Healing

Okay, now I want to help you understand where the fear of facing your emotions can come from. This is about the significance of what's known as the "empathetic witness" or, more often, the deeply felt, crushing absence of one. This is intrinsically linked to, and lies at the root of, the trauma stories we created when we experienced our painful encounter(s). These are the narratives that we carry with us and that shape our adult lives.

To put it simply, when you experienced something traumatic (when you felt vulnerable, unsafe, or under threat) – something that is still subconsciously impacting you now – that supportive person wasn't there. There was no one within your reach to comfort you and give you a feeling of being safe, validated or seen. You felt alone. The empathetic witness didn't exist.

An empathetic witness is that person we needed when we were having that struggle, that trauma, that horrible experience that made us want to shrivel up inside. The one that made us so fearful, we had to retract or retreat into a place that only we could get to. Imagine if someone were there, validating you and saying, "It's okay. I've got you. I'm going to hold your hand." What if they embraced you in a big hug, assuring you, "You're going to be all right. You're going to get through this." How do

> "The 'empathetic witness' is not necessarily somebody who can change the child's situation but who can mirror, validate, and accept that child's feelings and emotions. That's how you protect people."
>
> – Alice Miller

you think things would have turned out for you? Do you think your life would have had a different outcome?

Imagine a child, small and vulnerable, facing a terrifying experience. A loud argument between parents, a harsh word, a physical blow, a moment of utter helplessness. In that moment, what they desperately need is an empathetic witness. Someone to say, "I see you. I hear you. You're safe. It's okay to feel this way." Someone to hold their hand, to offer a warm embrace, to whisper, "You're going to be all right."

But what happens when that witness is absent? What happens when that child is left alone, their cries unheard, their fear dismissed? They recoil, retreating to a place where no one can reach them. They internalise the shame, the blame, the unbearable weight of their experience.

Let's be honest. We all yearn for a life bathed in love and compassion, a life of peace and balance. Yet, to be fair, we all carry within us the echoes of grief, rage, and loss – the swirling aftermath of our trauma, no matter how big or small we feel it is. But as we've tenderly explored before, trauma isn't merely the event(s) themselves; it's the internal narrative, the fear-based landscape created in our minds because we faced that event alone, without an empathetic witness. Without soothing, supporting words of safety or validation.

Now, let's imagine a different scenario. What if, in those moments of terror, a child had someone to hold them? "I'm here. You're not alone." What if they felt afraid, but were immediately assured they were safe, loved, and supported? That child would learn that their feelings are valid, that they are worthy of love and protection. They would develop a sense of safety and security, a foundation for healthy relationships. As an adult, they would be more emotionally balanced, more resilient, and more capable of handling life's challenges.

The good news – because I like a bit of good news – is that we absolutely can learn how to become our own empathetic witness in adulthood.

We can go back and nurture that child, connect and have a dialogue with that child from the viewpoint of the woman we are today, or even with the voice of our Future Self. We can nurture that little girl who was left alone and experienced that horrible, horrible thing. We can use our own words to soothe ourselves.

> "You yourself, as much as anybody in the entire universe, deserve your love and affection."
> – Buddha

This is the power of self-soothing, the transformative act of becoming the empathetic witness we never had. When we offer ourselves compassion, when we validate our own experiences, the trauma begins to dissipate. The weight lifts, the fear subsides, and we reclaim our inner peace.

> So, my friend, get ready; this is what I will teach you how to do. You can transform how this trauma sits inside of you.

The False Self

Without an empathetic witness, can you start to see how the trauma narrative explodes in your mind? The fear, the hurt, the anger, the invalidation … the list goes on and turns into something very damaging. At this stage of life, in the early developmental stages of your brain, the pain can be just too much to cope with. Your brain can't organise these thoughts into rational ones; it's not developed enough to do that. Your delicate psyche shuts down in the process, and the mind creates a "false self", a new persona to hide behind, to mask the pain and suffering you feel.

The trauma narrative becomes suppressed, constricted. It's a fierce protection response to the absence of soothing, loving support and validation. All tucked away behind a shiny, adaptive, impenetrable mask. And sometimes, not even the person wearing the mask knows she's wearing one.

My friend, do you wear a mask in the outside world? It is okay if you are.

However this has played out for you, I want you to know you have the power to rewrite your story. You can become the empathetic witness you always needed. You can offer yourself the love and validation that will heal your deepest wounds.

> You can, through your own compassion and love, make a difference.

12.
The Adult Experiences

Commonly Unrecognised and Unmeasured Experiences
The Lasting Impact of an Absent Empathetic Witness

My friend, I want to talk to you more about the lasting psychological impact of not having someone there to validate your pain. Perhaps you've never thought about it in this way, but the absence of an empathetic witness during a moment of terror or overwhelm can create a narrative that shapes your entire adult life.

Imagine you were a little girl, say, ten years old. You might have seen your mum being hit by your dad. Perhaps you were the one being screamed at or hit, neglected, or maybe you were violated. Whatever the event, it left you terrified and alone. When you looked for comfort, for someone to say, "I see you, this is not okay," there was nobody there. Instead, you were told to "stop being dramatic," that it was "none of your business," or that you were simply "making it up." Anything but words of support.

That single experience, that moment of invalidated terror, can manifest in your adult life in several common and painful ways. Here are some psychological manifestations for you to appreciate.

Crippling Anxiety and Hypervigilance

As an adult, you might always be on edge, waiting for something bad to happen. Every loud noise makes you jump, and it feels impossible to relax. This constant hypervigilance is a direct result of the initial shock and vunerability you felt in what should have been a "safe place." A feeling that was dismissed as "dramatic" or "unimportant." Your nervous system, stuck on high alert, continues to believe that danger is just around the corner, leaving you feeling exhausted and anxious.

Intense Distrust of Self and Others

When your truth was denied, it shattered your ability to trust. You may have developed a deep fear of intimacy, keeping people at a distance before they can get close enough to hurt you. You might also struggle to trust your own feelings and instincts, leading you to feel disconnected and helpless, as if you have no control over your own life. This comes from that painful moment when you were told that your emotions weren't real.

Internalised Shame and Self-Blame

You may carry a heavy weight of guilt and shame, believing that what happened was somehow your fault. This narrative of self-blame is a direct link to the messages you received as a child. You may have learnt to hide your feelings, believing they were a burden to others, and that it was your fault you were feeling this way. That toxic shame can become a constant companion, silently criticising you for simply being you.

Emotional Dysregulation and Numbing

Because you lacked someone to validate your feelings and create safety in moments of vulnerability, your emotions can feel too big and scary to handle in your adult life. Because you weren't given the tools to process them, you might either have sudden, explosive outbursts of anger or of sadness, or you might completely shut down, feeling numb and disconnected from your life. This is a common survival mechanism. When your emotions were a source of pain and invalidation, the easiest way to cope was to turn them off entirely, leaving you feeling disconnected from yourself.

Severe Difficulty Advocating for Yourself

When your voice was silenced and your fear was dismissed, you learned a very painful lesson: your needs don't matter. As an adult, you may find it incredibly challenging to speak up for yourself. You might avoid conflict, fail to negotiate for fair treatment, and allow others to take advantage of you. This can leave you feeling powerless, invisible, and resentful, all because you were taught that your needs were a burden, and your feelings were "dramatic."

 Chronic Repetitive Patterns

You might find yourself unconsciously recreating the very scenarios that caused your pain. You might be drawn to people who are emotionally distant, who dismiss your feelings, or who tell you that you're "too sensitive." This isn't because you want to be in pain, but because the familiarity of the trauma feels safer than the unknown of a healthy, loving relationship. You're trying to resolve the original wound by replaying it, hoping for a different ending this time.

For You to Think About

These are just some of the ways that an absent empathetic witness can play out in our adult lives. Let's assume you missed out of having an empathetic witness, okay? Had you met a compassionate presence who simply said, "I believe you. What happened to you was not okay", your adult life and destructive behaviours would have been significantly different. Such a response would have provided a container for your pain, allowing your fragmented memories to be processed and integrated. It would have reinforced the message that your feelings were valid and that you were worthy of care and protection.

This external validation would have become an internal resource, preventing the core narrative of unworthiness from taking root. It would have enabled you to develop healthy coping mechanisms and trust your own emotional compass, rather than resorting to self-sabotage and repeating the trauma.

That single moment of invalidated pain can create a ripple effect, shaping everything from your relationships to your sense of self. The good news, though, is that once you see this pattern for what it is, you can start to change the narrative. You can finally become the empathetic witness you always deserved. That's exactly what I'm going to teach you to do for yourself. In my books, this is a must-have life skill.

You see, my friend, even from this deeply rooted pain, healing is absolutely possible. By becoming the empathetic witness you never had, you can begin to subtly heal those deep wounds, reclaim your sense of self-worth, and finally enjoy life turning out a bit differently for a change.

Still here, holding your hand ... not letting go!

13.
A Life Changing Skill

Becoming Your Own Empathetic Witness
The Steps for Healing What is Keeping You Stuck

First, let's give you some love. Take a breath, exhale, then sit back up again, and try to curl the edges of your mouth up, just for a moment. Wrap your arms around your shoulders and hug yourself. I know this has been a lot to consume.

I'd like to welcome you to this safe space, to open another door and take the next steps of this Change Experience journey, making a deep, much-needed connection within. Think of this as your personal starter pack, your guide to becoming your own compassionate ally, your own empathetic witness.

This isn't just an exercise. It's that handy crowbar you've needed to get things moving. It's a chance to turn inwards, to listen to your message centre, and to offer yourself the love and understanding you've always deserved. The door is wide open here now, my friend, exposing those hidden chambers within, where the stories of past traumas may still reside. And with a brave, glorious step forward through this door, we'll begin to heal the wounds long held captive within your younger self.

The beautiful thing is you can do this anywhere. Perhaps you'll find yourself nestled in a comfortable chair at home, with a warm blanket draped around you. Or maybe you'll choose the soft embrace of your bed, the grounding support of a yoga mat on the floor, or the peaceful feel of the outdoors. The possibilities are as endless as your imagination.

> **"She stood in the storm, and when the wind did not blow her way, she adjusted her sails."**
> — Elizabeth Edwards

What truly matters is that you find a space where you feel comfortable, where you feel safe and grounded, and most importantly, where you know you won't be interrupted. This is your time, and your private conversation with the most important person in your life: yourself.

You have this power within you, my friend. You do. You possess the most beautiful, transformative energy to do this work. And once you've connected with your younger self, I want you to allow that experience to flow through you, to make space for the emotions that arise, to honour every feeling that surfaces. This is a deep unfolding, a release, a journey back to wholeness. If you need to cry, let it all out.

> When I first did this, I had bowling-ball-tears streaming down my face.

Be Your Own Empathetic Witness

Getting Ready – Part 1

Before we dive into the heart of the exercise, let's take a moment to think about what it means to be your own empathetic witness. Let's lay down some stepping stones, some nice and easy reminders that will guide us along the way.

Acknowledgement: Acknowledge, within, that trauma isn't simply what happened to you. It's what you carry within you. It's the story you hold inside, often shaped by the suppressed emotions that swirl within your subconscious mind. In your heart space, ask yourself: "Can I feel okay with this concept? Does it resonate with me?"

◎ **Connection:** In your quiet time, have a little chat with yourself. Recognise that your heart holds the capacity for a vast tapestry of emotions? You are a woman of depth and feeling, capable of experiencing love and compassion, betrayal and rage, grief and loss. All these emotions are not only normal but also natural parts of your human experience. In your private space, ask yourself: "Can I feel okay with this truth?"

◎ **Trust Yourself:** Do you believe you can nurture this relationship with yourself? Can you become more intentional in this relationship? Can you openly and willingly try to connect with your Inner Child who experienced so much alone? Can you ask yourself: "Do I feel okay with this intention?"

◎ **New Skills:** Can you open yourself up to the possibility that it's never too late to become the empathetic witness your Inner Child so desperately needs? Yes? Then, believe, with every fibre of your being, that you are no longer alone, helpless, or without support. Can you embrace the opportunity to learn and practise the skills that will allow you to connect with that little girl? Can you find the words to offer her the supportive, the loving touch, the reassurance that she needs? Now, ask yourself: "Can you sign up to this belief?"

◎ **Grounding:** When you feel overwhelmed and yearn for support, who do you turn to? What soothing words of comfort do they offer you? Can you hear their voices in your mind? Can you speak those words aloud to yourself? As you do, remember to breathe deeply and ground yourself. And then afterwards, check in: How do you feel? Does this bring you a sense of ease? In your quiet space, ask yourself: "Can I feel okay with doing this?"

IMPORTANT NOTE: Being prepared is always going to give you better outcomes. Because, my friend, when you do these exercises and meditations, intense feelings can sometimes surface right at the beginning. These feelings can be overwhelming, and I certainly don't want you to stop doing this important work just because you might stumble at the first hurdle. It's a place of vulnerability, and I ask you to please honour that.

Getting Ready – Part 2

Okay, this is the next round of preparation to becoming your own empathetic witness, to healing those precious parts of you that may still carry the weight of the past. This is again, me stepping this out for you so you can get the most out of this exercise.

- **Find your cosy spot.** Pick a comfortable place where you won't be disturbed – your favourite chair, your bed, or even a soft mat. Gently close your eyes and settle in by simply noticing your breath.

- **Give yourself permission.** Say it out loud or in your head: "It's okay to be here. I am worthy of this time. This is all for me." Drop any doubts or worries at the door.

- **Block out enough time.** Don't try to squeeze this in right before you need to rush off to meet someone. Give yourself a proper buffer so you can truly go inward without a deadline.

- **Make time for afterwards.** Once you're done, have a peaceful space ready for yourself. This is a time to simply sit and be with whatever comes up. Allow yourself time to feel. Respect the voice that comes from within.

Getting Ready – Part 3

Nearly there. You're going to be so super ready! Follow these last remaining steps to ensure you have a powerful experience connecting with your Inner Child.

- **Be Open:** As you breathe, try to clear your mind. Let go of the day's worries and to-do lists. This is a time for you, and only you.

- **Connect with Your Inner Child:** Warmly invite your Inner Child to join you in this space. Imagine her there, perhaps as she appeared at a specific age, or simply as a feeling or a presence within you. (I often visualise her sitting under my old familiar tree, but you can create your own setting.)

🔗 **Trust Your Inner Messages:** Know, deep in your heart, that you already possess the capacity to connect with her. You have the words she needs to hear. Trust yourself to speak from your heart and offer her the validation, comfort, and reassurance she so deeply needs.

🔗 **Lean Into the Experience:** As emotions arise, lean into them. Don't push them away. Notice and name each emotion, acknowledging it with kindness. Reassure yourself that you are safe in this moment and that this is a beautiful and necessary release.

🔗 **Remember Your Safety:** Always remember that nothing can harm you during this exercise. You are creating a safe and sacred space for yourself. You are in control, and you are protected.

> **IMPORTANT NOTE:** I appreciate that it can be hard to read and do this exercise at the same time. If you would like to close your eyes and listen to my voice, you can access this meditation via the resources page on my website: **www.fleurelizabeth.com**. Or find it on my YouTube channel.

Healing and Connection Meditation Exercise
Meeting Your Younger Self

My dear friend, here we are ready to take a walk back to your former self, to meet the colours of your child within, and to offer her the love and understanding she's always needed and deserved.

Let's Begin

Now, in your safe space, read through this (or listen to my voice online):

I want you to imagine yourself walking down a path. It's a path you know well, a place that feels safe and familiar to your heart. Feel the warmth of the sun on your face, the strength in your body as you walk. Sense the ground beneath your feet – the soft grass, the crunch of gravel, or the smooth pavement. Listen to the beautiful sounds that surround you – the birds singing, the leaves rustling, the soft breeze whispering secrets.

Notice everything around you.

See the trees reaching tall towards the sky, the vibrant green of the grass, the delicate beauty of the wildflowers.

And then, just ahead, you see it – a magnificent tree. A big, glorious, old, beautiful oak tree, its branches covering you like a loving umbrella and cocoon of safety.

And nestled beneath that tree, you see her. Your former, younger self.

I want you to go to her.

Walk towards her with a heart full of love and tenderness.

Let her know that you are here. And when you sit down beside her, tell her, with all the love in your heart, that she is not alone anymore.

Let her understand, deep within her soul, that you are here to be with her, to love and support her.

Now, think about what your younger self needed to hear in those moments. Really allow yourself to connect with her needs, with the longings of her heart.

Let your younger self tell you about her experiences.

Listen to the words she speaks to you. Hear the emotions behind them, the unspoken feelings.

I want you to truly connect with that, to feel what she felt.

And then, as your adult self, as the strong, wise woman you are today, give her the words she (you) needed to hear so long ago. This is the part where you need to create the words that resonate with you, that are meaningful to you. It is these personal and soothing words that will be the critical ingredient.

Tell her the comforting words she needed to feel safe and seen. *(This is the part when you use your own comforting words to talk to your former self.)*

Give her the words of validation, the words that say, "I see you. I hear you. Your feelings are real, and they matter." Give her the words of wisdom to let her know that she will be okay, that you are with her now, and that you will guide her through this.

If you need to, tell her that it was horrible. Tell her that what she went through was not pleasant, that it was painful, but that she has strength, that she has support, that she has love – your love – to help guide her through it all. Use whatever words resonate with you, words that will make your younger self feel safe, cherished, and understood. What would have made you feel safe at that moment?

And then, wrap your arms around yourself, as if you are giving yourself the warmest, most loving hug. As if you are embracing her, your younger self.

Let your body feel the connection. Let your heart feel it too. Allow all the emotions to come.

Allow all the emotions to pass through you. Make room for the feelings coming up for both you and your younger self. Validate them. Say to yourself, "It's okay to feel this way. I'm here, and I'm listening."

Know that you are both in a safe place, a place of love and acceptance.

Know that you have the ability – the beautiful, powerful ability – to give your younger self the empathy and the love that she needs, that she has always needed.

Then, sit with her for a few minutes, imagine holding her hand, and give her the love she deserves.

And then, when you are ready, exhale deeply. Release. You can stay there in that space for a few more moments if you need to.

Okay, that's it. Now it's your turn to try it. When you are finished, open your eyes, ground yourself, and come back into your current space. I want you to gently get up and move around. Shake off any lingering energy. Because you've just unearthed a lot of energy, a lot of emotion that you allowed to surface.

If at any time you need to release sounds from your mouth – a sigh, a groan, a cry – please do so. If you cough, gasp, or cry, whatever happens, allow the physical manifestation of that energy release to make its way out of your body.

> This is a beautiful and brave place to be. You are doing amazing work.

REMEMBER: You are in your own safe place. I'm holding your hand in spirit. And you are holding your own hand, offering yourself the love and compassion you so deeply deserve. Repeat this as many times as you feel you can manage. Each time you "travel back" to rewrite the narrative in your inner, locked-away world of the past, you will activate thought-provoking change in your outer, current and conscious world. Your Future Self is thanking you!

• • •

After the Exercise

First things first: afterwards, please be sure to drink plenty of water.

You have already taken huge steps forward by reading all of this. It creates change within you, even if you're not aware of it yet. Be patient with yourself, too, please. Doing this Inner Child work is major metaphoric heart surgery, you know.

> **"Each night when I go to sleep, I die. When I wake up, I am reborn."**
> – Mahatma Gandhi

This is where a woman's true power resides to make changes in her world.

Be conscious that this exercise can bring up emotions, even for a few days after, and that's perfectly okay. Let it flow. Allow whatever arises to surface without judgement.

Try this again when you feel safe. Go back to a different time when you know you experienced something unsettling, and sit with your former self, and tell her everything she needed to hear back in that moment.

 **SO, THE MESSAGE HERE IS THIS:** This is also an exercise you can revisit again and again, as many times as you need. Each time, you can delve into different moments, different experiences where you felt unheard and unseen, where you longed for an empathetic witness to validate your pain and your fear.

You can journey back to those circumstances, sit beside your younger self, and quietly ask her to share the details of what she experienced. And then, with empathy and compassion, simply soothe, and love her. Validate her. Connect with her.

> And trust that things will start
> to change from here.

My friend, this is your life's work!

The Change Experience you are going through – is undoubtedly a commitment to your own peace and emotional health for the rest of your life. This work requires you to be mindful of all your colours – your scars, your triggers, your vulnerabilities – and to be aware enough to catch yourself when you stumble, even when everything seems rosy. These challenges will come up and test you all the time, but how you respond is the most important thing.

This work is not a death sentence; it is a part of your love language to yourself – and it's your responsibility to protect that love.

14.
Reflection Time

Your Process to Look Within
Understanding Your Wise and Wonderful Inner Child

Using your journal and in your favourite space, get ready to reflect and work on some self-validation. Perhaps now is a good time for you to start validating and offering the soothing words your Inner Child needed to hear and set her free. Release her. That precious part of you holds so much knowledge, so many answers to the questions you carry within. She's still there, you know. She lives within you, and you are a part of her, forever connected.

So, let's create a space for her. I would like you to sit with her, as this reflection is about just you and her. Let's invite her to share her experience, to reveal the stories she holds. By doing this, you'll gain such astute insight into what drives your behaviours, what has shaped your life, and perhaps what has held you back.

Throughout your life, those old wounds, those "scars", as I like to call them, might reopen. They can trigger behaviours, reactions, and feelings that seem to come out of nowhere. But they do come from somewhere. They're whispers from your Inner Child – gentle or sometimes not so gentle – reminders that she's still there, longing to be heard, longing to be healed. She's asking for your help, your understanding, your love.

When you embrace your Inner Child, you're embracing all of yourself. Those parts you might have pushed away, denied, or even forgotten. In this loving awareness, in this deep connection to your own truth, you'll discover the beautiful gifts of freedom she has to offer you. So let her speak.

 **A SMALL REMINDER:** This is a reflection of you. Approach it with the utmost compassion, my friend. This is about self-discovery, about connecting to your truest self, not about judgement or criticism. Be kind to yourself, as you would be to a dear friend.

If, at any point during this reflection, you start to feel difficult thoughts or emotions arise, please pause. Take a moment. Use the grounding techniques we've talked about to bring yourself back to centre: 4-7-8 Breathing, Dropping Anchor and Name and Tame. They are in the Appendix, remember.

You are in control here. You decide what you're ready for, what you're comfortable exploring. This is your time, your space. You know your own capacity, so please honour that.

> Remember, it's absolutely okay to stop at any time. You can always come back to this when you feel more settled, more ready.

Let's Begin

Now, let's dive in. This is your time to open your heart and mind to this evolutionary process of self-discovery.

> Remember to read your answers aloud
> so you hear yourself speak the words
> so you believe what you say.

1. **Creating a Safe Space:** How can you create a truly safe and nurturing space, both physically and emotionally, to listen deeply to what your Inner Child is trying to communicate with you? What does that space look like? Feel like? What will make her feel comfortable and heard?

2. **Understanding Your Needs:** What is it that you, as the woman you are today, need to understand within yourself to communicate your needs effectively in your relationships, your work, and your life? What messages did you receive as a child that might be holding you back now?

3. **Embracing Her with Love:** Imagine your Inner Child is right here with you. How can you embrace her, physically or metaphorically, and offer her all the loving words of validation, reassurance, and acceptance that she so deeply needs? What does she long to hear from you?

4. **Accessing Your Inner Know-How:** How can you access the deep-rooted knowledge within yourself, the insights that your Inner Child holds, and give her (and yourself) the love, compassion, and support you both deserve?

How can you change your narrative that she once held about you? The narrative that perhaps has kept you from moving forward into your daily life?

5. **What Have You Learned about Yourself so Far on this Journey?** How could this new understanding make a significant difference in your life moving forward? What shifts do you feel happening within you?

6. **Journalling Your Change Experience:** Now, take some time to write down your thoughts, your opinions, and your ideas. Let your pen flow freely across the page. What is the narrative you want to create about yourself today, about who you are as an emotionally resilient woman? Don't censor yourself. Just let the words come.

•••

After the Reflection Questions

Okay, this is something you may have to do a few times, maybe even regularly. There is generally a lot to unpack in our record books. If you have the faith and belief that this is a beautiful and ongoing process, and set your intentions for creating the right outcomes, you will see the results unfold; there is no doubt there.

Be patient with yourself. Be gentle. And trust that your Inner Child is guiding you every step of the way. Your work here is embracing your boundless truth. Your self-awareness will help you create a beautiful heart space for healing. Allowing communication, love, acceptance, and compassion to flow will unlock your cycles of unconscious behaviours. Get ready, you just may start to feel a new kind of glow from within.

You are doing such a wonderful job! I'm so proud of you for taking another step forward.

A Resilient Woman = Know-How

15.
Emotion is Your Friend

Unpacking Your Emotional World
Learning About Patterns and Predictability

Alright, my friend, are you comfortable there? Great. I would like to ask you something. Have you ever felt like your emotions are a bit of a mystery, or that they just happen to you out of the blue? If the answer is yes, then good, I am going to help you change that. Don't be afraid, just be willing to learn.

Now, we enter a deeply personal part of our journey – a roadmap into understanding your emotional world. This isn't about just talking about feelings; it's about getting to the heart of what they're trying to tell you. I use the phrase "emotional blueprint" because it suggests that emotions aren't random: there are predictable patterns and connections such as triggers, behaviours and consequences that can be mapped and understood.

It's only by understanding these predictable patterns that you can move from feeling like a passenger in your own life to being the one in the driver's seat. This isn't about controlling your emotions, which can feel impossible anyway. It's about recognising how they function as your own deeply personal guidance system.

When we unpack this layer by layer, we start to see that our reactions aren't random or chaotic. Instead, they're predictable signals, each one offering a valuable message. This journey from avoidance to understanding allows you to finally appreciate that your emotions aren't forces to be feared or suppressed. They are allies to be understood, leading you to a welcome sense of peace and a more authentic, joyful life.

> Okay, ready, let's get into the
> meat and potatoes of this!

Numbing Our Emotions

My friend, I want to talk about something I've seen in my own life and in the lives of many others: the temptation to numb our emotions. It's so easy for us to reach for something to quiet our feelings, isn't it? Whether that's a pill, a drink, or any other distraction, it's often an attempt to find a quick fix for the difficult parts of life.

I've watched so many people I care about choose a path of numbing their emotions rather than taking the time to understand what those feelings are trying to tell them. It's a challenging journey to face our inner world and do the work of self-discovery, and I know it's not their fault. We live in a world where medicine is a profit-making business, and pharmaceutical companies have done a brilliant job of normalising the idea that numbing ourselves leads to a better life.

I know that medication can be incredibly helpful and even lifesaving for some people, but I worry we've become emotionally lazy. It's become too widely accepted to simply pop a pill when life gets a bit hard. What if, instead, we saw those tough emotions as signals? What if we listened to them and learned to understand ourselves better? That, to me, is where true healing and empowerment begin.

Avoiding What We Need to Heal

So, why do we sometimes find ourselves avoiding our emotions? My friend, I know how it is. Sometimes, manoeuvring through your feelings can feel like walking through a minefield. Although there are many reasons why you might instinctively want to push them away, often it's because you're just trying to protect yourself.

Here are some of the big ones that I see come up time and time again. As you read these, if any of this sounds like you, just respond with "yes, that's me" out loud.

🔍 **Shielding Our Hearts:** Feelings like sadness, fear, and anger can hurt. Deeply. And after everything you've been through, sometimes you just want that hurt to stop. So, you might try to lock those feelings away, just to get a break from the pain. Does that sound familiar to you?

🔍 **What We've Been Taught:** Society can sometimes send you messages that you need to be strong and always have it together. Showing your emotions, especially the vulnerable ones, might feel scary, like you're going against what's expected of you. Have you ever felt that pressure?

🔍 **Our Own Way of Protecting:** When you've experienced trauma, sometimes your emotions can feel overwhelming. Disconnecting from them might be how you learned to cope, a way to keep going when things felt too much. Can you relate to this?

🔍 **Lost in the Noise:** Life gets busy, doesn't it? Sometimes, you're moving so fast that you don't even realise what you're feeling. Or maybe you don't quite know how to put a name to those feelings. Has that ever happened to you?

🔍 **Worrying What Others Might Think:** It's natural to worry about being judged for your feelings. You might be afraid of what others will say or how they'll react. Do you ever hold back your emotions because of this?

As these characteristics settle, you might find yourself thinking, "That's me." If so, a great next step is to explore those thoughts in your journal. You don't have to have all the answers right now. Sometimes just the act of writing helps you understand what's been simmering beneath the surface.

SO, THE MESSAGE HERE IS THIS: It's tempting to push our emotions aside, but that quick fix often creates bigger challenges down the road. Keep thinking of your emotions as messengers, each one trying to deliver an important message to give you the reason for change. When we stop listening to them, we begin to feel disconnected from ourselves – we've stopped listening to our inner coach, almost like walking off the field to go play for the other team.

I know that feeling of being completely overwhelmed. And, if it is feeling a bit much, my friend, this is the time to reach out and use your tools. Take a moment to do your 4-7-8 breathing technique and quieten your mind by naming your thoughts. You have what you need now to calm yourself, so do that. Remember, this journey is a marathon, not a sprint. (These tools are in the Appendix, as reminder, okay!)

> What you are avoiding is the one
> thing that will set you free!

Emotions Are Your Signals
Always Communicating and Guiding

I hope you're now getting the picture that your emotions are incredible guides, constantly giving you insights into the layers of your life's colour and complexity. Yet, I wonder, my friend, how often do you ignore them simply because they make you feel uncomfortable or come at an inconvenient time?

You're in the middle of a meeting, or at a friend's house for dinner, and there's no escape. You have to accept these feelings as the signals they are.

For example, frustration might signal that a current approach isn't working, nudging you to explore new ways of doing things. Sadness could indicate a deep need for connection or to give yourself some love, guiding you to seek support or prioritise what matters most to you. Fear can highlight potential risks, but it can also reveal hidden desires and untapped potential, encouraging you to step outside your comfort zones.

And that emotional meltdown when things are working out exactly as you planned? I know it feels overwhelming, but it's encouraging you to stop and ask yourself why you're pushing against something that isn't right for you. It may be time to question your motivation and then question why you are really doing it.

In a world that often values rationality and productivity above all else, emotional awareness can sometimes be dismissed as woo-woo, fluffy or even a weakness. I appreciate that you can be up against it at times.

Our avoidance, while completely understandable, leads us to suppress feelings like sadness, fear, or anger, in the hope they'll just disappear. But they don't. Instead, they linger, impacting our wellbeing in substantive ways. By turning away from our emotions, we miss out on crucial information about our needs, desires, and boundaries. They are vital feedback loops, alerting us to potential challenges and hidden opportunities. Ultimately, ignoring them creates a disconnect from our truest selves, making it difficult to move through life with clarity and purpose.

The real beauty of truly listening to our emotions is where self-confidence develops, and trusting yourself truly comes into play. Later, I'm going to give you some new tools on how to embrace real empathy for your past and trust yourself moving forward.

Pay attention – this is the path forward, my friend, step after step, removing those strangely ever-present roadblocks out of the way. If you want this change, you have to do the work. If you want to get unstuck and become more authentic in who you are, then get cosy with these emotions of yours, okay? They don't stink. They won't fart in bed, but they will keep you warm at night, if you let them.

> Keep this mantra with you: Life is never a straight line, but it's worth every twist and turn to reach a place where you absolutely trust yourself and experience true love from within.

Managing Your Emotions
Why Emotional Regulation Has Felt so Hard Until Now

To develop a new perspective and better understand your emotional blueprint, I want to help you fully appreciate what it means to emotionally regulate yourself. Perhaps you've found this incredibly difficult up until now. Trust me when I say, struggling to keep emotions in check or balanced is a universal experience for women who have navigated trauma. I was absolutely rubbish at regulating myself, so please rest assured, you are not alone.

The good news is, we are here now, together, courageously trying to understand how your past might be affecting you today. Okay, yes, the "regulation" part may sound like a big word, but let me spell out its meaning for you. Emotional regulation is the ability to manage and respond to your emotional experiences in a healthy and flexible manner. That doesn't sound too scary, does it?

Think of it like this: Instead of your emotions controlling you, you learn how to navigate them. It's about having the ability to hit the pause button when you feel overwhelmed, so you can choose to respond consciously instead of reacting on impulse. At its heart, emotional regulation is about finding a sense of inner peace and balance.

Right now, you might find it tough to catch yourself when you feel something uncomfortable, scary, or enraging. One minute you feel that something is "off," and the next, you react – boom! That's perfectly okay. It's completely normal. In those moments, you likely struggle to have the flexibility to respond with consideration, to be mindful of where you are and who you are with. You might feel like you lose your sense of self and simply react without a filter, perhaps with a burst of rage, saying things you don't mean. Or you might lose yourself in a flood of tears in a public place where people are present and watching you. It can feel as if you have absolutely no control over that instantaneous emotional response.

Now, I know that for many of you, especially if you've experienced childhood or complex trauma, this can feel like an enormous challenge. You might feel like you haven't had the chance to develop healthy coping mechanisms. Trauma can, unfortunately, lead to hyper-vigilance, emotional numbing, or intense emotional reactivity, as your nervous system becomes dysregulated. It's like your inner alarm system is constantly on high alert. The brain's stress response system can become overly sensitive, making it difficult to modulate emotions and return to a peaceful baseline. This can feel like a rollercoaster, with intense emotional swings, a reliance on unhealthy coping strategies, and even a significant difficulty identifying and labelling your emotions. These responses often stem from a lack of safe, consistent, and supportive emotional experiences in those formative years.

I remember reading the book *The Body Keeps the Score* and finding so many connections to my own life within its pages. There's a particular passage from the author, Dr. Bessel van der Kolk, that speaks to this truth so insightfully:

> "Traumatised people chronically feel unsafe inside their bodies: The past is alive in the form of gnawing interior discomfort. Their bodies are constantly bombarded by visceral warning signs, and, in an attempt to control these processes, they often become expert at ignoring their gut feelings and in numbing awareness of what is played out inside. They learn to hide from their selves."

This, I believe, is a universal truth for anyone who has suffered from trauma.

The Gifts of Emotional Regulation

The skill of emotional regulation we'll be working on together is absolutely within your grasp. When you embrace it, you'll feel an incredible sense of calmness settle inside you.

Just imagine a life where your emotions aren't crashing over you, but instead, guiding you. Instead of reacting on impulse, you'll find yourself responding thoughtfully. Your relationships will become so much deeper because you'll be able to communicate more clearly and authentically, and certainty in your decisions will feel clearer too, no longer clouded by fear or impulsivity.

This is how we really start to understand ourselves, gaining a quiet knowing of our needs and desires. And perhaps for the first time, happiness won't just be a fleeting moment but a more consistent, grounded experience. It's that kind of joy that comes from knowing you're living in alignment with your truest self – finally experiencing what that really means for yourself, not just reading it on the page. A genuine happiness that comes from within, not from those quick dopamine hits of sugar, wine, drugs, sex, or anything else.

The work we're doing together is the bedrock of your Change Experience. Eventually, with enough practice, these skills will become second nature. They're the keys to unlocking all those unwanted automatic behaviours we've been talking about, allowing you to progress on in life. In some ways, it's like going back to being a student, being open and willing to learn. But, make no mistake, it will be a rewarding journey, I promise you.

As I always say, learning and mastering new skills takes time, so please do remind yourself of that when you feel impatient, or if you mess up or fall over. That will happen because it happens to all of us. I really want to get you into the habit of reinforcing and validating that you are doing wonderfully just by exploring this side of yourself. I truly hope you can see that.

> How nice would it be for you to be able to stop yourself and think before you react?

Five Easy Steps to Emotionally Regulate

1. Learn to "Hit the Pause Button"
The first step is to create a physical and mental space between a trigger and your reaction. When you feel a strong emotion – like anger, panic, or sadness – rising, please don't react immediately. Instead, hit a mental "pause button." This might involve taking a deep breath, counting to ten, or simply telling yourself, "I need a moment before I respond." This small act of pausing interrupts

that automatic, impulsive reaction and gives your rational mind a chance to catch up. The goal, my friend, is to create a gap where you can choose a conscious response instead of just reacting on autopilot.

2. Drop Anchor

This powerful tool I have shared with you before, helps you stay grounded when you're caught in an emotional storm. Think of it like a boat in rough seas; you can't stop the waves, but you can drop an anchor to keep from being pulled under. The steps are simple:

- **Acknowledge:** Carefully notice what's happening inside you. Acknowledge your thoughts, feelings, and physical sensations without judgement.
- **Connect:** Ground yourself in your body. Feel your feet on the floor or the weight of your body in your chair. Focus on your breath, feeling the air move in and out.
- **Engage:** Look around you and notice your surroundings. Then, shift your focus to what you're doing in the present moment. Continue with your day, even while the difficult feelings are still there.

This technique is all about staying present and engaged in your life, even while experiencing inner turmoil. (It is in your Appendix, remember.)

3. Identify, Name and Tame Your Emotions

You can't manage what you can't identify, can you? So, a crucial step here is to build a vocabulary for your feelings beyond just "good" or "bad." Grab a feelings wheel or a list of emotions online. When you feel something, try to name it. Is it sadness, or is it grief? Is it frustration, or is it rage?

By putting a name to what you're feeling, you're separating yourself from the emotion and starting to truly understand it.

Once you've named it, you can begin to tame it. Taming doesn't mean making the emotion go away, but rather managing its intensity so it doesn't overwhelm you. You can do this by taking a breath and saying, "I feel anger right now, and I can handle this." This conscious response puts you back in the driver's seat. (The Feelings Wheel is in your Appendix, remember, if you need help expressing your emotions.)

4. Validate Your Feelings

Once you've named and tamed the emotion, the next step is to validate it. This is about becoming your own empathetic witness, remember? Say to yourself, "It makes sense that I feel angry about this", or "It's okay that I'm sad right now". You are giving yourself the compassion you may not have received as a child. Validation doesn't mean you have to act on the feeling; it just means you're accepting it. This simple act of self-compassion really helps calm your nervous system and removes the layer of shame that often accompanies big emotions.

5. Practise Healthy Self-Soothing

When you feel overwhelmed, you need tools to calm yourself down, don't you? This is where healthy self-soothing comes in. Think of things that comfort you and make you feel safe. This could be anything from drinking a warm cup of tea and listening to calming music to taking a bath or going for a gentle walk. The key is to find activities that genuinely soothe you without causing long-term harm. By intentionally engaging in these practices, you're teaching your mind and body that you have the ability to calm yourself down, which truly builds your inner strength and resilience.

Labelling Your Emotions
Give it Form and a Name

You know, you are going to be learning so much about understanding your emotional blueprint in these pages. I want to help you appreciate what labelling emotions means and why it's going to be helpful to you to develop a new perspective in your emotional world. It might sound a bit formal, but it's just about getting to know your feelings better. It's like when you meet someone new, and you want to learn their name so you can connect with them. It's the same with your emotions! So, can we talk about what it means now?

 First, it's about tuning in
It's about taking a moment to really check in with yourself. What's going on inside? Are you feeling a flutter in your chest, a tightness in your shoulders, or maybe a sense of lightness? It's paying attention to those little signals your body gives you and recognising that they're tied to how you're feeling.

 Finding the words for the emotion
Once you've noticed those feelings, it's about giving them a name. Not just a general "I feel good" or "I feel bad" but something more specific. Like, "I feel a bit anxious about that meeting" or "I'm feeling really joyful about this sunny day". It's like putting on your detective hat and figuring out exactly what's going on inside. You can say it out loud, write it down in a journal, or even just think it to yourself. The important thing is to acknowledge it. (This is in your grounding tools, too!)

 Get specific about what it is
Instead of just saying "I'm upset", try to pinpoint what exactly you're feeling. Is it sadness? Frustration? Disappointment? It's like choosing the right colour when you're painting. Each emotion has its own shade, and being specific helps you understand it better.

🔍 Calming the inner emotional storm

Get into the habit of naming and watch calmness develop. When I name my emotions, it's like taking a deep breath and calming my nervous system. It's like acknowledging a little spark before it turns into a wildfire. Putting words to those feelings can help them feel less overwhelming. This is your homework to practice, okay?

🔍 Knowing myself better

It's building a relationship with yourself. The more you label your emotions, the more you understand your patterns and what triggers different feelings. It's like getting to know a dear friend. Intimately.

🔍 Speaking your truth, perhaps for the first time

When you know what you're feeling, you can express yourself better to others. It's having the right words to say what's in your heart. This has made such a difference in my relationships!

🔍 Making clearer choices, consciously

When you are aware of your emotions, you can make decisions from a calmer place instead of being swept away by them. It's like navigating a forest with a clear map rather than simply wandering and hoping you don't get lost.

🔍 Lessening the load

Acknowledging your emotions stops them from building up inside and becoming too much to handle. It's like letting steam out of a kettle so it doesn't explode.

🔍 Processing and moving on

Labelling an emotion helps your brain process it. It's like closing a chapter in a book, so you're ready to start the next one.

> In essence, my friend, it's all about being kind to yourself and giving yourself permission to feel whatever you're feeling.

> Naming those feelings is a powerful step forward in taking care of yourself and piloting the beautiful, sometimes messy, journey of life.

A Bonus at the End

For some extra support, in the Appendix, I have included some more practical tips for understanding emotions as a valuable inner compass, not something to fear. As we will explore, emotions are vital signals, serving as motivation and pathways for communication with others and our own selves. Learning to "lean into them" as we would a new relationship allows us to recognise their powerful purpose. This section provides tools to transform emotions from intimidating forces into sources of wisdom and guidance for a more enjoyable life. Look out for:

Your Emotional Compass: Navigating life's journey will shift your perspective and start seeing your emotions as a friendly compass, softly guiding you through life's twists and turns. They're not the enemy; they're valuable messengers.

Understanding the Function of Emotions: When you've spent a lot of time avoiding your emotions, it's easy to lose sight of the messages they're trying to send you. It's easy to forget that every single emotion has a job to do. So, think of this as a little guide to what some of those feelings are trying to tell you.

> Check this out when you have finished all your work here. I wouldn't want you to miss out on any good bits!

16. Reflection Time

The Courage to Reclaim Calmness
A Guide to Listening to the Language Within

Let's dive into a series of questions designed to help you connect with your emotional blueprint. This is a space for you to be truly honest with yourself, without any judgement. It's all about knowing yourself better and giving light to the parts of you that you may be hiding away from. These questions are designed to provoke the thoughts that will give you a reason to change, build the desire to do the work, and create a deep trust in your ability to build a better life.

Let's take a moment, just you and me, to really dive into what's been stirring within you. Grab your journal and let's explore these questions together. Write your answers down, but don't stop there.

> **Are you still reading them aloud?** I hope so! That's the secret sauce, remember. It's the starting point for any lasting change. By allowing your own words to be heard by your brain, you're not just writing a new narrative – you're making it effortless and real.

Let's Begin

Understanding the Message

1. Let's begin by reflecting on a recent trigger, event, or scenario that has troubled you. Thinking back over the past month, what were the top three emotions you felt that were the most challenging? Without any judgement, simply name them. (Remember you can use the feelings wheel to help you connect to the feelings you struggle with.)

2. Now I want you to connect with why you found these particular emotions so difficult. What stories are you telling yourself about why you might be avoiding them? The stories we tell ourselves often hold the key. Do you feel these emotions are stirring up an old wound that needs a little tenderness – one you've avoided because of fear? Could you now use your new skills to embrace this story and soften its presence in your world?

Your Automatic Patterns

3. What automatic behaviours tend to kick in when you're feeling these emotions? What do you find yourself doing almost without thinking? These are the patterns you often overlook, but they hold so much insight for where you can start making changes.

4. Now, let's explore the consequences. What has been the cost of these automatic behaviours? Take a moment to be honest with yourself and see how they have impacted you, your relationships, your work, and your health. How did they impact you and those around you?

Reprogramming Your Response

5. What if you could be in control and reprogramme your behaviours? Let's take that one troubling scenario and re-imagine it. If

you could go back to that moment, what would you do differently? How can you choose to act within your values, instead of outside of them?

6. What do you think your emotions could be trying to reveal to you about this situation? What is it you need to connect to that you might be avoiding? This is the brave internal dialogue you need to have with yourself. Trust what it is telling you, sister.

7. Okay, let's ask this in another way. If you were to give these emotions a voice, what would they say to you, honestly? What would they want you to know about your role in this scenario? This isn't about blame, but about taking ownership and hearing their message.

A Placid Path Forward

8. Now, how can you show yourself some love and allow yourself to sit with that message? First, remember to use your 4-7-8 breathing to calm yourself. Then, drop an anchor to ground yourself in the present moment, and respectfully name and tame the emotion, giving yourself permission to feel it and be safe in its presence.

To honour all your amazing work here, go get yourself a warm cup of tea, or wrap your arms around yourself for a nice warm hug. Tell yourself the words you need to hear, like, "I am safe" or "I'm okay to be friends with this feeling". This is your kind acknowledgment of all the courage you've shown today.

•••

After the Reflection

My friend, I have taken it upon myself to be your sideline cheerleader for today!

I want you to hold onto this truth: You are not broken. That image of "flowers growing through concrete"? That's you. That's the essence of your spirit, pushing through and blooming even when the ground feels hard.

This process, looking inward, takes so much courage. You've shown that today, by facing parts of yourself with honesty and vulnerability. Be so, so proud for giving yourself this gift of reflection and for honouring your own story. You are inherently strong, incredibly resilient, and brimming with potential. More than you know.

It can be so tricky to navigate all this challenging emotional stuff – believe me, I've been there. While it is an important part of the Change Experience journey, it's also completely okay for things to be messy and imperfect while you walk this path with me. Normalise that.

> Whatever you wrote down in this reflection, accept it as a part of who you are. It simply means you're human.

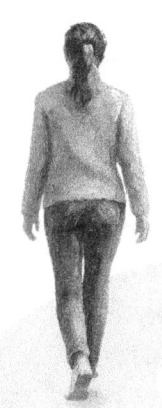

The Patterns of Trauma

17.
My Trauma Experience

Hiding the Shameful Parts of Myself
The Unconscious Dance of Repetitive Cycles

Okay, I think we've already agreed that this is a safe space, just us, to acknowledge some truths together, right? I'd like to share this with you now.

I've come to see my repetitive cycles as an unconscious broken record player, replaying old wounds repeatedly. It's almost like a quiet, desperate hope that this time, the story will end differently, and the song will be sweeter. I realised it wasn't a choice, not really. It's more like a pattern woven into my very being, where the familiar feeling – the comfortable-uncomfortable – strangely feels safer than stepping into the complete unknown. For someone like me, who experienced childhood trauma, this showed up in ways that were both heartbreaking and confusing.

My father left my mother when I was 12. One day he just moved out. But it wasn't the clean break it seemed. My mother, in my young eyes, was a beautiful, caring, loving woman. In my adult years I awoke to see her clearly as a master manipulator. She made Dad out to be a monster. She blamed him and painted a horrible picture of what a terrible man he was. Young and vulnerable, we all believed her. The truth was, he left because she had an affair. She played the victim beautifully, and he was cast out – shamed, and isolated from us. But to me, he still abandoned me. I had no idea what was happening behind their closed doors. He would write and call me once a week. This was my childhood blueprint of a relationship: a father I was told not to trust, but who was present enough to be a lifeline yet never fully there, just out of my reach. I replicated this in my adult relationships.

I found myself drawn to partners who were emotionally distant, mirroring the neglect and abandonment I knew as a child. I had many long-distance relationships with men over the phone. They felt intellectually stimulating and deeply connected, yet they were always with men who were never quite in my reach. They mimicked the fantasy I held of the relationship I yearned for from my father – playing the masculine support role, the intellectual powerhouse, and adoring who I was. But, sadly, they also all lacked the trust I had lost in him.

I kept them at arm's length, unable to hurt me from a distance, and to be honest, they were never truly connected to who I really was. I only ever showed them what I wanted them to see, never any of my true vulnerabilities. Yet, these connections with physically and emotionally unavailable men always left me feeling not good enough, like I wasn't successful in society's eyes. It hurt, yes, but there was this unsettling sense of "home" in that pain – a subconscious tug to try and mend the past by reliving it.

As an adult, I faced further trauma in abusive relationships with men who would build me up and then tear me down, playing out the other masculine role models in my family of origin who had abused me as a child. I began to rely on the times they would build me up. I would give away my power to them and feel helpless, unworthy, and desperate. This compulsion clouded my judgement. How was I doing this when I felt like I was such a together and fabulous woman? (Well, my false self definitely thought she was.) Somehow, I kept getting into the same situations. I'd brush aside red flags or ignore that gut feeling when something felt off. It's like my heart was drawn to people who echoed the manipulative behaviours from those past traumatic relationships in my family. Even when my mind knew it was harmful.

Another cycle that always confused me so much was my work compulsions. To be a star one minute, and then the enemy, a target, and a scapegoat the next. Because I was the scapegoat in my family, and criticism and belittlement were part of my story, I gravitated toward work environments where I was constantly undermined. I would rise to the occasion to win their affection and excel, but then be king-hit by a cannonball and have it all come crashing down. I would complain about it, but never leave; I'd stay and suffer more pain. It was as if something in me was trying to help me finally conquer that narrative and pain by making me face it again and again.

For years, I carried so much shame about those parts of myself, the shame in my behaviours – desperate behaviours for love, to survive financially, to be accepted, to numb all the pain of the past – that I never wanted to admit what happened to me. When I was building my skills and becoming a "better human," as I used to call it, I denied this part of myself existed; I was so ashamed of her. It was like she, or those years of my life, didn't exist. I was embarrassed by her, and I was embarrassed by myself.

> **"Your brain is like Velcro for negative experiences but Teflon for positive ones."**
> – Dr. Rick Hanson

I made so many mistakes, so many horribly shameful mistakes that I beat myself up for. In my desperation to keep up appearances and not show the outside world I was struggling so much, I trusted the wrong people, I hurt people I loved, betrayed their trust, and I hurt myself in the process. No wonder I felt so alone.

It's as if my whole being was wired to replay that old trauma script, desperately hoping to rewrite the ending. I was missing the key to the locked door that would finally let me in to find some peace or resolution. It took me a long time to get it, but once I did, those scenarios stopped showing up in my life.

It was only when I learned the skill of acceptance that I truly was able to accept that part of myself, that delicate part, and be humbled by her presence in my life. She was me, and I was her, and we had to agree that she was on my team. She was doing the best she could with the capacity, tools, and resources she had at the time. No matter what choices she had made in the past, she was still worthy, a woman to love, then and today.

I'm no longer ashamed of her; I understand where her behaviours came from. I have forgiven her and myself for banishing her to the dark corners of my mind. And when I reached this point, I wept, and I grieved the lonely sadness she endured to have to live that way. My former self and I are now best friends again, living harmoniously together as one whole human.

> She's now a fundamental part of
> my love story with myself.

The Five Days of My Life

This is when the story that I shared at the beginning of the book became my mantra. Now, with a lot of work and commitment to rewiring my old narratives and catching my patterns, I choose to walk down a different path. And – you guessed it – always, always, always, living by my values, surefooted in my authentic self.

Day 1 – I walked down a path; I fell into a hole.

Day 2 – I walked down the same path; I fell into a hole.

Day 3 – I walked down the same path; I fell into a hole.

Day 4 – I walked down the same path; I walked around the hole. Ah!

Day 5 – I walked down a different path.

Oh goodness, the peace I feel within myself now – I've never experienced it before in my life. It's quite remarkable. I feel like I've evolved into a completely different woman. Looking back at all the things I did and the woman I was, I have immense empathy for her, but the woman I am now is worlds apart from her. The evolution of life is magnificent! So yes, I'm very proud of this work and I feel honoured to share my stories so authentically and vulnerably to help other women get to where I am in life now – to be real in order to heal.

I hope you can find some meaning in these words that may inspire you to find your own courageous step forward towards acceptance of your past shame.

> Ha, I think I just found a new one liner
> I will use – "Be real in order to heal!

18.
Repetitive Cycles

Patterns Etched Within
Unpacking Your Unconscious Scripts

Those pesky automatic behaviours, those things we find ourselves doing over and over again. My word, it can be utterly exhausting, can't it? "When is this ever going to stop?!" If you've ever asked yourself that, you're in the right place.

I know, I know ... the idea of unravelling more of your emotional blueprint can feel so overwhelming, like trying to swallow an elephant whole. Trust me, I've been there. That's why I want to break this down into manageable pieces and give you a new perspective on why this happens.

A crucial aspect of healing is recognising those repetitive patterns we all fall into. These repeating patterns are what we call repetition compulsion. Essentially, it's an unconscious drive to re-enact past hurts, perhaps with a glimmer of hope for a different outcome this time around.

> ### *Here's a simple way to look at it:*
> - Imagine your brain is a computer that stores memories.
> - Trauma creates a glitch in its software, leaving a painful memory fragmented and unprocessed.

- Your brain, in its attempt to fix the glitch, unconsciously tries to recreate the situation.
- It's like hitting replay on a bad movie, hoping it will turn out better this time.
- But it doesn't work. Instead, it keeps you stuck in a cycle of hurt, and you find yourself in the same situation, reacting in the same ways, even when you know it's not good for you.

That's repetition compulsion. It's your brain's misguided way of trying to heal, but it ends up keeping you in a cycle of pain.

The Lasting Impact on Your Brain

Think of your brain as a vast, intricate network of pathways, constantly adapting based on your experiences. When trauma strikes, it's like a sudden, jarring earthquake that disrupts those pathways, leaving deep fissures and reshaping your inner landscape.

Here's a look at what happens in your brain when this occurs:

- Your amygdala – your brain's emotion and fear centre – becomes hyperactive, much like my groodle, Peach, on "Chief of Security" duty.
- Your hippocampus, which is responsible for organising and storing memories, struggles to make sense of the overwhelming experience, leaving traumatic memories fragmented and unprocessed.
- This is why trauma can make us feel so stuck. It's not a neatly filed memory; it's still alive and present in your nervous system.

The Cycle of Repetition

Because those traumatic memories are fragmented and unresolved, your unconscious mind seeks to make sense of them, to heal the wounds. It's like trying to complete a puzzle with missing pieces, desperately searching for a way to fit them together. So, you unconsciously recreate those traumatic situations, hoping that this time, you can control the outcome and finally find a resolution.

It's a heartbreaking paradox: you're drawn to the familiar pain because it feels safer than the unknown, even though it keeps you trapped in a cycle of suffering. Even when you know it's not working and you see the pattern, those old neural pathways are so strong, so deeply ingrained, that your brain defaults to them. It's like a well-worn track, easy to follow, even when you desperately want to walk a new path.

But here's the most important part: you can learn to rewrite the script. By understanding what's happening, you can start to make new, healthier choices and break the cycle. This isn't easy, but it's the path forward. It's how you get unstuck and become more authentic in who you are.

Why Change Is Possible

This is why the rewiring of your thoughts is so critical to your healing process, my friend. It can take a while to sink in but understanding and recognising how your brain holds onto trauma is a crucial step towards making changes in your world. Believing that you have the ability to change the narrative, is essential.

This is your time to acknowledge the old narrative and begin introducing the new one. This means living consciously setting intentions every day, being true to yourself

> **"There is nothing stronger than a broken woman who has rebuilt herself."**
> – Hannah Gadsby

(understanding your vulnerabilities and nurturing them), having clear boundaries, and asking for what you need. Woah, that's a mouthful, isn't it? But in time, this should all become your new normal soon.

Do repetitive cycles feel familiar to you? By sharing some of my own deeply personal experiences, I hope to give you permission to lean into your own stories. You see, when you realise you're not alone in this, the journey feels so much less daunting.

19.
The Hooks of Your Inner Stories

When Your Beliefs Drive Your Reactions
Making Liberated Conscious Choices

So, let's address those thoughts that get caught in a loop, replaying the same old stories in your head. When we get "hooked" by emotional triggers, our perspective gets skewed, and we start treating our thoughts as hard facts without questioning where they came from.

Things like:

- **Feelings of not being enough:** "I can't get anything right; I'm a failure." "I'm out of their league." "I'm too difficult to love." "I don't deserve good things."

- **Feelings of being alone:** "No one will listen to me." "I don't belong here." "I'm too sensitive."

- **Feelings of hopelessness:** "It's hopeless, I can't do it." "I'll never move on from this." "I'm so far behind everyone else."

- **Blame:** "It's all my fault."

Sound familiar? I wonder, is any of this true about you, or is it just a narrative? We might try to push through, gritting our teeth and soldiering on, but these fear stories often drive our automatic and sometimes unhealthy behaviours. So, let's find out how we can change this narrative, shall we?

What It Means to be "Hooked"

When I say you're getting hooked, I mean you're caught by a story you've created – a repeating narrative based on past experiences that your subconscious holds onto. Your mind believes this story will play out every time you face something similar. These fear stories are perceptions, judgements, the rules and all the reasons you give for things you believe to be true. They're all things you've created that keep you stuck in the past, becoming part of your core belief system. This is why understanding the values instilled by your family of origin is so crucial – that environment can be hard to shake without conscious awareness of the "who," "how," and "why" behind it.

Beyond family imprinting, getting hooked is also a major reason why you might avoid living by your true values. You're used to operating on autopilot, without much thought. And to be honest, it can feel like you're not fully in control in these moments. But here's the good news: I'm going to guide you in discovering how to make changes and regain control. This is what we'll master together. First, let's break down four key areas to understand how you create these narratives.

The Areas to Reclaim Control

Judgements: The judgements you hold about yourself, your life, and others create self-sabotaging narratives that control your behaviour and prevent you from becoming the person you truly want to be.

The Past, Present, and Future: By bringing conscious awareness to the stories, you repeat about your past, the anxieties you project onto your future, and the worries that hook you in the present, you can change your perspective and make a conscious choice to live fully in the now.

The Reason for Things: By shining a light on the reasons and barriers you've been conditioned to accept without question, you can understand what's truly holding you back from becoming the person you want to be.

The Rules: By examining the unspoken rules you live by, you can determine if they still serve you or if they're simply old, fear-based beliefs holding you back from living a life of freedom.

Decoding Your Default Settings Exercise
Unmasking Your Inner Hooks

To truly connect with what's going on inside, take some time to write your responses in your journal. Don't rush; just let the thoughts flow. When you're ready, read what you've written out loud. By now, you're likely witnessing firsthand how incredibly powerful hearing your own voice speak these words can be. You are starting to feel a far deeper connection within yourself, bringing forth a clearer awareness of what you're experiencing in different situations.

Your role in this is to take this new awareness and use it to make changes and conscious choices. This is your time to walk down a new path on your Day Five. You can no longer ignore it when you're reacting automatically based on past experiences. Now, you can empower yourself to choose a different path – one that truly aligns with what matters most.

Let's Begin

Judgement

How you see yourself and your life? First, let's talk about the judgements you hold. Take a moment to think about what you're judging within yourself and your life.

1. **What do you judge about your appearance?** What do you see when you look in the mirror? How do you feel about your skin, your hair, your body, your breasts, your behind?

   It's crucial to be honest with yourself here, because this honesty is key to understanding the stories you create. Your self-perception is likely much harsher than reality.

   While this is true for everyone, the difference is that others likely aren't belittling, judging, and blaming themselves for every little thing, especially for physical attributes they can't control.

2. **What other judgements do you hold about your life?** What negative self-talk do you catch yourself saying? Write them down – knowing these is knowing where you need to work on creating a new narrative.

   - "I'm a failure at my job."
   - "I should be further along in my life by now."
   - "I can't do anything right with money."

3. **How about judgements about relationships, work, performance, or how you show up in the world?**

   These judgements create narratives that can hook you and pull you away from the person you want to be.

   Here's an example: Your first boyfriend left you for someone else and the story you created is that she must have been smarter, taller, prettier, sportier, and so on. Now you expect every partner to leave you, based on this past experience. You start behaving as if it's inevitable. Ironically, this behaviour creates negativity in the relationship, and eventually he does leave, validating your original belief.

Can you see how your thoughts can control your behaviour and, ultimately, who you become?

This isn't a fun exercise, I appreciate that, but it's about bringing conscious awareness to the narrative you have on repeat in your mind. This is what you need to be aware of so you can catch yourself the next time it happens. These are the things that hook you, propelling you into those automatic behaviours that take you away from living by your values, and, yes, that prevent you from experiencing joy, peace, and becoming your Future Self.

• • •

Strategy: Rewriting Your Judgement Narrative

So, how do we begin to change those narratives?

Ready to give that inner critic a kick up the bum? I thought so. It's time to build a new skill – one of the most powerful things you can learn. It's about stopping the endless chatter and starting to talk back. Let's make a deal with your brain: no more nonsense. Here's a simple, three-step strategy to take control.

1. Is This Narrative a Fact, or a Story?

The first step is to simply notice your negative thought without judgement. Once you've caught it, ask yourself this simple, powerful question: "Is this narrative a fact, or is it just a story?" The facts are the facts. A story is an opinion you've created based on those facts.

2. Gather the Evidence

Now, I want you to act like a detective. Search for evidence that proves your fear story is not the whole truth. What's one example that contradicts your narrative? If your narrative is "I can't get anything right," what's one small thing you got right today? It could be as simple as making a good cup of tea or arriving at a meeting on time.

3. Rewrite Your Narrative

Finally, it's time to intentionally rewrite the story. Take your negative thought and shift it into something that's more balanced and truer. It doesn't have to be perfect, just a step in the right direction. For example, if your old narrative was "I'm a failure", your new one could be "I'm a work in progress and I'm taking steps to improve".

The Past, Present, and Future

Next, let's explore the stories you have in the past, present, and future. You can't change what's been done, but you can absolutely change your perspective on it.

The Past

1. **What's the one event, mistake, or embarrassing moment that consistently hooks you?** What is the "song on repeat" saying?

2. **When you think about a time someone hurt you, or a time you hurt a person, what emotions still linger?** What message is that feeling trying to send you?

3. **Who did you trust that you should not have, and what was the consequence of that?** What is the story you still carry about that experience? Think of just one experience.

The Present

1. **What in the present moment creates anxiety for you?** What's happening right now that hooks you?

2. **When you are talking with someone, how easy or difficult is it for you to remain in the present moment?** What distracts you?

3. **What's the story you're telling yourself about your life right now, and how is it keeping you from making the changes you want to see?** For example, are you telling yourself a story that you're too busy, which stops you from prioritising your own health and healing journey?

The Future

1. **What are you so afraid might happen in the future that hooks you with "what ifs"?** What about the future scares you when you think of letting go of control?

2. What is it about the future that makes you think your life will be different then than it is now? What is the fantasy you have about the future that you are avoiding creating today?

3. Are you projecting a fear story, based on the past, into the future? What assumptions are you spending time on when you can't predict the future?

・・・

Strategy:
Your Tools to Turn It Around

That's the most powerful part of this work, my friend. Once we shine a light on the narratives, we can begin to flip the script. The strategies you've provided are excellent and serve as the perfect tool to help you turn these stories around.

1. For the Past: Cultivate Compassion

You can't change what happened, but you can change your relationship with the past. When that old story comes up, gently acknowledge it without judgement. Then, consciously remind yourself that you did the best you could with the awareness and tools you had at the time. Can you offer that part of yourself some love and compassion, perhaps by giving yourself a warm hug? This doesn't excuse what happened, but it honours the healing journey you are on.

2. For the Present: Choose Your Next Right Action

When an emotion hooks you in the present moment, remember the three-step strategy you have learnt. Use your 4-7-8 breathing to calm yourself, then drop an anchor to ground yourself in the present moment. Now, respectfully name and tame the emotion. Then ask yourself this simple question: "What is the next step I need to take that is right for me?" This empowers you to respond consciously, rather than reacting on autopilot.

3. For the Future: Focus on What You Can Control

When a fear story about the future tries to take over, ask yourself, "What can I control right now?" You can't predict every outcome, but you can take one small action in the present moment that aligns with your values. If you're worried that you don't have time to heal, for example, your one action could be to set aside just five minutes to write in your journal the supportive words your Inner Child needs to hear. This small step in the present is where your power truly lies.

The Reason for Things

The next area to consider is the reason we give ourselves for inaction and for remaining stuck. These reasons often function as our primary blockages to change. We all have a list of reasons why we should or shouldn't do something, creating excuses often without even knowing why. We might put up barriers "just because" someone told us to, and we believed them without questioning it. We just go along, even if something feels wrong, because we've been conditioned to, and maybe we want to avoid rocking the boat.

1. **The "Just Because" Reason:** What is one thing you want to improve in your life right now? Now, what's the first reason that pops into your head for why that change won't work for you right now?

2. **Your Personal Barriers:** What is the biggest barrier you find yourself making when you are trying to change? What stops you from not responding so automatically when you are triggered?

3. **The Unspoken Reasons:** What are the reasons you give yourself for not doing the exercises in this book, and for not answering these questions? Are you "too busy," or are you telling yourself it's "too hard" to make these changes?

> Regardless of whether your reasons are valid, writing them down helps. You might just discover some insightful truths about yourself.

• • •

Strategy: The Three Whys

When you've identified a "reason" or a barrier, ask yourself this simple set of questions to appreciate where it came from and move through it. Think of it like peeling back the layers of an onion.

- **The First Why:** Write down the reason you've given yourself. Now, ask yourself, "Why do I believe this is true?"

- **The Second Why:** Your answer to the first question will probably lead to another reason. Now, ask yourself again, "Why do I believe that?"

- **The Third Why:** Keep going until you get to a fundamental belief about yourself or the world that you've never questioned before. Once you get to this place, you can ask yourself, "Why can't I change this now?"

This simple, repeated act of asking "why" helps you get to the root of the "just because" reason, exposing the false narrative that has been holding you back. Yes, you might cry a little (it is like peeling an onion, after all), but trust me, clearing out those blockages to change is worth every bit of release.

The Rules

Lastly, let's talk about the unspoken rules we live by – the box we put ourselves in. "I can't do that, it's against the rules." I'm not talking about laws or company policies here, but the personal rules you live by. I want you to question who made these rules? Did you set them yourself, or did someone else set them for you? Your parents, your community, your partner?

Often, we're conditioned to live a certain way, and, like good little soldiers, we fall into line. But now is your time to take on the liberating task of assessing whether these rules still serve you. This isn't about becoming a rebel and simply breaking rules; it's about working out what works for you now, in a way that feels real and human.

1. **Uncover Your Personal Rules:** Think about all the unspoken rules you follow in different areas of your life: at home, at work, in your relationships, and even in how you present yourself. What rules have you created out of fear, shame, anger, or lack of confidence? Write them all down. Don't hold back – think about the way you dress, how you socialise, or even how you do the shopping.

2. **Evaluate and Choose:** Now, look at your list and ask yourself, "Is this a rule I want to live by? Is it right for me? Is it necessary anymore?" Take your time with this and dig deep. Find the rules that are weighing you down and note the ones that uplift and ground you. What do you want to keep, and what do you want to let go of?

We're often unaware of sticking to patterns that no longer serve us – things that restrict our growth or confine us. By bringing conscious awareness to them are more steps forward on the path to emotional freedom.

• • •

Strategy: Your First Act of Liberation

Now that you've identified your rules, let's close with an act of conscious and healthy rebellion.

This isn't about changing everything at once; it's about reclaiming a little bit of your emotional freedom, right?

1. **Choose One:** From your list, choose just one rule that you're ready to let go of – one that feels heavy and restrictive.

2. **Take a Small Step:** For that one rule, take a tiny, gentle step to break it. If your rule is "I must always respond to every message immediately," let one message wait for an hour, then see if you can wait for two hours, or even the next day. If your rule is "I must never ask for help," ask a friend to help you with one small thing that is important to you.

3. **Notice How It Feels:** As you take this very brave step, pay close attention to the emotions that come up. This is your chance to witness your inner world and see that even if it feels uncomfortable at first, you are safe to feel that way. You are learning that you can handle it, and that's more golden moments of emotional freedom.

This small, conscious act of liberation is where you begin to rewrite the rulebook for your life.

To Wrap This Up

This Change Experience journey of self-discovery of delving into judgements, past narratives, hidden reasons, and unspoken rules isn't always easy. But it's surely giving you a new perspective, right? It requires courage, vulnerability, and a willingness to face the parts of ourselves we might prefer to ignore. But I promise you, the emotional entanglement and freedom that I keep banging on about is worth every moment of introspection.

By understanding these hooks, by acknowledging the stories we've told ourselves, we begin to dismantle the barriers that have kept us stuck. This isn't just about change. It's about taking back the control that those old narratives have held.

And that, my friend, is where you start to feel and experience what it means to be truly liberated. Once you start this process, you will find that life will never be the same again.

> And, that is a good thing, right? Henry Ford once said, "When everything seems to be going against you, remember that the aeroplane takes off against the wind, not with it."

20.
Getting Yourself Unhooked

Moving Beyond the Old You
What Your Resist, Persists

Every weekend, I have a debrief on life with my dear friend Anna. We can talk for hours about life, love, our philosophy on healthy living, and the simple things that give us joy. (I'm not joking, this is how we talk!)

When we pull apart scenarios that come up in my life, our conversation always has an element of, "The old me would have done this, but here's how it's playing out now." I love how it feels to appreciate that my behaviour and approach to life are so different now. I see challenges and triggers with new eyes, with considered responses, and love discussing how better outcomes always come from more conscious and values-based choices. I wanted to share with you some more ways I've learned to make this evolution of self, because it's so common to feel a vast gap between the reality you have today and the one you want to have.

The Gap Between Who We Are Vs. Who We Want to Be

In today's world, with so much exposure to people's seemingly perfect successes, the pressure of keeping up with the Joneses is immense. Our inner dialogue of "I just don't measure up" naturally pulls us towards negative thinking and harmful self-talk. This gap between us and them is another source of pain.

Emotional triggers and mistakes are a normal part of life, and we can learn from them. It's important to acknowledge the pain and realise that many women experience similar feelings. By doing this, you validate your experience as normal. It's okay to feel this way, but it's also important to remember that you don't have to stay stuck in this place. You only need to be willing to accept where you are and take the steps to move forward.

However, we are all individuals, and that's crucial to remember. Please don't spend your precious energy comparing your pain, conflicts, or mistakes to anyone else's. You are unique, with your own DNA, childhood experiences, parental values, and life experiences that shape your responses to everything. Knowing this logically won't necessarily stop your mind from cycling through its patterns, but it will help you name, notice, and unhook yourself from the painful cycle.

The Power of Acceptance and Action

But the thing is, my friend, you must do the work. The key is to unhook yourself by recognising and validating your pain and the events that caused it. Then you can begin to replace the emotions surrounding it with positive, forward-thinking steps and a vision for your future. Of course, this pain hurts, I know it does. This stuff can be really hard, and I'm not denying that. It's normal to feel uncomfortable. Acknowledge that you are human and that your feelings are valid.

The critical things you're aiming for here are:

- Slowing yourself down enough to practise self-compassion.
- Being flexible with yourself and your emotions.
- Catching yourself and stopping the impulsive behaviours.

Your brain has a default setting that tries to make sense of your situation. However, when you're triggered, emotions can override this sense-making mechanism and throw you off course. Again, this is your subconscious taking over, pushing you away from the person you want to be and keeping you stuck in the automatic reactions you've developed over time. These reactions can become so ingrained that they feel like personality traits. This exercise will help you change those patterns.

Whilst this might sound formal or clinical, I would encourage you to start to see this as a way of sense-making and flexibly responding to your emotions – something you might not feel capable of doing today.

These skills are a gift to yourself, as they are creating new neural pathways in your brain. You'll start to get better at making sense of your experience, becoming more flexible, cultivating a kinder inner voice, and truly learning what it means to love yourself. Your task is to build these skills of change and watch how life expands and evolves for you.

> **"What you resist, persists. What you accept, transforms. Acceptance is a key flexibility skill in mindfulness practices. This reminds you that, for thoughts, feelings, urges and sensations you can't change, it's best to accept them."**
>
> – Russ Harris

Who know, perhaps when you're triggered, you just might stop using those coping responses, whether it's with food or drink, or anything else in your arsenal.

Changing Reactive Patterns Exercise
The Power of Acceptance in Action

Here's an awareness strategy to practise so you can unhook yourself from emotional triggers when they arise or when you've made a mistake that you're struggling to accept.

Let's Begin

1. Acknowledging Pain

Notice and name it. Notice and delicately acknowledge the painful thoughts and feelings. Approach your pain and respond to yourself with kindness and love, the same kind of love you would offer someone you care about who is suffering.

Feel yourself be present in a moment that really hurts. Be present and connect with the moment in a non-judgemental way, simply noticing the pain that is showing up.

Acknowledging is the first small step towards acceptance.

2. Letting Go of Self-Judgement

We all have minds that are quick to judge. You are not alone as we all have a strong inner critic. Voices that say, "I am weak, and I am stupid. I am undeserving". This inner critic can be harsh, cruel, and unrelenting at times.

This is normal and how the brain works. The human mind has evolved to be a judgement machine. Knowing this about yourself is vital and accepting that you can't stop these thoughts from arising is key.

If you can normalise it and accept that self-judgement is common, you'll stop fighting against it. This makes it easier to unhook yourself from the negative self-talk. Just let it pass on by!

3. Acting with Kindness

The core of self-compassion is kindness. Compassion for others and self-compassion both involve extending kindness.

As you've learned, your values are your deepest desires for how you want to treat yourself, others, and the world around you. When you live by your values, you commit to acting in alignment with them. You need to be flexible. You're working on identifying behaviour patterns and determining what actions you need to take when you get triggered.

Therefore, if you sense a trigger coming, you can choose how to respond, guided by your values. Ask yourself what a kind person would say about this. Think of your kindest, most compassionate friend, and consider what they would say, how they would act or react, and what their perspective would be.

Being open to this means letting go of inner judgement. When you practise this, you're not shifting blame or being that harsh inner critic who tells you that you're wrong. You're transforming into a kind, loving, and compassionate person, learning the benefits of treating yourself with love.

Eventually, as you replace judgement with kindness, that kindness will override the negative self-talk and become your default. Although there's work to do, it's as simple as saying, "I want to do/be this, not that".

> Doing simple things for yourself can be highly effective. Give yourself a hug. Kind self-touch is a powerful way for the brain to register love, compassion, and kindness of spirit. Say to yourself, "You did a great job today," every night before you go to sleep.

In this act of kindness, consciousness and connection with your mind and body are key. The tone of your voice is very effective in enabling this. Think about a kind person talking to you – their lovely, soft, warm, inviting tone. You can use your words to soothe yourself and that Inner Child reacting to the situation. Use the words and the voice you wish you had heard as a child when you needed validation. (You are learning this skill in this book.)

> **Question:** How do you feel about practising acts of kindness towards yourself? How do you feel about working on silencing the inner critic and using your voice to soothe?

4. Acceptance: Making Room for What Is

I'm introducing this now, and then I'll be talking about it more in the coming pages, because it's so effective for change; it needs a bit of airplay, in my books!

The practise of acceptance is a powerful tool for so many things in the healing process, including creating balance, inner peace, and a new inner narrative. It's often underestimated, but conscious acceptance doesn't mean passively giving in to a situation or trauma. It means acknowledging what happened and making room for the painful thoughts and feelings that arise and pass. You are no longer in denial, trying to sugar-coat your past with a false persona. This is also a huge part of self-kindness and self-compassion.

Like all humans, your default setting for painful thoughts is to try to get rid of them, to block them out, assuming this is the best way to move on. But you can't go around this; you must go through it. The emotions, thoughts, and feelings that come up through a triggering event are your private experiences.

> **This is the function of acceptance:**
>
> - To better manage the emotions that arise.
> - To recognise and acknowledge everything that comes up.
> - To know that you can make conscious changes to how you react in the future.

When you make room for these emotions, when you bring them into the light, you take away their power to control you and set off impulsive behaviours. The "Name and Tame" technique is a great way to consciously accept your thoughts and feelings.

...

Putting "Name and Tame" into Practice

When you notice a recurring story in your head, acknowledge it and give it a name. For example, you can say to yourself, "This is my overwhelmed story" or "My I'm not good enough story" or "My I'm fixated on the past story". Whatever the thought may be, give it a name. Then thank your brain for sending it to you. Let it wash over you for a while and accept that it's come to say hello and will soon pass through.

> **When you build this skill enough to manage these four things consistently, you honour yourself and your pain.** Remember, this is all about practising self-compassion and kindness. You can use some fun language and tones to do this, so you don't sound "judgy" with yourself. Humour is a great healer!

Practise Kind Deeds to Do for Yourself

My friend, try to simply practise one or two minutes of kindness thoughts (or you can sit quietly in meditation) in the morning or evening before bedtime. *I call it "have a little chat with yourself" time.*

Be gentle and go easy on yourself when you make mistakes. Practise kind self-talk and focus not only on the words but also on the tone of your voice. Practise words like, "I see you are in pain", "I care about you" and "I am here for you".

Do little things that show kindness to yourself. Draw on the kindness you show to others and redirect it inward. And make sure you spend time with people who care about you. Do this for two weeks, and then try to carry on for a month and I promise you things will change. You will start to feel such a massive shift in your inner world.

> **Then, reflect on this:** What past experiences of kindness have you witnessed or experienced that you can draw upon for inspiration, that you can now make your own?

Bye bye, nasty inner-bitch-face-talking you down! Hello, feeling good, from within.

Your limitless potential

I want you to really believe and trust that your potential is absolutely limitless. There is a vast ocean of strength and resilience living right inside you, and your capacity for change is not a question of "if", but a certainty of "when". The power to shift your current adult experience, to move past your pain, your feeling of being stuck, or your frustration for not having what you deeply want in life – is completely within your grasp. As I've said before, what you resist, persists. Trust that you already have the capacity and the know-how. Now, reach in and grab hold of that woman who is there, always there, waiting within you to heal your past so you can evolve and grow. Trust that. I mean it.

Please let that sink in ...

Triggers, Behaviours, and Consequences

21.
Sticky Cycles

Everything is a Pattern
Understanding Triggers, Behaviours and Consequences

Throughout these pages, you may now be noticing a recurring theme emerging: the cyclical nature of our experiences. I often share with those dealing with pain and feeling lost amidst this repetitive chaos that the message is in the mess! What I mean by this is that when we suppress difficult emotions, our lives tend to become complicated. Messy.

When something persistently resurfaces in our lives, it carries a message. We are safe to agree with that now, yes? And what we shy away from often leads to disarray, and ironically, what we avoid is precisely what we must embrace to find resolution. Correct? As you become intimately acquainted with your patterns of evasion, I hope you are starting to believe that true transformation is not so impossible.

The Challenge of Looking Inward

I'd like to ask you what have you uncovered so far that you perhaps haven't acknowledged before? Are you starting to see where you have felt ensnared – or caught – in a loop, where the same challenges and setbacks keep reappearing? I am here to tell you, sister, this is a universal human experience. The key is that until we are willing to confront what we are avoiding and understand the root cause, these patterns will likely continue to repeat. It's a fact of our psychology, and perhaps, the way the universe operates.

Can you also acknowledge that there are serious barriers that get in the way of self-reflection and introspection? You might have found that while doing these exercises. You might even be staring at the page and feeling completely blank.

> That, my friend, is a barrier, too.
> It makes this whole healing journey
> pretty damn hard at times.

It can be incredibly challenging to look inward these days, because our world is so focused on the external. We communicate through online platforms, constantly bombarded with messages about what's "right" or "wrong" and what our friends are doing. It's a vast screen of other people's ideals, making it extremely difficult to listen to our own inner voices and depend on our intuition. In an ideal world, we'd all be asking ourselves, "How can I become more conscious of the patterns in my life that may be triggering me and throwing me off course?" But in the real world, not many of us do that, do we?

The Path to Change

The encouraging news is that making a change to step away from these cycles is entirely within your reach. From here, I will guide you through connecting with your patterns, so you can anticipate your triggers well in advance. This will empower you to slow down those automatic responses. Then, equipped with your Liberation Toolbox (this gem is coming in the final chapters) filled with self-empowerment tools and an embrace of practising acceptance, you will be fully prepared to stay aligned with your path, armed with everything you need.

Triggers: Those Little Sparks That Ignite Our Reactions

Okay, let's really settle in and start to talk about triggers. We all have them – those little things that, seemingly out of nowhere, can send us spinning. Think of them as tiny sparks that light up a fire within us. They are the "hooks" that snag our attention, unconsciously, and suddenly we're on an emotional rollercoaster. The good news is, they are a very normal part of being human.

Sometimes, a trigger is external, like a critical comment from a colleague or a social situation that makes us feel uneasy. Other times, it's a sensory trigger – a song, a particular meal, or a physical touch that takes us back to a painful memory.

Identifying your own unique triggers is like discovering a secret map to your inner world. It's another first brave step towards understanding that part of yourself that needs some love and taking the reins of your reactions. By realising that triggers can come from all these different places, we can begin to understand our reactions and get to know ourselves better with a new perspective.

 ### Behaviours: Your Automatic Response

The why behind your actions: To put it simply, a behaviour is your automatic reaction to a trigger. These responses can be physical, emotional, or in your thoughts. Every behaviour serves a purpose, whether it's to seek comfort, avoid pain, or seek validation. They all arise from some influence in your life – sometimes it's one specific thing, and other times it's many things at once. The skill of identifying these influences will help you act and move away from destructive behaviours.

Examples of Behaviours

- Emotional eating or drinking
- Withdrawing from social interactions
- Putting things off or avoiding tasks
- Responding with aggression or defensiveness

- Seeking constant reassurance
- Self-criticising

Understanding Why You Do What You Do

When you notice an automatic behaviour, ask yourself these questions to gain insight:

- What need is this behaviour fulfilling (e.g., comfort, escape, control)?
- Is this behaviour helpful for me in the long run?
- What emotions drive this behaviour?
- What are the short-term gains?

Consequences: The Ripple Effect

You know the expression, "cause and effect", right? This is the same. Every behaviour has a ripple effect, resulting in outcomes that affect your life, mental and physical health, and happiness. These outcomes can be payoffs (benefits) or costs (detrimental effects). Often, we repeat patterns because the result reinforces the behaviour, sometimes without us even realising it (I will explain).

I think we have all seen that a trigger can lead to a cycle of shame and self-loathing, making you feel absolutely rubbish and leading you to seek out a quick fix – that temporary high or comfort in food or drink. Sadly, what you may not appreciate is that this can reinforce the very behaviour you want to avoid.

Other times, a behaviour might offer a temporary payoff, like relief, which can be counterproductive and increase the behaviour. A temporary payoff could be avoiding a difficult situation, unpleasant thoughts, or feelings of anxiety. This could look like avoiding social events, cancelling plans, or simply blanking someone. While avoidance might bring relief in the moment (yes, avoidance is a quick fix, too!), it can lead to other feelings like loneliness and insecurity, creating a new set of emotional reactions that will have their own consequences.

A simple example of how a behaviour can play out:

Trigger: Feeling stressed and overwhelmed at work.

Behaviour: Eating a large amount of comfort food or drinking four beers when you get home. (Function: seeking temporary relief from stress.)

Consequence: Not sleeping well, waking up sluggish and tired, having an even worse day at work the next day.

Understanding the Payoffs and Costs

Understanding the consequences of your behaviours is the first step toward making better choices.

 ### Payoffs (Benefits)

- Temporary relief from emotional pain
- A sense of being in control or making you feel secure
- Avoiding difficult situations

 ### Costs (Detrimental Effects)

- Feelings of guilt, shame, or regret
- Health problems (both physical and mental)
- Damaged relationships
- Increased anxiety or depression
- Further emotional isolation

The Reinforcing Power of Consequences

- Short-term payoffs can often reinforce negative behaviours, even if there are long-term costs

- For example, emotional eating provides immediate comfort but can lead to guilt and weight gain, continuing the cycle
- That temporary feeling of relief can be a very strong reinforcer

Stopping the Cycle

The key to making change is to break the cycle. Here are a few simple strategies to help you do that:

🔍 **Identify the Costs and Payoffs:** List the costs and payoffs of your unwanted behaviours.

🔍 **Challenge Negative Thoughts:** Replace self-defeating thoughts with more realistic and compassionate ones.

🔍 **Develop Healthy Coping Skills:** Practise healthy ways to manage your triggers and emotions, such as mindfulness, deep breathing, or exercise.

🔍 **Practise Self-Compassion:** Be kind to yourself, especially when you make mistakes.

🔍 **Set Values and Goals:** Define your core values and set goals that align with the life you want. This will help you make choices that reflect what's truly important to you.

Just so you know, we'll be doing a lot of work on helping you get what you want in life – by building skills for goal setting and executing on those personal desires – in Book Three: *Liberated Connection*.

> Remember that the feeling of "failure" is also a trigger in itself.

Acting in Line with Your Values

By understanding your triggers, behaviours, and consequences, you can make conscious choices that align with your values. When a trigger appears, you'll be better equipped to choose behaviours that move you towards your goals, rather than away from them.

> **For example:**
>
> **Value:** my physical and mental health
>
> **Trigger:** feeling stressed at work
>
> **Behaviour (New):** taking a short walk or practising deep breathing
>
> **Consequence:** reduced stress, improved focus, and a sense of feeling good inside and out

By understanding and working with this cycle, you'll gain the power of perspective, befriending your emotions and creating a more fulfilling and balanced life.

Let's move on to something truly powerful: a deep dive into your triggers. Think of this as an opportunity to understand what truly stands in the way of your peace and joy.

> By getting to know them, you're not just identifying challenges – you're creating a clearer path to the life you want to live.

22. Those Damn Triggers

Your Inner Alarm Bell
Understanding the Messages in More Detail

Trauma, whether it feels big or small, leaves an imprint. I think that message is pretty clear now, don't you agree? So, work with me on this: imagine it like a sensitive alarm system within you. Sometimes, seemingly ordinary situations can set off a cascade of emotional and physical reactions. These reactions are what we call "triggers" – specific stimuli that, consciously or subconsciously, remind us of past experiences. Recognising these triggers is another step towards healing and reclaiming your inner peace.

When you feel triggered, when something feels deeply uncomfortable, that's your inner compass speaking to you. It's signalling that there's something unresolved from a past trauma experience. These triggers are powerful guides. In my own experience, when these unresolved issues are addressed and acceptance takes place, the triggers lose their power and no longer throw me off course. In fact, when you embrace your triggers, they point you in the direction of your own healing, your liberation, your freedom from feeling stuck.

> Change begins with awareness: When you start to make the subconscious patterns conscious, you can start to change them.

I get it; you fear those little stings, those triggers that make you want to recoil. I once did too. But I am here to tell you confidently, my friend, they're not your enemies; they are messages. If you let them, and if you are patient enough to hear, they whisper – or sometimes shout – about the parts of you that long for healing. They're invitations to lean in, to explore the shadows you've been avoiding. I know it can be scary. Trust me. I truly do. But imagine, just for a moment, that behind that discomfort lies a pathway to a truer, freer version of yourself. So, in other words, that pain you've been running from? It's often a map, guiding you towards a deeper understanding and a more bona fide existence.

On the other side of your fear, there's a liberation waiting, a lightness you may not have felt in years. (I love the word "liberation"; it's only now that I experience it, that I can completely love its essence and genuine meaning. I'd love you to experience that too!) So, breathe, be kind to yourself, and dare to listen to those whispers. You might just find the courage to rewrite your story.

To help you get a little more comfortable with your triggers, I'd like to explore the different types of triggers that can create reactions, anxiety, and emotional storms in your life. From there, I'd like us to work on some practical strategies to help you ground yourself when you're feeling knocked around or anxious. Is this okay for you? Do you feel ready to approach this together?

> **"The most beautiful people we have known are those who have known defeat, known suffering, known struggle, known loss, and have found their way out of the depths. These persons have an appreciation, a sensitivity, and an understanding of life that fills them with compassion, gentleness, and a deep loving concern. Beautiful people do not just happen."**
>
> – Elisabeth Kübler-Ross

What Is a Trigger?

A trigger is your emotional response to a particular event, memory, or experience in your conscious world. It's a reaction from a part of you that has yet to heal, and if you can find the courage to explore the messages inside it, you'll discover a powerful opportunity for healing and peace. And then, just like that, poof, that trigger no longer exists in your life. It no longer has a hold on you or evokes a reaction that once felt like a heaviness, a darkness, an emotion you'd rather avoid.

Your triggers are ignited through your physical senses: sight, sound, smell, taste, and touch. The important thing here is to simply acknowledge what a trigger is for you. A helpful awareness tool is to highlight which sense your trigger is associated with. For example:

- A specific scent may remind you of a person or a past event.
- A particular touch may remind you of a way you were touched before.
- A taste may remind you of a time you were treated in a way that hurt you … and so on.

Each of these sensory experiences causes a particular behavioural response.

The less time you spend caught, stuck, and hooked in amplified emotions – playing out destructive or unhealthy behaviours in your life – the more time you must direct into more meaningful moments. This allows you to achieve your goals and step forward into a life of happiness, fulfilment, and balance.

The Triggers List

To help you gain a deeper understanding, we're going to dive into some common triggers that can pop up in our lives. Remember, understanding these isn't about blaming ourselves but rather about gaining that incredible superpower of awareness, so we can be kinder to ourselves when these moments hit. I've put together a "Triggers List" to outline some different scenarios, and my hope is that this information will truly resonate and potentially touch those previously out-of-reach places within.

> **NOTE:** Choose the triggers that you have experienced before. You can either circle them here on the page or take your favourite journal and write which ones you feel you have come up against in the past. Putting them on paper helps you allow room for them in your mind.

This is about you, your Change Experience, and your journey. Be kind with yourself as you explore these triggers. It's all part of the beautiful, messy, and utterly human experience of being you.

This might feel uncomfortable and create some anxiety, so please remember to use the Dropping Anchor exercise to ground yourself and the 4-7-8 Breathing exercise to slow down your anxiety and create some peace within.

Let's Begin

1. Family-Related Triggers

These are those moments tied to our family, whether it's the one we grew up in or the one we've created. Sometimes, old dynamics can sneak back in and stir things up.

- **Common Responses:** You might find yourself feeling trapped, invalidated, or a deep sense of being unsupported, like those old feelings are resurfacing.

- **Examples:** Think about family gatherings where you feel that familiar lack of emotional support, almost like stepping back into a challenging past.

Or perhaps a child's tantrum might unexpectedly trigger a wave of heightened anxiety or even vivid flashbacks if your own childhood involved difficult experiences.

2. Love/Relationship-Related Triggers

Our intimate relationships, beautiful as they are, can sometimes hold little landmines from past hurts.

- **Common Responses:** These can bring up a strong fear of abandonment, a deep feeling of invalidation, a potent sense of vulnerability, or even distrust and a general feeling of unease.

- **Examples:** Imagine a conflict with loud voices or aggressive tones that can instantly reactivate old wounds of feeling dismissed or unheard.

Even something as simple as a partner's sudden shift in mood might trigger those deep-seated fears of abandonment or rejection, especially if you've experienced betrayal before.

3. Mental Health-Related Triggers

Sometimes, our own internal landscape can become a trigger, bringing back echoes of past struggles.

- **Common Responses:** You might experience feelings of hopelessness, a rush of anxiety, or even full-blown flashbacks and panic attacks.

- **Examples:** Going through a period of low self-esteem or anxiety can sometimes feel like an old trauma is resurfacing, bringing with it that familiar sense of despair.

Or, surprisingly, a particular song or even a scent might instantly transport you back to a traumatic event, triggering intense emotional reactions.

4. Feeling Out of Control

These are those moments when it feels like the ground beneath you has shifted, and you're no longer in the driver's seat.

- **Common Responses:** A deep sense of helplessness, intense anxiety, and palpable fear, as if you're losing your footing.

- **Examples:** Any situation where you feel powerless can become a weighty trigger, activating that deep-seated fear of being unable to influence your circumstances.

Uncertainty or unexpected changes can quickly bring on anxiety, mirroring past times when you felt things were unpredictable and unsafe.

5. Social Triggers

Handling social situations can sometimes feel like walking through a minefield, especially if past experiences have made us wary.

- **Common Responses:** You might feel overwhelmed, a surge of anxiety, or even a strong sense of panic and distrust.

- **Examples:** Crowded places or big social gatherings can quickly make you feel unsafe, bringing on a wave of anxiety.

Perhaps encountering someone who reminds you of a past abuser can immediately trigger feelings of fear or deep distrust, even if the person means no harm.

6. Work-Related Triggers

Our professional lives, unfortunately, aren't immune to triggers, especially when power dynamics are involved.

- **Common Responses:** You might experience anxiety, fear, a sense of helplessness, or feelings of inadequacy and worthlessness.
- **Examples:** A demanding boss who uses a particular tone or phrase might trigger that familiar anxiety or fear you felt with a past abuser, even if the situation isn't dangerous now.

Receiving critical feedback can sometimes reactivate those painful feelings of inadequacy, especially if you've been subjected to constant criticism in the past.

7. Authority Figures

People in positions of power can sometimes unknowingly tap into old fears, especially if past experiences involved controlling or abusive figures.

- **Common Responses:** A deep-seated fear response, a feeling of vulnerability, and a penetrating fear of abandonment.
- **Examples:** Just being around a boss or teacher might spark fear, reminding you of past encounters with controlling figures.

Power dynamics – situations involving power imbalances, control, or coercion can be highly triggering.

Witnessing or even experiencing anger, even if it's not directed at you, can activate that internal alarm system, reminding you of times when anger felt unsafe.

8. Environmental Triggers

Our surroundings can sometimes hold echoes of the past, bringing back intense emotions without warning.

- **Common Responses:** Intense emotional flashbacks, feeling overwhelmed, hypervigilance, and deep distress.

- **Examples:** Being in a place that looks or feels like somewhere a trauma occurred can instantly bring back a flood of intense emotions.

Loud noises, bright lights, or even certain textures can be incredibly distressing if they were present during a traumatic experience.

9. Anniversaries and Holidays

These significant dates can sometimes carry a heavy emotional weight, bringing up memories of past pain.

- **Common Responses:** Intense emotional distress, sadness, anxiety, and a profound sense of loss.

- **Examples:** Dates that mark traumatic events or periods of neglect can unexpectedly trigger a wave of intense emotional distress.

Any situation that reminds you of a time you felt trapped or unable to control your environment can be deeply unsettling.

10. Triggers Related to Sexual Assault

These are particularly sensitive triggers as they connect directly to experiences of deep violation and a loss of safety.

- **Common Responses**: Intense fear, anxiety, distress, a feeling of being exposed or vulnerable, and potentially flashbacks or a sense of re-**traumatisation**.

- **Examples:** Even a soft, unexpected touch can be deeply unsettling if it reminds you of past unwanted physical contact.

Sexual innuendo or even certain conversations can be incredibly distressing, bringing back memories of the assault.

11. Layered Triggers (Combining Complex Trauma and Sexual Assault)

When complex childhood trauma and sexual assault intertwine, the triggers can be incredibly potent, hitting multiple sensitive spots at once.

- **Common Responses:** A sense of being re-traumatised, deep insecurity, blame (often internalised), intense fear of losing control, and intense anxiety.

- **Examples:** Feeling silenced or disbelieved can be incredibly painful, especially if your childhood also involved your experiences being dismissed.

Situations where you feel blamed can be deeply triggering, reactivating not only the sexual assault trauma but also those childhood feelings of being responsible for adult problems.

12. Physical Health-Related Triggers

Our physical health can sometimes unexpectedly tap into deeper emotional wounds, especially if past trauma involved physical harm or medical distress.

- **Common Responses:** A strong sense of vulnerability, fear, anxiety, and potentially flashbacks.

- **Examples:** Physical pain or illness can easily trigger a wave of vulnerability, especially if your past involved physical harm.

Certain medical examinations, procedures, or environments, like hospitals, can bring on anxiety or flashbacks if you've experienced medical trauma before.

13. Spiritual Health-Related Triggers

Our spiritual path, which should ideally bring comfort, can sometimes hold triggers if past experiences involved spiritual manipulation or abuse.

- **Common Responses:** Feelings of guilt, shame, despair, and uncomfortable isolation.
- **Examples:** Hearing religious teachings that focus on guilt or shame can be deeply triggering if your past involved religious abuse.

Feeling disconnected from your sense of purpose could trigger despair, especially if trauma shattered your faith or sense of meaning.

14. False Self-Related Triggers

These are those moments when we feel like we're not being our true selves, often a coping mechanism from past trauma.

- **Common Responses:** Internal conflict, a sense of living a lie, deep exhaustion, and resentment.
- **Examples:** Being praised for something that feels inauthentic can cause a real internal struggle, making you feel like you're not being true to yourself.

Feeling pressured to constantly appear strong or happy can lead to exhaustion, especially if past trauma forced you to suppress your real emotions.

15. Sensory Triggers

Our senses are powerful gateways to memory, and sometimes, a simple sound, smell, or sight can transport us back to a traumatic moment.

- **Common Responses:** Intense flashbacks, sudden panic attacks, and a visceral sense of re-experiencing the past.

- **Examples:** Specific sounds, smells, or textures that were present during a traumatic event can immediately trigger vivid flashbacks.

Even certain lighting or weather conditions can resemble the environment of a past traumatic experience, bringing those feelings back.

16. Media/News Triggers

In our constantly connected world, what we see and hear can sometimes trigger us, especially if it mirrors past traumatic experiences.

- **Common Responses:** Intense emotional distress, sudden flashbacks, and heightened anxiety.

- **Examples:** News reports or fictional stories about violence or abuse can easily trigger flashbacks or emotional overwhelm.

Scrolling through social media and encountering triggering content can lead to a quick surge of anxiety.

17. Gaslighting-Related Triggers

Gaslighting is a particularly insidious form of abuse because it directly attacks our sense of reality. Any situation where your perception is questioned can be a powerful trigger.

- **Common Responses:** Intense self-doubt, confusion, a chilling sense of losing touch with reality, and significant anxiety.

- **Examples:** Being told that your clear memory of an event is "incorrect" can make you question your own mind and feelings.

Hearing phrases like "You're too sensitive" when you know your emotional response is valid can reactivate past experiences of invalidation.

18. Narcissistic Relationship Triggers

When you've dealt with a narcissist, certain dynamics can instantly trigger old fears and feelings of worthlessness.

- **Common Responses:** Intense hypervigilance, deep fear, a feeling of helplessness, and a resurgence of past trauma related to manipulation.
- **Examples:** Sudden shifts in someone's behaviour, like moving from intense affection to cold detachment, can instantly trigger that hypervigilance you learned with a narcissistic individual.

Even subtle disregard for your boundaries can reactivate those painful feelings of being controlled or manipulated.

19. Parental Mental Health Triggers

Growing up with a parent who struggles with a mental health disorder can create a deeply unpredictable and chaotic environment. This kind of instability attacks your fundamental sense of safety and reality, and anything that mimics that experience can become an unwanted trigger.

- **Common Responses:** Deep-seated insecurity, a very un-fun lack of trust, a constant anticipation of betrayal, a feeling of disgust or intense anger, and a chilling sense of losing touch with your own reality.
- **Examples:** Experiencing a parent's sudden, unexplained mood swings can trigger a constant state of hypervigilance, as you never know when the emotional landscape will shift.

Seeing charm used to deceive others can evoke a deep sense of distrust, especially when you realise that the same facade was used to make you feel responsible for their general happiness.

20. Psychopathic Intimate Partner Triggers

If you've experienced a relationship with a psychopathic partner, anything that hints at isolation or manipulative tactics can be a potent and frightening trigger.

- **Common Responses:** Intense fear, a chilling sense of being unsafe, paralysed helplessness, and deep confusion.

- **Examples:** Encountering someone who shows a shocking lack of remorse after causing harm can trigger intense fear, reminding you of your partner's capacity for cruelty.

Witnessing manipulative tactics like triangulation or mind games can bring back overwhelming feelings of confusion and being controlled.

Okay, that was big. Well done. Put the book down now and go do something that makes you feel good. Call a friend or do something from your rewards list.

Just reading through that list can be a trigger in itself!

...

Mental Health Check

My friend, before we go on, let's take a moment for a focused mental health check.

This work can be tough, and I want to make sure you're feeling okay to continue. Please pause and ask yourself if you are ready to proceed. If you're feeling unsettled, that is completely normal and okay. There is no rush here.

If you need to, please practise a tool we've learned, like **Dropping Anchor, Name and Tame,** or the **4-7-8 Breathing** exercise. Find what feels comfortable for you and use it to feel a little more grounded before you move on.

When you do feel ready to continue, remember this: Don't be scared of this process. The good news is that by learning to recognise your triggers, you're not just uncovering challenges – you're learning how to manage them, and that's the key to a much more peaceful life.

If you need to, take a break. Go for a walk, get some fresh air, have a glass of water, and come back to this when you're feeling refreshed.

23.
Your Trigger Playbook

Connecting the Dots
A Map to Your Patterns

Perhaps you can't immediately connect with what triggers you, and that's okay. Identifying your triggers is truly a journey of self-discovery, my friend. It's about lightly peeling back the layers to reveal the places where your past still echoes within you. We're going to create a visual map of your understanding – turning the unconscious into something you can see, understand, and work with.

To get you primed and ready, I'd love for you to take a moment and reflect on the past week, or perhaps the last month. Think about a circumstance where you were triggered, leading to unwanted behaviours, which resulted in a consequence you'd rather avoid. You may even start with something simple, like food or drink. When you slow down and pinpoint each of those moments, you start to gain such a deeper understanding of your own actions.

> It's like taking the reins back in your life, and I promise you, it feels absolutely amazing.

Your Trigger Cycle Map

Step One: Pick a Trigger
Take a moment and simply choose a trigger that you can remember from the last few weeks, or longer if needed. Don't worry about being perfect. Just choose the one that comes to mind most easily.

Step Two: Find the Root
Now, ask yourself where this trigger might have come from in your past. What was the first memory you have of something like this happening to you as a child? This is your nugget of gold – where you can focus on realising and healing that experience.

Step Three: Identify the Behaviour and Consequences
For that trigger, I want you to write down what behaviour most commonly happens for you. What do you do, what do you say, and how do you react? Next, look at the consequences of that behaviour. What happens as a result? Be completely honest here – we're looking at the full picture, good and bad.

Step Four: Reflect on Your Values
Take a moment to reflect. Are these behaviours in line with your values? Are they how you truly want to respond, or are they reactions that you feel are not aligned with who you are? Simply answer Yes or No for each one.

Step Five: Act
How are you going to take action to change? What small step can you take to shift this pattern? What would you do differently the next time you encounter that trigger? It doesn't have to be a huge change; even a small shift can make a big difference.

Step Six: Do It Again
Once you've completed this exercise for one trigger, choose another one. This time, read it all out loud to yourself. Hear your own words. Sometimes, hearing our own thoughts spoken aloud can help us come up with the bright ideas we need to make changes in our world.

For You to Ponder

Once you've completed this exercise, sit with it for a while. Let your internal messages and insights flow. Consider this your practice run, and know that you can revisit it to continue to refine this skill. Take a moment to acknowledge that you're building greater connections, deeper self-awareness, and new confidence in making discerning choices. The next section will help you hone these skills.

? AND ONE LAST THING: When you feel yourself wanting to shy away from an emotion that is bubbling up inside, can I ask you to do this one thing, please? Ask yourself, "What is the message this is trying to communicate to me, and where did it start?" Then, just let that sit and see what comes to you. You don't have to force an answer; just listen.

Once you've done that, I give you full permission to go take a break from all of this and go back to being human again.

> You've done the work; you've earned it.

More Bonus Questions in the Appendix

I've added some extra learning opportunities there, and truly, I want you to have every chance to grow and build these new skills. Life throws curveballs – relationships, work, health, grief – and those big emotions can be tough. This is where you can explore more about your triggers.

In the Appendix, you'll find reflective questions that will get you thinking about how all the parts of your life connect. We'll explore:

- **Your Tribe of Support:** Those people who light you up and you can always count on. We'll appreciate them together.

- **Identifying Different Triggers:** We'll look at triggers in relationships, work, health, and family. Because they show up everywhere, right?

- **Moving Forward:** We'll talk about taking small steps, inviting growth, and creating ease. It's about building a future that feels good.

I've included this section because everything in our lives is interconnected. Understanding one area often sheds light on another. Acknowledging your triggers is a sign of strength, and journaling can help you explore even further.

My biggest hope is that the Appendix helps you find your own wise solutions in the future, and that you move towards a path that feels more legitimately yours, fulfilling, and just ... *more you.*

By the way, I've kept this in the Appendix because you've already done so much work here. I want to give you some space and a chance to revisit this when you've had time to process everything.

> No need to flick ahead through the pages now, okay! I really don't want you to miss out on any good bits here!

Become Trigger Positive

The message here from me is to keep working on what triggers you.

You might find another one from the list, or you might just connect to what is triggering you in the moment. Get used to identifying your patterns and breaking it all down, so you can work out where you want to make some changes in your life. Here are some things to consider:

1. What situations have triggered you? When was the first time you ever experienced that feeling?

2. What behaviours immediately followed? Were they internal, external, private, or public?

3. What were the consequences, in terms of costs or payoffs? Be honest with yourself here.

4. Who were the people involved? Notice who tends to appear in these moments when you engage in automatic behaviours, whether they be risky, destructive, or unhealthy habits with food and drink.

5. What would you do differently next time? Knowing what you know about yourself and what your values are, how could you choose a different path? Imagine you're giving advice to a dear friend – what would you tell them?

6. How could you find calm and balance within yourself after the chaos of this trigger? What are your go-to strategies for self-soothing? What brings you back to centre? What fills your cup?

For the Benefit of Your Change Experience

Keeping a diary or using a journal is a powerful way to trace those past triggers and patterns. It's your personal roadmap to seeing those patterns emerge and having your own Aha! moments. Through this work, clarity will become your wonderful gift – a clear map of the tracks you have taken, over and over again, is truly invaluable. The answers you're looking for are already inside you, just waiting to come to light.

In my humble opinion, this is another one of those must-have life skills for making change.

...

24.
Is Your Reality Being Twisted?

Unpacking Gaslighting
Perhaps a Link to Your Automatic Reactions

While life throws countless triggers our way, I want to focus specifically on gaslighting and the many forms it can take. Why? Because, my dear friend, this incredibly hurtful and demeaning experience can be such a powerful driver of automatic and destructive behaviours. It can really wreak havoc on our lives, and it can be a deeply damaging trigger when we turn to things like food and alcohol to cope.

It's sadly common for people like us, sensitive souls with big hearts, to be subjected to gaslighting or to become scapegoats. I want to shine a light on the different phrases, terminologies, and styles of gaslighting that you've likely encountered. Because with knowledge comes awareness, with awareness comes action, and with action, we can create real and lasting change in our lives.

Creating awareness and understanding the breadth and widespread consequences of gaslighting can help you be better prepared for when it happens again. When you're exposed to such an experience, you

> **"Gaslighting is a type of psychological abuse aimed at making victims seem or feel 'crazy,' creating a 'surreal' interpersonal environment."**
>
> – Paige L. Sweet (Harvard University), The Sociology of Gaslighting

can make a choice about how you behave. Perhaps you won't respond in the ways you always have, now with these new tools and skills you've gained. That would make me smile!

> Remember the work you did with the "Choice Point" in Book One? This is where you use it.

Gaslighting – What Is It?

Simply put, gaslighting is someone deliberately twisting your reality, making you doubt your own sanity. It's not just a disagreement; it's a calculated attempt to control you by making you question your memories, perceptions, and feelings. You see, the act of gaslighting isn't always a big, dramatic blow-up. It's often in the little things – the tiny cracks that start to appear and slowly widen until you're not sure what's real anymore. It's like a slow leak in your tyre; you don't always realise it at first, but eventually, you're left stranded, wondering how you got there.

Gaslighting is incredibly subtle. It's those little comments and dismissive glances that gradually erode your sense of self, making you feel like you're losing your mind. And that, my friend, is exactly what the gaslighter wants. They might say things like, "You're remembering it wrong" or "You're always exaggerating". They'll pretend not to understand, refuse to listen, and twist your words until you're questioning your own sanity.

> **"The worst part about gaslighting is that it undermines your self-worth to the point where you're second-guessing everything."**
> – Dana Arcuri

 **NOTE:** Clinically, this is now considered a form of mental abuse.

A Devastating Consequence

Gaslighting isn't just a psychological term; it's a real, devastating experience that can drive us to unhealthy coping mechanisms. When our reality is constantly questioned, our emotions become a tangled mess. We might reach for a bottle of wine or that extra slice of cake – anything to numb the pain of feeling paralysed and invalidated. It's a desperate attempt to soothe the chaos inside.

For example, after a particularly intense gaslighting episode where your partner, parent, or boss insists you imagined a critical conversation, you might find yourself mindlessly snacking, seeking comfort in the physical sensation of food, or downing some tequila – anything to distract yourself from the emotional turmoil.

I want to be clear: It's not about arguing or trying to reason with them because, my friend, you can't win a game where the rules keep changing. In fact, you are not even on the same field. It's about recognising the manipulation, grounding yourself, and saying, "No, this isn't my reality". Sometimes, the best thing you can do is simply walk away. Remove yourself from the situation until you can gather your thoughts. Take a deep breath, remind yourself of your truth, and know that you are not alone. You deserve to feel safe, validated, and heard.

> **"Trauma must be regarded as a virus that can still be triggered years later; and when it is triggered, it produces unhealthy responses."**
> – Peter Levine

Later, I am going to help you become familiar with the common phrases gaslighters use, so that you can start to be more aware of the patterns and see the manipulation before it takes hold. And remember, you are not losing your mind. You are strong, and you are worthy of a life free from mind games.

Gaslighting as an Emotional Trigger

My friend, let's agree that you're carrying a backpack filled with painful memories, maybe old wounds from childhood, or some horrible event, or maybe a previous abusive relationship. That's why you are here, correct? Now, someone starts gaslighting you. It's like they're poking at those old wounds, those sensitive spots in your backpack. And it hurts. But they deny ever inflicting this pain. They're making you question your reality, and that uncomfortable feeling you get mirrors the uncertainty and fear you felt during those past traumas. Your body remembers those feelings, even if your mind doesn't consciously recall every detail. So, when someone says, "You're imagining things" or "That never happened", it's not just a simple disagreement. It's a direct hit to those vulnerable places, triggering a flood of emotions – fear, doubt, anger, helplessness. It's like a flashback, but instead of a visual memory, it's an emotional one. Your nervous system goes on high alert, thinking you're in the line of potential danger again, even if the current situation isn't physically threatening. It's your body's way of saying "This feels familiar, and it's not safe".

Your nervous system misinterprets the gaslighting as a confirmation of your deepest fears – that you are unworthy, unlovable, or fundamentally flawed. And that, my dear, is how gaslighting can become a powerful emotional trigger, sending you spiralling into old patterns of fear and self-doubt.

The gaslighter's tactics denying your experiences, twisting your words, and invalidating your feelings – echo the past issues you faced, making you feel trapped and helpless. In a desperate attempt to regain control or numb the overwhelming pain, you might turn to familiar coping mechanisms, even if they're ultimately destructive. Food, alcohol, or any other numbing technique you deploy become temporary escapes, offering a fleeting sense of comfort and oblivion. This was my experience too, and that of many millions more.

A Real-Life Story

Let's talk about someone I know; we'll call her Penny. Penny grew up in a home where her emotions were constantly dismissed. If she cried, she was told to "toughen up". If she was excited, she was told to "calm down". Her feelings were never validated, never acknowledged. This left a deep wound – a belief that her emotions were somehow wrong or invalid.

Now, years later, Penny is in a relationship where her partner often says, using humour, things like "You're overreacting" and "That's not how it happened. You're remembering it wrong". Each time he says these things, it's like a punch to the gut. It's not just a disagreement; it's a reopening of that old wound from childhood. That familiar feeling of being dismissed and of being told her reality is wrong, floods back. She starts to doubt herself, her memory, her sanity. "Am I crazy?" she wonders. "Am I just making things up?"

The emotional turmoil becomes unbearable, and in those moments of desperation, she finds herself reaching for a bottle of Shiraz and a whole packet of 70% dark chocolate late at night. The wine and chocolate are masterful in numbing that agonising feeling of being invalidated, of feeling like she doesn't matter. She knows, deep down, it's not the answer and it's unhealthy, but each time, she still says, "Stuff it, I want this".

She resists and she suffers, and then she complains about it, promising her girlfriends that tomorrow she is starting a new routine of self-care and working on changing this mess she is in. But in that moment, she knows that's a lie, too. She knows she's just feeding them a story to keep them listening to her. Deep down, she knows that tomorrow nothing will change. She doesn't know how to stop the way she is being treated or how to show up differently to the subtle gaslighting manipulation. She can't question him, as he will just shut her down so cleverly telling her to have another drink and lay of the drama. Feeling helpless and believing him, she stays in her relationship and continues to give her power away to this man. In a constant state of fight or flight, her nervous system is wired permanently on red alert, and she is stuck, drinking on a daily basis.

The emotional assault is so powerful, and the feeling of being caught in that cycle is so familiar, it feels like another addiction she suffers from. For now, she carries the belief she is an alcoholic, over and over, repeating the same pattern, a truckload of shame, bolted to her heart.

IMPORTANT NOTE: An example of the importance of the root cause: So often, people are labelled as an "alcoholic," when in reality, they are a victim of gaslighting. Their unhealthy behaviours are simply a coping mechanism for the abuse they are experiencing. I believe that when we can avoid labels as much as possible, the healing process can be far more effective, as we can focus on addressing the root cause of the problem.

Spotting Their Moves
Unmasking the Four Ways Gaslighting Twists Your Reality

Oh, sigh. Gaslighting. I know just hearing the word can feel heavy, can't it? It's a loaded term, and honestly, it carries a lot of pain for so many of us. But here's what I've learned, and what I want to share with you: When you truly understand gaslighting, when you see it for what it really is, you start to reclaim your power. It's like gaining a kind of inner warrior strength, a way to protect yourself and say, "No more". If even to yourself. Understanding these patterns, these specific ways that gaslighting shows up, is a huge step towards healing and taking back your own life.

Let me help you appreciate this masked, ugly beast by breaking it down into the familiar ways it can show up in our lives. Gaslighting, as a particularly manipulative form of psychological and emotional abuse, often manifests in four distinct ways: outright lying, the manipulation of reality, scapegoating, and coercion. My goal is to walk you through these forms so you can recognise them and feel empowered to stand up for yourself against them. Let's take a closer look at each one.

 ### 1. Outright Lying – The Web of Deceit
For me personally, outright lying has always been a huge trigger. It feels like a betrayal of trust, a violation of something sacred. Gaslighters are incredibly skilled at this; they can be so smooth and believable. But the truth is, they're lying to cover their own bad behaviour, to avoid accountability.

In a relationship, they might pretend that betraying someone is the worst thing imaginable. They'll say it with such conviction, with such a show of sincerity, that you almost don't want to question them. You start thinking, "How could someone say that with such feeling and then be lying? Surely not!"

WATCH OUT! If you do question them, they often double down on the lie. They might take it even further, turn up the heat on you, and make you feel responsible for even bringing it up. Please know this: don't feel like a fool. It's human nature to want to believe people, especially those we love and trust. It's human nature to want to trust the people we choose to have relationships with.

When someone says to you, "It's not me; it's you", it's incredibly difficult to challenge their integrity in that moment. So often, we end up believing the lies because the gaslighter is so skilled at deflecting and putting the blame on us. They often use humour, which makes it even more confusing. Questioning them feels almost impossible, and that's how they get away with it. In those moments, sometimes the best thing you can do is to walk away, to create space for yourself.

Example: You're curled up on the couch with your partner, watching a movie where someone's being cheated on, and he whispers in your ear, "I would never, ever cheat on you", his voice full of conviction. "Infidelity is the lowest of the low." You believe him. You trust him. You feel safe in his arms. But then, you find a stray earring under the passenger seat of his car, a text message coming through late at night, each night, a gut feeling that something's just not right. When you confront him, his eyes widen in mock horror. "Cheat on you?" he gasps, his voice laced with indignation. "You're being insecure. It's all in your head. I would never do that." He twists the narrative, making you feel like the unstable one, the one with trust issues. He spins a web of deceit, denying the undeniable, making you doubt your own intuition.

2. Manipulation of Reality – The Slow Erosion of Truth

The manipulation of reality is a particularly insidious form of gaslighting. It's like a slow, steady chipping away at your sense of self, your confidence, your very understanding of the world. It often starts with a simple question about something you've said, about how you feel, or about your opinions. A seed of doubt is planted by denying your experience or feelings. They might say, "I need clarification on that," which subtly undermines what you know to be true. Over and over again, they deny your feelings or your words, to the point that you start to doubt yourself. Tick, tick, tick … boom. Your confidence is gone. Your reality becomes blurred in this constant ripple effect.

What happens, sadly, is that it eats away at your self-esteem and your confidence. This thing that you thought you knew you just aren't sure about anymore because the gaslighter is so subtle. They can be kind and nice one moment, and then they'll push you away the next. It's a mental struggle because they pull you close, which feels good, and then they subtly push you away. But they deny pushing you away, leaving you feeling confused and questioning yourself.

Then the cycle begins again. They'll draw you close, giving you that fleeting feeling of validation, and then they'll push you away again, leaving you uncertain and vulnerable. You become dependent on them for validation, and you lose the strength to challenge them.

Example: You're at a party, feeling lost in the crowd, and your partner is completely engrossed with someone else, leaving you feeling invisible. When you express your hurt, he dismisses your feelings, saying you're "overly sensitive" or "making a big deal out of nothing". Or maybe you see him deep in conversation with another woman at the bar, but he insists you're "mistaken" and he "barely spoke" to her. These subtle denials and dismissals chip away at your confidence, making you question your own perception of reality. He's manipulating your truth, planting seeds of doubt that grow into a tangled mess of insecurity and self-blame.

A question for you:

Have you ever felt like you lost yourself with someone?

3. Scapegoating – The Blame Game

Let's talk about scapegoating. This is often familiar to those who have experienced abuse. Perhaps you were the one who was scapegoated in your family, in social settings, or even at work. You're nit-picked, criticised, and blamed for things: "See what you did?" "What have you done now?" Often, you have played no part in the situation and have done nothing wrong. But the gaslighter puts the blame on you, and you start to believe that it's your responsibility when it's theirs or someone else's. Why? Because you know the truth, so they do this to keep you small.

You can end up in this situation because your sense of reality is unsteady, and you may not have the strength to say, "Enough! That's not my fault". Once again, your reality is distorted. You start to believe these negative portrayals of yourself. Scapegoating can be subtle or aggressive, and it can be delivered with passive aggression. But the bottom line is this: If you're constantly being blamed for something you know you didn't do or something that isn't your responsibility, you're likely being scapegoated. Be aware of that.

Example: You've just finished presenting the new marketing campaign, weeks of work, all flawlessly practised and delivered. Your boss, Mark, the bully whose desperation for a promotion is palpable, leans back in his chair. He doesn't smile; he simply offers a slow, critical frown. "This isn't what I was looking for," he says, his voice flat and dismissive. "The messaging is all wrong, the visuals are weak, and frankly, it's just not good enough." Your heart shatters, and the brilliant energy you brought into the room evaporates completely. You know you put your all into this campaign, carefully considering the target audience and meticulously crafting every detail. But here's the thing: you later find out that Mark had already decided to hire an outside agency for this project, regardless of your pitch. He set you up to fail, intentionally creating a scenario where he could criticise your work and justify his pre-determined decision. He even goes on to praise the agency's work, highlighting how "fresh" and "innovative" it is, making you question your own abilities and feel like you're not good enough. It's a cruel combination of gaslighting and scapegoating, leaving you feeling betrayed, undermined, and deeply insecure about your professional skills.

Now, you may ask, isn't scapegoating a form of gaslighting?" While both are manipulative, the behaviours in gaslighting and scapegoating have different goals. Gaslighting is a form of psychological abuse that makes you doubt your own sanity and reality, while scapegoating is a way for someone to deflect their own blame and responsibility by unfairly targeting you.

> ### Here is a simple comparison
>
> **Gaslighting** makes you feel like you're losing your grip on reality. It's about denying your perception, twisting events, and making you question your own memory. Its goal is to make you rely on the manipulator for your sense of truth.
>
> **Scapegoating** makes you feel like the problem. It's about unfairly blaming you for something you didn't do so that the other person can avoid taking responsibility. Its goal is to deflect blame and guilt.

My friend, one makes you feel **confused and disconnected from reality**, and the other makes you feel **blamed**, but both are designed to control and manipulate you.

4. Coercion – The Charm Trap

The fourth type of gaslighting is coercion, which is a particularly interesting form of manipulation because it often involves charm. The gaslighter gets you to collude with their bad behaviour, making you feel like it was your idea, that you're a part of this, and that you have to do something about it. They try to make you the one who carries out their dirty work. It's very clever, a real mind game.

They've manipulated you into being part of their plan, and if things don't go their way, they can become aggressive. They might bully you into thinking you aren't holding up your end of the bargain. Every day it can shift from subtle, charming manipulation to something quite uncomfortable.

You end up feeling stuck and doing what they want because you feel trapped. You feel like you're doing something wrong. The charm can be very powerful, or the aggression can be intimidating. It's their way of getting you to act against your own will. But you do it because you feel you must, because you feel like it's the only way out.

Example: You're having coffee with your friend, and she starts talking about someone you both know, Sarah. She's not being outright nasty. In fact, she's got that sweet, concerned tone she always uses when she's about to stir up trouble. "I'm really worried about Sarah," she sighs, her brow furrowed with worry. "She's been acting so strangely lately, and I think she needs to hear what people are saying. You know, for her own good. Could you maybe just casually mention it to her?" She makes it sound like she's genuinely concerned, like she's just trying to help Sarah out. But your gut is screaming. Something feels off.

You know how Sarah feels about gossip, and you know your friend knows it too. It's like she's trying to use your good intentions as a cover for her own not-so-innocent motives. It's that classic gaslighting coercion, twisting your sense of empathy and loyalty to manipulate you into being her messenger, even if the message is far from kind. And you're left feeling pressured, uncomfortable, and wondering why you're suddenly caught in the middle of her manipulative game.

> Ever felt like someone sounded like they were a friend, when they really weren't?

Their Words, Your Reality
Recognising the Common Phrases That Bend Your Truth

Have you ever felt a nagging sense that something just isn't right in a relationship, but you can't quite put your finger on it? You're not alone. If you're noticing signs like denial, minimisation, blame-shifting, isolation, withholding, confusion, doubt, constant criticism, projection, or even those intense bursts of affection known as "love bombing", you might be experiencing gaslighting. It's so important to become familiar with these tactics so you can recognise them when they appear.

> When I first started exploring this, I was genuinely surprised by the sheer range of manipulative language out there. It was eye-opening to realise how much my own reality had been twisted.
>
> For years, I carried the weight of so much blame and the shame of it. Too often, I was the scapegoat in my own family. When I finally came across the concept of gaslighting and saw those common phrases laid out, it was like a lightbulb went on. So many of them resonated deeply, and I realised I had been internalising blame that wasn't mine to carry.

We're about to dive into the specific phrases that gaslighters often use. My hope is that as you read through this, something clicks for you too. When you hear these expressions and they feel familiar, you'll start to see the patterns you've been caught in. You'll be able to say to yourself, "Ah, okay. I see what you're doing. I see you". And in that moment, you begin to reclaim your power. (And, yes, if you need to add a little colourful language there, go right ahead!)

NOTE: Reading this for the first time can be confronting, so use the grounding techniques. You also might need to sit with these ideas for a while, and that's perfectly alright.

Common Gaslighting Phrases

When someone tries to make you doubt your own reality, it can be so confusing and hurtful. But, with a new perspective on where this hurt is coming from, things can start to change. I've put together this list of common phrases that might sound familiar, but are designed to help you connect to what may be triggering you.

Take your time with these and maybe circle the ones that really hit home for you. If it helps, jot down a name beside a phrase – sometimes that can bring clarity. This is about recognising and understanding, so you can build up your inner strength.

It's okay if some of these phrases feel scarily familiar, and it's also okay if some don't resonate with your experiences. We're each on our own journey. But let's dive in, so you can start to feel more empowered and protected.

Let's Begin

"You're making that up."
You are being confronted with an accusation of lying. When you try to defend yourself, all your words will be used against you in the argument, which will lead to you being shamed.

"You're overthinking it."
This is a way to undermine you and make you feel small. The gaslighter is intent on having you believe you make too many assumptions with no basis in truth.

"It was just a joke!"
This is coercive and manipulative gaslighting and a cunning way to put you down. On a deeper level, it makes you question your ability to decide whether something is the truth or not.

"You're overreacting."
Similar to the above, you are being invalidated and confronted with the suggestion that you are not able to discern what is right and real for the situation. This makes you question whether your reactions are justified.

"Everyone agrees with me."
The fictitious army of people who also agree that you are wrong – this is a highly effective way to put you down and make you feel small. The gaslighter wants you to feel outcast and believe they have support while you do not.

"You always have to be right."
This is classic deflection and projection all at the same time. A gaslighter always wants to be right, so to blame you is a deflection of their behaviour. Ugly stuff.

"We already talked about this – don't you remember?"
The aim here is to make you weak and question your sense of reality. This is how they do it. They make you question your memory about whether something did or didn't happen. It is calmly done and very clever, so watch out for this.

"I did that because I was trying to help you."
Playing the helper card is like playing a victim card – it is a scheming way to manipulate you into feeling guilty for having emotions about something they did.

They will generally push you into thinking you don't have enough self-esteem to allow someone to help you. Which creates huge self-doubt.

Sadly, you will then start apologising for how you behaved. When you did nothing wrong but disliked their bullshit.

"I did that for you. It is what you wanted."
A gaslighter spins what happened, so you feel like it was something you somehow asked for. Yet, it is what *they* wanted. Then, they will convince you that you are confused, stressed out, and don't remember correctly.

"This is how you treat me after everything I've done for you?"
This is the coercive turn to make you feel extreme guilt. You are taking responsibility for their bad, crappy behaviour, and they get to throw the victim card at you.

"You're crazy."
The big ambition here is to have you question yourself. This can lead to low self-confidence and anxiety. This can also increase your vulnerability to more of their manipulative ways.

"This is why you don't have friends."
Isolation is a key tool for a gaslighter. It makes you feel weak, undervalued, and vulnerable.

"This is your own fault."
Watch out for this – a true gaslighter loves to twist the blame onto you, to make you feel confused and disoriented, hesitant to defend yourself, and ultimately cause you to doubt yourself.

"That's not what I meant."
A gaslighter does not like confrontation, so if you try to suggest that they hurt you, they will swiftly baffle you with a spray of denial and change the meaning of what you know you heard. They will calmly suggest that your interpretation of things can be off at times, as if the problem is with you. Watch out for that.

"You're too sensitive."
If you ever try to stand up for yourself, a gaslighter may use this one against you to make you feel small. To make you feel invalidated and like your opinion or feelings are not worthy of recognition.

"Get your facts straight."
No gaslighter likes to be wrong; remember this. They use this phrase to cast blame and question your ability to discern the truth. You look bad, not them.

"I don't know what you want me to say."
Such a cop-out – this is how a gaslighter will avoid accepting responsibility. Leaving you to hold all of it.

"How dare you accuse me of that!"
This is a very bold tactic – it makes you feel small and makes you immediately want to apologise. It is doubling down on their lie, which is super hard to question, so you end up questioning yourself.

"You have no clue."
This is a cute little belittling comment that makes you doubt yourself. Often said with charm and humour, it shoves you into a secondary place of not knowing the truth.

"Don't worry about it right now."
This is a deflection exercise; it gives the gaslighter time to gather themselves because you have caught them out. This is also to suggest your concerns are not valid.

"You never told me that."
But you know you did. This is the same old trick to make you question your memory. The smooth calmness of the way they say it to you, as if they have no recollection, is mind-boggling, so it is hard to challenge.

"You're being paranoid."
This is another bold move of a gaslighter. This is when they will go deep into a position of deflection to hide their wrongdoing.

No matter what you know, the gaslighter calls it paranoia and says that you need help. They work cleverly to make you feel like your emotions are way off course, and you really do not know what you are doing. It makes you question whether you can make fair judgements or not.

"Let's forgive and forget."
Yuck, this is the slimy gaslighter's way to make you feel guilty for what they actually did. It is also designed to cast doubt on whether you can offer compassion or forgiveness, so you feel like your morals or values are called into question.

"I think you need counselling."
The classic way to quickly make you feel small. And at the same time, invalidate your experiences. They will work you into a place where you question whether it is normal to have your emotions.

"You have an active imagination."
This is a sneaky belittling technique to keep you stuck in a place of feeling off balance. It is designed to frustrate you as well. So, you plead your case, which will never hold sway against their manipulative words.

"You think you're so smart."
Quite the opposite; this is a horrible way to tell you they think you are stupid, and a tactic to make you feel invalidated and undermined.

"You're not making any sense."
This one is purely to make you feel like your reality is in question.

"Why are you trying to confuse me?"
This one is a manipulative double play – normally, they are trying to confuse you, so they fling this at you to deflect. Often, it is how they gain time to think about their next move.

 **IMPORTANT NOTE:** Reclaiming your power is about taking a stand within yourself. It's about deciding what your truth and your reality are and owning them. But to do that, you need to clear away the "misinformation" you've been subjected to. Go back and define your own values, the ones that truly resonate with who we are. The ones you chose in Book One: *Project Clarity*. This is where you find your basis to work from.

• • •

A Little Reflection

Take a moment with this and check in with yourself. If any of these phrases ring a bell for you, know that it's completely okay to sit with whatever feelings arise. This isn't about blaming anyone; it's simply about bringing conscious awareness to the ways you may have been manipulated. You might find it helpful to explore these feelings in your journal, giving them the space they need to breathe. If these phrases don't resonate with you, that's a wonderful thing. You are one of the fortunate ones to have been protected from these forms of manipulation, and that is a blessing to be celebrated.

Please remember that you are not alone on this journey, and your feelings are always valid. The truth is your foundation, and you have the strength to reclaim your story, protect your reality, and empower yourself with every step forward. You are strong enough to stand in your truth.

*You are strong enough to stand in your truth.
I want you to believe that.*

25.
Taking Your Power Back

Your Go-To Responses for Gaslighting
Navigating Tricky Waters with Strength and Self-Compassion

Okay, first things first: this is another form of skill building. And, secondly, let's just agree that none of this is easy, right? It's not. But we absolutely need to learn how to protect ourselves, don't you think? My friend, managing a relationship with a narcissist or gaslighter can feel incredibly overwhelming, like walking through a minefield blindfolded. I know that feeling, that sense of utter disorientation. If possible, I wholeheartedly advocate for disengaging, for not showing up for these individuals.

But let's be honest with each other – that's not always a feasible option, is it? Sometimes, these people are woven into the very fabric of our lives, making complete detachment seem impossible. So, I've gathered a few skills for you to practise, tools you can use in those moments when avoiding or detaching isn't immediately within reach. And please, above all else, hold this close to your heart: your safety, your overall balance and ability to experience happiness – these are absolutely, undeniably paramount.

> **"Gaslighting of the soul: They do everything to dim your light, and then they ask you why you're not shining."**
> – Unknown

Gaslighting Responses

As we've discussed, gaslighting is a deeply unsettling tactic, a cruel twisting of reality that can leave you feeling utterly disoriented, questioning your own sanity. *And, as you would well know,* direct conflict with someone who thrives on manipulation can be incredibly draining, leaving you feeling like you've run a marathon without moving an inch.

I've been there, and I know how destabilising it can be. When someone attempts to manipulate your perception of the truth, it becomes absolutely vital to stand firm in your own reality, to anchor yourself in what you know to be true.

> **"Someone who gaslights you is trying to talk you out of your experience to alleviate their shame and responsibility for an issue. It's a tool to control and manipulate you."**
> — Henry Cloud

Here are ten responses you can keep in your back pocket, ready to use when faced with gaslighting. They're designed to be delivered with both strength and, just as importantly, deep self-compassion. You deserve that kindness, especially in these challenging moments.

In these early stages, I wholeheartedly advise against getting pulled into a "validate me" tug-of-war. Remember, our goal here isn't to seek their approval or understanding anymore, right? Instead, we're focused on a single one-liner to protect your precious energy, get you out of a situation, and shield you from those emotional storms that can erupt when you feel disrespected or manipulated.

🔍 **"I understand you see things differently, but I know what I experienced/remember. I'm not going to argue about it."** This is about setting a boundary, a gentle but firm line, without getting drawn into their distorted reality.

🔍 **"I'm not willing to have this conversation if you're going to invalidate my feelings/experiences."** This clearly states your limit, and more importantly, it protects your precious emotional balance.

🔍 **"I'm noticing that my reality is being questioned, and that's not something I'm comfortable with. Let's change the subject."** Here, you're pointing out the behaviour directly, but without accusation, and tactfully redirecting the conversation.

🔍 **"I'm not going to try to convince you of my truth. I know what I know."** This reinforces your self-trust, that inner knowing, and refusal to be pulled into their game.

🔍 **"I'm going to step away from this conversation. I need to take care of myself right now."** This is about prioritising yourself and your mental health while removing yourself from a potentially harmful situation.

🔍 **"I've written down/recorded what happened, so I'm confident in my memory."** This provides external validation for yourself, a way to remind yourself of the truth, and shows that you won't be easily swayed.

🔍 **"I'm not interested in debating my perception of reality. My feelings are valid."** This acknowledges their differing view but firmly maintains your own truth, your own feelings.

🔍 **"I'm going to trust my own judgement on this. I don't need you to agree with me."** This reinforces your autonomy, your self-reliance, and your right to your new perspective.

🔍 **"I don't need to justify or explain myself to you."** This removes the obligation to defend your feelings or actions, an obligation that is never truly yours in the first place.

🔍 **"This conversation is making me feel confused and uncomfortable. I need to end it."** This is honest, direct, and acknowledges the emotional impact, allowing you to end the interaction with integrity.

Now, a small reminder, from my heart to yours: my intention here isn't to suggest you engage in a confrontation with the gaslighter or narcissist.

Honestly, from my own experience, that rarely leads to anything positive. It's their game, and you simply cannot win by playing by their rules. To truly find your peace, you need to create your own game, one where you set the terms, where you define what's acceptable. So, my friend, sometimes the bravest and most loving thing you can do for yourself, the most empowering act of self-care, is simply to walk away.

 **SO, THE MESSAGE HERE IS THIS:** you are not responsible for someone else's behaviour. You are, however, responsible for protecting your own inner peace, your own sense of reality. These responses are tools, little helpers, to assist you in doing just that. You are strong, you are incredibly capable, and you absolutely, without a doubt, deserve to be treated with respect.

> Trust that quiet voice within. Listen to your gut, and know deep down in your heart that so many of us have stood right where you are now.

Gaslighting Protection Skills

Traversing the tricky terrain of gaslighting and dealing with those who might have narcissistic tendencies can truly feel like walking on eggshells. These skills I'm sharing take some practice; I understand. But I want you to know, this is all within your reach, okay? So, bear with me.

🔗 Give it Ten Seconds – The Don't Respond Immediately Rule

When someone says something that makes you feel that familiar pang of discomfort, try this: pause for ten seconds. Yes, just ten seconds. It might feel a bit awkward at first, but trust me, it's incredibly powerful. You're creating a vital space between their words and your reaction. It's a way of saying, "I hear you, but I'm not going to engage on your terms." Your body language speaks volumes here, too; it communicates that you won't be feeding into their need for control or aggravation. It's about taking your power back, one pause at a time.

🔗 Trust Yourself and Listen to Your Internal Dialogue

One of the most powerful tools you possess, my friend, is your own intuition. I want you to truly learn to trust that gut feeling. If something feels off, if their words and actions don't align, or if you sense a deep unease, please, please pay attention. Your inner voice is your most reliable guide. You know those old wounds you carry? Gaslighters have an uncanny ability to find and poke at those sensitive spots, stirring up those old feelings of fear, doubt, and helplessness. That's precisely why it's so important to be extra kind with yourself and fiercely protective of your emotional space. Think of it as creating a cozy, safe haven within yourself.

🔗 Healing Grows with Awareness

In the beginning, as you start to recognise these patterns and find your footing, please don't feel pressured to fight back. Trying to justify yourself or argue with someone who's gaslighting you can often be counter-productive, especially in these early stages. The most crucial step is simply acknowledging what's happening. See it, name it, and then set a firm boundary. Protect your precious energy like the treasure that it is. You are worth protecting.

🔗 Create Space from Manipulative Loved Ones

It's so easy to confuse our need for connection with what can be conditional, manipulative "love". Emotional manipulation is one of the most confusing forms of control because it often disguises itself as love. So, when someone who supposedly loves you gaslights you, take a pause. Create some space. Take that ten-second break. And then, if you choose to, ask them to repeat what they just said. This often makes them think twice about their words and their control tactics. Creating space also helps you recognise when you're being manipulated. It gives you the chance to ask yourself, "Is this truly looking after my needs?"

REMEMBER THIS, MY FRIEND: You are not obligated to engage in their manipulative games. Set boundaries like a strong, protective wall around your heart. Limit your interactions, keep conversations brief and factual, and never, ever hesitate to say "no" to requests that make you feel uncomfortable. Your "no" is a complete sentence.

Keep Records at Work

If you ever feel at risk at work, document everything. Keep a record of conversations, emails, and any instances of gaslighting or manipulation. This can help you stay grounded in reality and provide evidence if you ever need to take further action. It's about having your own back.

Look for Support

While I believe in the work we're doing here, you need real-life support too. Reach out to a therapist, a trusted friend, or a support group. Having someone who understands and validates your experiences, someone who can offer guidance and encouragement, can make all the difference in handling these challenging situations. You're not alone, and you deserve to feel safe, empowered, and at peace.

Check in with Your Future Self

As you build your confidence, clarify your values, and become more certain about the kind of behaviours you want in your life – the behaviours that will lead you to the life you truly desire – dealing with these gaslighting situations will become much more manageable. Imagine your Future Self, strong and at peace, and let that vision guide you.

Bye-Bye, Nasty Past

Interestingly, what often happens when you start setting healthy boundaries is that those who've been drawing energy from you simply start to fade away. You'll be different. You'll stop reacting in the ways they've come to expect. You won't give them the fuel they need to feed their ego.

Eventually, those narcissists and gaslighters will stop showing up because you've stopped showing up for them. And, honestly, what a welcome relief that will be! It's a place of peace, empowerment, and true freedom, and I'm so excited for you to reach it. I know you can do this; with this new perspective on gaslighting, you can.

Good chat, lady – All power to you!
Yep, I'm still holding your hand.

26.
My Trauma Experience

Calling Lifeline
Coming to Terms with My Truth Helped Me Heal

It took me over thirty years to truly understand that what happened to me was real, that I wasn't making it all up. It was a heartbreaking realisation, a painful acknowledgement of my truth, but it was also incredibly liberating. Honestly, I didn't even know what gaslighting meant until 2016 when my therapist explained it to me. It was then that I realised I had been continually gaslit for most of my life. I would plead for help, only to be told there was nothing wrong with me.

I remember being told to stand in the middle of a paddock, and then they let the horses out. I was trampled, and it could have been fatal. When I cried, confused and hurt, I was told it was my fault for being in the paddock when the horses were out. It also took me a long time to understand the term "scapegoated." I was always the one blamed when things went wrong. If oranges were thrown off the roof onto cars or the neighbour's house, and a window broke, it was my family who did it, but somehow it was always my fault. I was always the one who threw the orange, even when I was just standing there, watching.

As a child, I wet the bed for years, night after night, because of the trauma of being sexually abused. I was shamed for it, told I was drinking too much before bedtime, or accused of sneaking into the kitchen at night. I'd be woken up with wet face washers thrown at me because that's what the bed was like – wet. I was constantly told my reality wasn't what I thought it was. Maybe I did sneak a drink in the night. Maybe it was my fault, and I deserved to be hit with wet face washers because I couldn't control myself while I slept. I was flawed because I would wee while I was asleep and couldn't control it, which made me the issue. But I didn't make any of this up. It wasn't just in my mind. I was forced to doubt myself, but the truth always comes out, and I finally realised these things did happen to me.

Urinary incontinence (enuresis) is the medical term for bedwetting, and it's much more commonly part of a wider picture of emotional or behavioural disturbances. So, whilst I was sexually abused, the emotional dysfunction in my house was undeniably a part of my issue as well.

When I was a child, under ten years old, and my parents were working nights at their restaurant, other family members would treat me like a human toy. I was chased, pushed against walls, covered with blankets, and then hit repeatedly. I was pinned down, spat on, and verbally abused. When my parents came home, I would tell them what happened, and they would laugh. "Oh, you're so dramatic!" they would say. "Stop being silly." They dismissed everything, saying nothing had happened and that I couldn't possibly be hurt. But the most painful gaslighting came when they'd say, "Well, you probably deserved it. You were being annoying, and you deserved it. That'll teach you."

My parents worked most nights, so this torture was ongoing. One night, after a particularly painful incident, I was desperate and vulnerable. I called Lifeline and begged the lady on the phone for help. She was caring, kind, and compassionate. I had never experienced that kind of compassion at home, and it made me uneasy. I grew up in a small town, and the Lifeline operators knew my parents. I waited for my parents to offer support, but it never came. Instead, I was punished, given more chores, given the silent treatment, and denied any attention. At dinner, I remember being spoken to in a snide voice. "Oh, you're such a funny little girl. What an amazing imagination you have. You're such a little dramatic one, aren't you? You're a born actress." Then life went on as if nothing had happened. That was my existence.

Naturally, after being called a "born actress" a thousand times, I wanted to become one. Every time I cried for help or said I was being abused, it was dismissed as me creating a scene, creating drama, creating the problem. Eventually, I started to believe it. I thought I was the problem. I thought I made it all up. And I thought these people, who could be so charming and fun after the abuse, and would try to include me, were just showing me how things were.

So, if I was creating fantasies, I discovered I could create good ones too: stories where I was happy, a princess, a winner, loved, admired, and adored. I would create little shows with my dolls, teddy bears, and Barbies. I was on stage, and people were watching my amazing show. I played out these fantasies in my head and in my garden. Sometimes, family members would catch me and laugh, ridicule me, and put me down. But these weren't just ordinary fantasies – they kept me company, they created a little glass box where I felt safe, and they helped me survive the terror of the life I was born into.

In my teens and adult life, if I ever challenged someone in the family unit about what they did and expressed my hurt, it would be twisted against me. The person I confronted would rally the rest of the family and play the victim, accusing me of being nasty, horrible, and going against the family. Then I would face a mass confrontation, be chastised for being a bad person, and I would blame myself and try to fix things.

Make no mistake, these people were so charming, and publicly very alluring. My family's value system was to keep up appearances. We had to play a role. We could never talk about anything deep or troubling. The status quo was to make everything light and breezy. Everything became a joke. We were conditioned to make fun of anything and everything. To pretend our pooh didn't stink. To act like, "Aren't we fabulous?" We didn't dare share or discuss family secrets. (What secrets? They didn't exist, right?) The motto was to "deal with it and move on", but we never really dealt with anything.

But they truly were masters at inflicting pain and suffering, and when I complained, they tore me down for having those emotions. They blamed me and played the victim.

So, I became conditioned. Look happy, keep smiling, be funny, and don't embarrass the family. I had to look the part. My mother's answer to everything was a one-dimensional, positive phrase, "Go with courage and a quiet mind, darling", and she said this after every challenge or drama. I came to hate those words.

We were the family that exemplified the phrase, "Envy someone until you reach their front door." On the outside, we were shiny, shiny, shiny. Everyone loved my mother, loved my family. But I don't think anyone would have believed what happened behind closed doors.

Our family values, for show, were honesty, compassion, and generosity. But our true values were denial, control, and shame. We were never allowed to feel pain, let alone discuss problems or pain. We lied constantly, never able to admit weakness or dysfunction. We were all toxically connected by this shameful, abusive behaviour. Even today, they maintain their innocence, denying anything toxic or painful occurred – true to form, gaslighting 101. They still play the victim and talk about me as though I have mental health problems and maintain there's nothing wrong with our family.

That used to hurt me a lot; I won't lie. It certainly did. But what I have come to learn and accept is that with denial, there is no truth. And it does not excuse them for the dark, hurtful, and abusive behaviour. That, my friend, is with them. They became that way because of their own trauma. Those are their personality traits to resolve, not mine. I don't carry that around with me anymore.

Accepting that gaslighting was the norm in our household wasn't about forgiving them, either. It was about seeing it for what it was and giving it a place in my past. The fact is that this is how my family secrets were kept. This was their learned behaviour: to avoid and deny. Nevertheless, it is heartbreaking to realise it's your own family, people you love, are bending your reality because they can't face their own.

I don't accept that behaviour from anyone anymore. I call it out immediately and stop anyone who tries it with me. It's rare now, but some people still try.

> Being on the other side of gaslighting – being a woman who is healed enough to stand up to it – I feel privileged to share this with you.

27.
Checking In

Let's Take a Moment to Pause
How Are You Feeling?

Okay, so by the time you've worked through to this section, you should really be feeling like you've got more of a handle on things. The whole point of diving into getting to know your triggers is to give you the power back.

With your newfound perspective, what I want you to walk away with is this:

You're Getting Yourself Now. You're starting to see what sets you off – those situations, people, or even just thoughts that can trigger big emotional reactions, especially when it comes to food and drink.

You're Tuning into Your Emotions. You're not pushing them down anymore. You're acknowledging how you feel when those triggers pop up, and that's a huge step in understanding yourself.

You're Spotting the Patterns. You're starting to notice when those same triggers keep showing up and how you tend to react. This means you can start to see them coming and maybe even head them off before they throw you off course.

You're Growing, Big Time. This isn't always easy stuff, but by exploring those vulnerable parts of yourself, you're creating space for real healing and positive change.

You're in the Driver's Seat. You're not letting your triggers dictate your choices anymore. You're taking charge of your reactions and making more conscious, intentional decisions.

Ultimately, this whole book is about giving you the tools to do some serious self-reflection. It's about understanding yourself on a deeper level and, most importantly, learning how to regulate your emotions so you feel more in control.

> **"To not deal with trauma is to be at war with yourself."**
> – Peter Levine

So, how does it feel? If it's a lot, well, that's okay. Take your time. The more this information percolates inside you, the more comfortable you will start to feel with it. New skills take time to build and develop, remember.

You are human. Your feelings are valid.
Always remember that.

Getting On with Life Now

28.
Your Liberation Toolbox

The Golden Nuggets of Change
Your Everyday Skills for Resilient Emotional Health

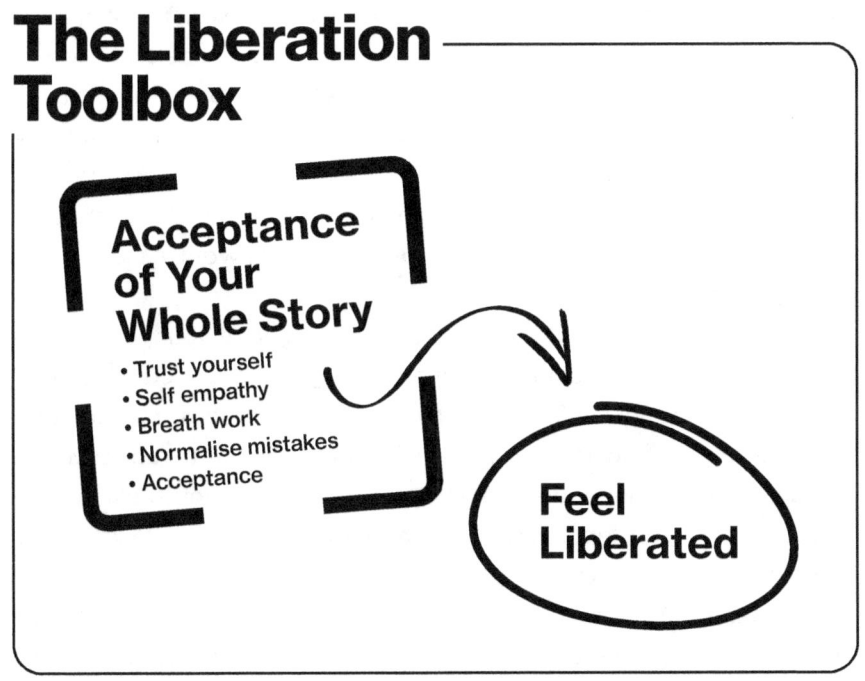

Can I ask you something seriously, for a moment?

? What do you think it would feel like if you woke up tomorrow and you trusted yourself, every gut feeling you had you listened to, took action and respected your inner messages?

? What if you loved the woman you are today, and held a warm empathy for your past experiences, and accepted them for what they were, no longer feeling like a victim?

? What if you smiled every time you made a mess or mistake, giggled in fact, because you knew that you were going to be better for it?

? And what would you feel like if you practised breathing to ensure your mind felt clear, you slept like a baby, and your lungs felt strong and your nervous system calm?

I think you would feel pretty liberated, wouldn't you? Well, I'm not making things up here; this is all possible, right here, right now. You better believe it.

Right then, come now, this is your next level of perspective, my friend. These skills I'm sharing with you, like a precious gift passed down from my own journey, are what I used to playfully call my "Warrior Princess Toolbox". I know that might feel a bit … intense for some, so I've changed its name to the "Liberation Toolbox". You can call it what you want, it's just about finding what resonates with you.

This is how you learn to let go, to release the grip of your past, before you get caught up in a troubling emotion or trigger. It's the releasing of your birthright to trust yourself, in order to make wise decisions, connected to your self-worth and core values. It's the key, my dear one, to rediscovering that untapped, rather powerful feminine energy within you. Making it the right time for you to step back out into the light and go get what you want, for your good self. Finally!

Yes, this toolbox is the prelude, in a way, to Book Three: *Liberated Connection*, where I teach you how to make use of this special energy you possess, how to turn lemons into lemonade, and finally see a clear, bright path before you. Yes, one book to go, with much more fun work to do there, not so much serious hard stuff like this one, I assure you. And yes, I acknowledge it may be slightly annoying to give you another hook to continue past the end of this book, but my friend, we are just not done here yet.

I know this might seem like a winding path, a long journey, at first. But trust me, as you begin to practise these tools, something magical happens. It starts to feel less like work and more like … coming home to yourself. It becomes intuitive, a natural part of how you navigate the world. You're creating space for yourself, reclaiming your power, and making conscious choices. You're no longer at the mercy of every passing thought, every wave of emotion, every sting of painful feelings.

With each element of this toolbox that you embrace, you're building a strong, resilient foundation, a sanctuary of inner strength, against those old, automatic behaviours that no longer serve you. And, yes, of course, you might stumble. You will likely take a tumble; the best of us have already. That's perfectly human. Just gently dust yourself off, with kindness and self-compassion, and keep moving forward. Keep walking that beautiful path of self-discovery towards the brighter future you so deeply deserve.

1. The Skill of Self-Empathy
How Empathy Regulates and Balances Your Emotions

My dear friend, let me be crystal clear: self-empathy isn't a luxury. It's a fundamental, non-negotiable skill for survival and a cornerstone of emotional resilience. If you've navigated rough seas in your past, it's time to build a solid, unshakable inner foundation.

The journey to truly understand and befriend our emotions, especially when our past carries the weight of trauma, begins with a powerful, transformative act: offering ourselves empathy. You see, when we learn to extend empathy inward, it's a monumental step towards mastering our emotions, emotional regulation, and ultimately, taking control of how we respond to the storms within us. It's a delicate yet incredibly potent process – a way of cradling our own hearts with the same loving tenderness we would offer someone we deeply care about.

You've likely spent too long at the mercy of your emotions, feeling like you're being tossed and turned relentlessly by their waves. Learning to validate your own experiences, accept the parts of the past you can't change, and take ownership of your journey with genuine compassion is not just a gentle act of self-kindness, it's a declaration of your inner power. It's the key that unlocks the door to emotional freedom, the bridge that guides you from fear to a place of true friendship with your inner self.

With self-empathy, your emotions transform from terrifying adversaries into understood, acknowledged and integrated parts of who you are. They no longer dictate your life but become valuable messengers, guiding you towards healing and wholeness. Within this skill, you need to learn to master three essential parts: self-validation, acceptance, and personal responsibility. This is how you reclaim your strength, my friend, and this is how you truly begin to live authentically.

The Three Pillars of Self-Empathy

1. Self-Validation

When we carry the weight of past trauma, our inner world can feel like a turbulent ocean. Often, we've been told, directly or indirectly, that our feelings are "too much," that we're "too sensitive," or that we need to "just get over it." This invalidation often echoes from within, a cruel refrain of the invalidation we experienced from others. This is where self-validation steps in. It's about acknowledging the truth of your experiences and the reality of your pain, without judgement. It's saying to yourself, "Yes, this hurts. Yes, this is difficult. And, yes, it's absolutely okay to feel this way". Think of it as creating a safe haven within yourself, a place where all your emotions are welcome, not banished.

2. Acceptance

Acceptance is another essential part of self-empathy. It isn't about excusing harmful actions or pretending the past didn't happen. It's about a quiet, steady acknowledgment of the reality of what occurred and the recognition that we cannot change what's already happened. You can accept the reality of what happened without having to forgive the inexcusable. Acceptance is the quintessential step in creating a new story, one where you are not defined by your trauma but by your resilience.

3. Responsibility for Yourself

Taking responsibility for yourself, in a compassionate way, is also crucial. This isn't about self-blame, not at all. It's about recognising your role in the patterns you've repeated and the choices you've made. It's about saying, "Given what I went through, given what I knew at the time, this makes sense." It's about seeing yourself with kindness, understanding that you did the best you could with the tools you had. This allows you to make new choices and to break old patterns – not from a place of shame, but from a place of self-understanding and growth.

Practising Emotional Empathy

When emotional regulation is rooted in self-empathy, it becomes less about control and more about being compassionately present with yourself. It's about being with your emotions, not fighting against them. Here are a few ways to use empathy to regulate your emotions:

When Overwhelmed by Fear: Instead of criticising yourself for feeling scared, try saying, "My body is reacting to perceived danger. It's trying to protect me. I understand why it feels so unsafe right now. I'm here, and I'm safe in this moment". Place your hand on your heart or belly and breathe deeply. This physical gesture reinforces your self-compassion.

When Triggered by a Memory: Acknowledge the pain without judgement. "This memory is bringing up intense feelings. It's okay to feel this way. My past experiences were real, and they still affect me." Ground yourself by noticing your surroundings: the texture of your clothes, the temperature of the air, the sounds around you. Push your feet into the floor and say out loud five objects you see around you. This brings you back to the present moment.

When Feeling Shame or Self-Criticism: Challenge the critical voice with openness and curiosity. "This voice is trying to protect me, but it's not being kind. Is this thought true? Is it helpful? What would I say to a friend in this situation?" Think of yourself as a child. What would you say to this child? What would you do for this child to make them feel safe and loved?

When Feeling Anger: Acknowledge the anger without judgement. "I am feeling angry; this is a valid emotion. I have a right to feel this anger. What does this anger need from me?" Journalling can be a great tool to process anger. Accept anger as a powerful energy that needs to be expressed.

My friend, this isn't about using fancy words that sound intimidating. It's about showing up and doing the work for yourself. And when you don't get it right, that's perfectly okay. We've already agreed that this journey is not about perfection but about progress. It's about learning to hold ourselves with kindness, to validate our experiences, and to accept the reality of our past while creating a more compassionate experience for our Future Self. It's about becoming our own safe haven, our own loving friend. And you, my friend, are more than worthy of that love.

2. The Skill to Appreciate Your Mistakes
Give Yourself Permission to Validate and Normalise Them

Let's face it. We all make mistakes. It's a natural part of life. It's time to normalise our mistakes. Relapse, falling short of a goal, struggling to maintain boundaries, or not sticking to a diet – trust me, you are not alone. In these scenarios, you can experience guilt, shame, or overwhelming feelings of failure. But it doesn't have to be that way!

> **"What a waste my life would be without all the beautiful mistakes I have made."**
> – Alice Bag

The most important thing in this process of change is to normalise mistakes. If you mess up, if things blow up, who cares? That's okay. Because you've learned something. You've seen a part of yourself communicating something important. You've observed a part of yourself that you can use to direct your path forward. My friend, there is so much capacity inside you that will help you learn from those mistakes. Allow yourself to try again. Don't ever think a mistake is terrible; it's an excellent learning opportunity. And whatever the outcome, it is progress.

Validation Is Key

Once you're on this journey of unhooking yourself from emotional turmoil, there's this wonderful notion called validation. It's a beautiful gift to tell yourself that you're worthy, that you're okay, that you matter, that it doesn't matter that you made a mistake, and it doesn't matter that something didn't go perfectly. Even if you don't fully believe it at first, keep at it. Keep validating yourself.

Remember, your subconscious repeats itself like a movie. It doesn't know the difference between what really happened and what you tell it happened. The more often you tell yourself you're okay now, the more your subconscious will believe it and replace that old judgemental voice with a new voice of self-worth. It also helps to close your eyes and smile when you do this, even if you don't feel like it. Try visualising yourself in your favourite place – a garden, forest, beach, water, field of flowers – and connect to your happy place with you at the centre, happy, twirling in the sunlight, dressed in your favourite outfit. I promise you this works, even if temporarily.

The body recognises positive energy. When you visualise like this, you create positive, high-frequency vibrations that are healing and soothing. And as I said, the more often you do this, the more it will stick.

We all have that inner critic. We all have that voice that tells us it's our fault. That voice that's mean and sniggers, telling you that you are not as good as someone else. That voice is the first to berate you when you missed the point, didn't follow something, or didn't pay attention. You know that voice that's always there to tell you how badly you screwed up. But it's all you. You're doing this to yourself. I'm not saying this to be mean. It's just how the mind works. And the only person in your mind is you. Well, enough already! That's the *old* you.

Here, you are learning that you are in control, and you can validate that what you did in any given situation was okay, based on what you knew at the time, with the tools, resources, and support you had. You have 100% permission to face up and say, "Yep, I made a mistake, and I'm okay with that". You are human. You are not an AI machine. And stuff just happens sometimes. Normalising your mistakes and validating yourself is the best gift you can give yourself. This isn't some trick. It's a physiologically, scientifically proven fact that the brain – the entire body – responds to positive energy, and this is what you're creating when you do this.

NOTE: When you connect to positive thoughts that make you feel happy and uplifted, you decrease the amount of the stress hormone (cortisol) in your body. And the brain then produces more serotonin, making you feel good and balanced. This helps you feel less anxious and more grounded.

The result of this validation – the kindness, self-compassion, and self-empathy you're extending to yourself – presents itself as a soothing feeling. Your gift includes learning from each situation. Observe what happened. Notice the trigger; notice the behaviour. See the pattern, so next time you can consciously walk down a different path while looking back at the person who once used to fall into that horrible hole of self-loathing.

And, my friend, I want you to believe you *can* catch yourself. You may catch yourself after the fact, but at least you caught the negative self-talk. You recognised it. Next time, you'll get closer to catching yourself as it's happening. Eventually, you'll catch yourself before you go down the wrong path. Tell yourself you're good. Tell yourself it's alright and just sit with that for a bit.

> If you did the things you are capable of, you would astound yourself. Show up and give it a go!

3. To Skill to Regularly Breathe
Get Comfortable with Power of Breathwork

You already know the 4-7-8 Breathing technique. I'm bringing it up again because it's incredibly relevant in those moments when we feel overwhelmed. I also want to share another breathing technique that can be a real game-changer, especially if you're prone to panic attacks.

When anxiety hits, our breathing changes. It's like our body's alarm system goes off, preparing us for something. We shift from a calm, steady state into hyperarousal, and our sympathetic nervous system kicks into overdrive.

 **NOTE:** The parasympathetic nervous system is in charge during quiet "rest and digest" times, while the sympathetic nervous system activates our "fight-or-flight" response when we're stressed.

When we get hooked by a stressor, an event, or a trigger, our breathing becomes shallow and rapid. We start taking in more carbon dioxide than usual. Our heart rate might increase as it tries to process this extra carbon dioxide in our bloodstream. And because we get even more anxious when we feel our heart pounding, it can create a vicious cycle, pushing our heart rate even higher. There might not be a tiger or bear chasing us, but our body reacts as if there were.

That's where the breathing techniques come in. The 4-7-8 method is simple: Inhale for 4 seconds, hold your breath for 7 seconds, and then exhale for 8 seconds. Repeat this four times. This helps slow down those short, shallow breaths and starts to ease the stress response, guiding us back to our parasympathetic nervous system – our calm state.

The Alternative Diaphragm Breathing Technique

This technique is particularly effective for calming yourself down when you feel a panic attack coming on. It helps regulate the amount of carbon dioxide you're taking into your lungs and balances your blood pressure, which might be working overtime to expel that extra carbon dioxide. It also brings a sense of peace to your mind, quieting all that swirling energy because you're focusing solely on your breath. This is also a wonderful tool for those nights when sleep just won't come.

NOTE: As I mentioned before, I can speak from personal experience here. I've been to the hospital several times during a full-blown panic attack, convinced my heart was about to explode. It was all triggered by initial anxiety and the resulting imbalance of carbon dioxide in my system, creating that ripple effect I described earlier. Now when I feel anxious, I use this technique, and I haven't had to call emergency services in a long time.

Take Back Control from Your Panic Attacks

I'd like to offer up something super-important about a crucial element in what actually brings about the panic attack itself: our breath. When panic attacks start creeping in, they often bring along this whirlwind of rapid breathing, which feels out of control, right? I know that feeling all too well.

When you are starting to have a panic attack, you are beginning what they call hyperventilation, which can create a knock-on effect called attenuated baroreceptor sensitivity that feels like more anxiety. This is a fancy way of saying your body is trying to get rid of toxins.

Basically, when we hyperventilate, we're in a state of rapid breathing. This causes the level of carbon dioxide gas in our bloodstream to increase. You can be taking lots of little breaths, but you don't feel like you are getting enough air into your lungs. This can make you feel dizzy and unsettled. You can feel tingles in your hands and up your legs, and you may get a flushed face. And then you feel like you can't breathe properly, like you can't catch your breath. Then your heart starts to race. Your heart is beating faster because it needs to process the carbon dioxide out of your system.

But here is the thing: At this point, you instantly feel like something is wrong with your heart, and so your anxiety then starts increasing, which then, in turn, also puts more pressure on the heart, and your heart starts pounding out of your chest. Oh, my word, it's a cluster of chaos, and very scary, but it all began because of the hyperventilation, way back at the start. In fact, there is nothing wrong with your heart at all; it's just doing its job, and rather well, in fact.

The remedy is to return you to a state of homeostasis. This means that you are balanced, your breathing can return to normal, and the carbon dioxide levels in your body are also back to normal.

Here's the good news: we can bring ourselves back to balance, to that lovely place of homeostasis. We can get our breathing back to normal and those carbon dioxide levels right where they need to be. This is where diaphragmatic breathing, or "belly breathing" as I like to call it, comes in.

Let's Get Grounded Together

Diaphragmatic breathing, or "belly breathing", engages the diaphragm, intercostal, abdominal, and pelvic floor muscles. This process calms your breathing hyperactivity, brings you back to equilibrium, and restores the correct blood flow in your system. This isn't about magically stopping anxiety in its tracks. It's about giving ourselves a tool to calm our breathing, to ground ourselves again, so we can better manage those anxious feelings. And, hey, sometimes that anxiety even fades away completely – which is always a bonus, right?

Try this exercise and see how it works for you. It is not a tool to stop anxiety; it is simply to help calm your breathing and allow you to ground yourself again, so you can better manage your anxiety. You may even find it goes away, so enjoy that, too.

A LITTLE NOTE BEFORE WE START: Please, please listen to your body. If you feel lightheaded, hold onto something or someone. Sitting down can be helpful. However, you may want to stand up to make pushing air out and into your lungs easier. Just do what feels right for you.

Let's break it down, step by step:

1. Breathe Out First – Clear the Vessel
Do this when you hyperventilate and feel like you can't breathe. Perhaps it sounds counterintuitive, but the trick is to expel the air out of your lungs by pushing with your abdominal muscles. You want to clear out the old air that you have been taking in whilst breathing intense short breaths, so you start with an empty vessel.

> **Tip:** Push the air out of your lungs through the nose, using the muscles below the rib cage – the diaphragm, and, yes, my gosh, make some noise with it! I always find that helps.

This will help empty your lungs and make breathing at a slower pace more possible. This is your ticket to allowing more fresh air into your lungs. Yes, it may feel strange, but bear with me.

2. Pause and Commence Slow Belly Breaths – The Magic of the Diaphragm
The technique: place a hand on your belly and slowly breathe in (inhale) through the nose, drawing the breath down towards the stomach. The stomach should push upward against the hand while the chest remains still. When you do this, the diaphragm moves down with each breath, which helps fill the lungs with the air you need.

This may feel odd, but you are making a conscious effort to engage your diaphragm, taking deeper breaths to help your lungs. You will notice your stomach rising and falling. It will also feel like an expanding or stretching sensation in the stomach rather than solely in your chest and shoulders.

Then, slowly release the air (exhale) through the nose, starting with the chest and finishing with the lower lungs, pushing the remaining air out using the diaphragm. Allow yourself to take a small pause for one or two seconds, and then take another slow breath in.

Exhale. Inhale. Repeat.

3. Regulate your Breathing – Find Your Rhythm

Take a slight pause. Then, take a deeper, slow breath in. Hold it for two seconds, then release it out again. Keep your hand on your tummy as a reminder to breathe using the diaphragm, not the upper chest. Pause for one to three seconds, then take a deeper, slow breath in. Hold it for two seconds, then release it out again.

Repeat this process until you feel you are getting the right amount of air into your lungs. Remember, you are aiming for slow and steady breathing.

Be connected and practise your self-compassion skills here.

NOTE: You may have seen some people using a paper bag to breathe in and out of. But doing this increases the level of carbon dioxide in the blood. It's up to you. I have always found that the paper bag method makes me feel claustrophobic.

4. Acknowledge Your Heart's Faster Pace – It's Working for You

Your heart is working hard to regulate the carbon dioxide levels in your bloodstream, so you may continue to feel lightheaded for a few moments during this, which can be expected. The racing heart can often feel like a panic attack is ensuing, but it is really the heart working like a steam train to eliminate the unwanted chemicals in your system. This can last between ten minutes and an hour or so. Everyone is different, so please just monitor yourself.

For me, learning this changed my life. No more calls to 000 to get emergency services here. Once I learned this, I stopped panicking. It gave me permission to allow my body to do what it needed to do, and I didn't need to panic about having a heart attack anymore!

HEALTH CHECK: Please check that you do not have any extreme chest pains, tightness in your chest, vomiting, or discomfort in the shoulder, arm, back, neck, or jaw. If you are experiencing any of these symptoms, please call your nearest emergency service.

> Knowledge, my dear friend, can be
> so powerful and liberating!

To Wrap This Up

When you're practising these breathing exercises, there's no room for judgement or criticism. You don't feel shame or terrible about yourself because you're so focused on your breath and your body. You can't concentrate on anything else. So, in that very act, you unhook yourself from the emotional storm.

In my own experience, taking control of my breathing brings a lovely sense of calm and peace. You reclaim your power in a big way, and honestly, it feels amazing. It's a truly wonderful place to be.

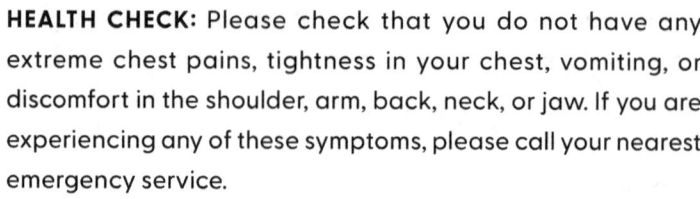 4. *The Skill to Champion Acceptance*
The Golden Ticket to Leave the Past Behind

Acceptance. It's a word we hear often, but truly grasping its power – that's where the magic lies. I want to share how acceptance can be your most insightful gift, your key to inner peace, balance, and changing those unwanted patterns, especially around food and drink.

Let's be real. Things happen. Ugly, painful things. Things we desperately wish we could erase. But the past is etched in stone; we can't change it. Acceptance isn't about condoning what happened. It's not saying it's okay. It's about acknowledging your present reality, the valid pain that arises. By doing this, you're permitting yourself to be fully human – to feel the hurt, the rage, without suppression. And that suppression? That's where the real damage occurs.

You can't change the past, but you can change how it affects you now. You can create a safe space for your whole self, your vibrant feminine energy, in a place of acceptance – a place of true peace.

This isn't easy. When I first started, I was confused, angry, and rather resistant. But as I embraced acceptance, the anger and pain lost their control over me. I learned to love even the parts I used to shame. Anger is powerful, but I realised that it's all just energy, communicating necessary information. By giving it space, it flowed, had its say, and left without leaving lingering triggers.

Here's another crucial point: acceptance does not mean forgiveness. Not at all. I truly believe you do not have to forgive someone to find a place of acceptance.

You can have the foresight to understand the situation, to see what happened in your past with adult eyes. With a new perspective, looking in, you are no longer the victim. You can see that the person, or people, involved were carrying their own issues, their own layers of complex and complicated past wounds. They were driven by their own inner voice, their own demons and hurt inner children. They were simply acting within the capacity they had at the time.

This is for all types of people, even the bad ones. Because every child is born innocent and pure. It is only when things happen to them, or they are exposed to or treated in a particular way, that they become evil or mentally dysfunctional.

I was raped, I was sexually molested, and trust me, finding acceptance for why those men did that was a very hard task. But through some deep work, I did it. I broke them down, with my adult eyes, and understood what was driving them and how their own inadequacies were a part of that situation's dynamic. This isn't forgiveness, it's accepting who that person was at the time. I know for a fact that one of the perpetrators was abused himself as a child, so this often plays out in their world – they do this to others. It does not make it right; it just makes it a pattern.

My mother and her manipulation? She was abused as a child, raped, and adopted. I don't have to forgive her to understand that these events caused her to develop a mental illness that she suffered from, which played out in extremely manipulative and narcissistic abuse patterns. Everything is a pattern. And so, I don't have to forgive these people. I just have to see them for what they are. And sister, I can tell you for certain, when I think of them (which I rarely do, now) I don't get triggered, I no longer raise havoc in my life, with food, alcohol, or silly behaviours that leave me feeling rubbish on the outside and in. Man, that is joy, right there. To have the freedom from the chains those memories had on my life – whoa, that is a massive change in my life. One that I am so grateful for.

So, you see, if I accept those truths about these people, and I accept that I was a victim of their past hurt, I am no longer sitting in the horrible, paralysing position of being a victim now. I see what happened at that time, but I am no longer a victim to them. Because I am here, a woman, with choice, with my values, with my health to be responsible for. I am accountable to every part of myself, every layer and colour that has flowed through my life – it is me, and I accept that. I no longer give my power away to them through this acceptance. Can you see that? Does this make sense to you?

Why Embrace Acceptance?

Mentally, acceptance breaks the cycle of rumination. When we fight our feelings, we fuel them, creating a loop of distress. Acceptance allows us to observe our thoughts and emotions without judgement, creating space. We realise we are not our feelings; they are simply passing experiences. We regain our power to choose, building resilience and coping with life's storms with greater ease.

Physically, resistance manifests as tension: clenched jaws, tight shoulders, racing hearts. Chronic stress from fighting our feelings leads to health issues. Acceptance promotes relaxation, deepens breathing, and calms the nervous system. Studies show it reduces chronic pain, improves sleep, and lowers blood pressure. When we stop struggling, we allow our bodies to heal.

> I'm going to talk to you more about
> healing your hypervigilance in the
> next book, Liberated Connection.

Over to you. Here's the heart of it: Does the idea of more peace resonate with you? Can you accept your thoughts and feelings about your experiences? It's a practice, a journey. And even small steps towards acceptance can lead to profound freedom.

Now imagine if you were willing to try this – to lean into acceptance. What if you allowed yourself to feel the discomfort, the rawness, without judgement? You might find, as I did, that the very act of acceptance loosens the grip that those old wounds have on you. You'd begin to experience that liberation I keep talking about, not as an abstract concept, but as a tangible shift in your inner landscape. You might discover hidden corners of yourself, strengths you never knew you possessed, vulnerabilities that, when embraced, become sources of deep know-how and strength. And maybe, just maybe, you'd find your little place of happiness. Not a grand, sweeping kind of happiness, but the quiet joy of noticing a sunbeam dancing on the floor, the peacefulness of a deep breath, the simple satisfaction of being present in your own life.

My friend, you might rediscover the meaning that felt lost, the sense of purpose that flickers when you allow yourself to be truly, authentically you. Acceptance isn't a magic wand, but it's a knowing hand guiding you back to yourself – back to a life where peace, joy, and meaning are not just possibilities but your lived reality.

5. The Skill to Trust Yourself
Enjoy the Liberating Feeling of Listening

Close your eyes for a moment and imagine this: you're standing at the edge of a vast, open field. Breathe in the fresh air. Feel the sun on your face. You've walked a long, winding path to get here, haven't you? A path marked by shadows, by echoes of past hurts that still whisper sometimes. For so long, you've turned to others for direction, for validation, for answers, because your own inner compass felt ... well, let's be honest, it felt a little broken, a little unreliable. But look at you now. You stand here, you have come this far, and perhaps something inside you is stirring. Perhaps another message that you are ready? Ready to rebuild your trust in yourself.

What does it truly mean, though, to trust yourself after navigating the complexities of your complicated history? Let me tell you, it's not about striving for some impossible, perfect version of yourself where doubt never creeps in. It's about something far more real, far more beautiful. It's about nurturing an unshakable belief in your own inner wisdom, in that quiet voice of intuition that resides within you. It's about recognising your inherent worthiness, the absolute truth that you are valuable, just as you are. It's about knowing, in the very core of your being, that you are capable, resilient, and utterly deserving of a life that reflects your truest, most candid self.

Now, imagine the ripple effect. Imagine the subtle, yet powerful, changes that begin to unfold as you step fully into this self-trust. You start making choices that resonate with your own genuine needs, not with the lingering echoes of past challenges and painful experiences. You set healthy boundaries, not from a place of fear or defensiveness but from a place of deep self-respect and self-care. You learn to ask for what you need, without apology, without shame, because you understand that your needs are valid, important, and deserving of attention.

You begin to live in alignment with your values, those guiding stars that light up your path. You learn from your mistakes, not with harsh self-criticism but with curiosity and compassion. You see each day as a precious opportunity to learn, to grow, to evolve into the woman you were always meant to be. You trust your gut, that quiet, knowing voice, and you listen to the messages your emotions are sending, understanding that emotions are not your enemies but wise messengers guiding you along the way.

You learn to tactfully, yet firmly, remove yourself from chaos, from the draining energy of toxic situations, because you understand that your peace, your balance, your ability to experience happiness from within, is non-negotiable. You trust that you are on the right path, even when the road gets bumpy, and you know, with a deep certainty, that even the most difficult times will eventually pass, leaving behind valuable lessons and even greater strength.

You trust that you can allow your emotions to flow, like the ebb and flow of the tides, without being overwhelmed or swept away. You use your grounding techniques – your anchors – to stay present, centred, and rooted in the here and now, knowing that even the darkest storms will eventually give way to calm. You trust that you know what is truly important to you, and you become fiercely protective of that. You trust that you can make healthy, loving choices for your balance, for your sleep, for your vitality.

This journey of self-trust, my friend, is not a destination to arrive at but a continuous, beautiful unfolding. It's a soft, graceful dance of self-discovery and self-acceptance. It's about remembering who you truly are, beneath all the layers of trauma and conditioning, and embracing that unvarnished, radiant self with boundless love and compassion.

> Repeat after me: "I am worthy. I absolutely have the capacity to trust myself. And loving myself will be the greatest love of my life."

Trust Yourself Checklist

A Gentle Guide

- ◯ **Listen to Your Gut:** Pay attention to those subtle nudges, those intuitive whispers. They are your inner compass, guiding you home.

- ◯ **Validate Your Emotions:** Your feelings are valid, always. Acknowledge them, allow them to flow, and trust that they hold valuable messages for you.

- ◯ **Set Healthy Boundaries:** Your mental health and balance are sacred. Learn to say "no" with grace, without guilt, and protect your precious energy.

- ◯ **Live Your Values:** Identify what truly matters to your heart and make choices that align with those values.

- ◯ **Learn from Mistakes:** See each day as a school day, a beautiful opportunity to learn and grow. Embrace imperfection and treat yourself with unwavering compassion.

- ◯ **Ask for What You Need:** Your needs are valid and important. Don't hesitate to ask for support, for help, for what your heart truly desires. Someone is always there.

- ◯ **Create Safe Spaces:** Surround yourself with people and environments that nurture your soul and uplift your vibration and spirit.

- ◯ **Trust Your Path:** Even when the road gets bumpy, trust that you are exactly where you need to be. Remember, when things get rough: "This, too, shall pass."

- ◯ **Ground Yourself:** Use your grounding techniques to stay present, centred, and connected, especially during challenging times.

○ **Prioritise Self-Care:** Nurture your body, mind, and spirit with loving, healthy choices.

○ **Celebrate Your Strength:** Acknowledge your incredible resilience, your courage, your capacity to heal and grow with your newfound skills and awareness.

○ **Be Patient with Yourself:** Self-trust is a beautiful journey, not a race. Embrace the process and take your sweet time. Treat yourself with endless kindness and compassion.

○ **Remind Yourself:** You are enough, beautiful to the core, curious, and possess free will.

Download this list from my website and keep it on your fridge! Let it all sink in!

...

To Wrap This Up

I truly wish I could be right there with you, speaking these words directly to your heart as you close your eyes. But since I can't, I would love you to do something in this moment. Read that section back to yourself, out loud, with your own voice. Let the words wash over you. Let them resonate within you. Hear the strength, the compassion, the truth in them, as if you are speaking your own reality into being. Because, darling, this is your reality today, and every day forward.

> **"There is a crack in everything; that's how the light gets in."**
> – Leonard Cohen

In Japan, they have this beautiful art called kintsugi. When pottery breaks, they mend the cracks with lacquer and gold, highlighting the imperfections, celebrating the history of the object. Kintsugi means "golden joinery" or "golden repair". Think of your journey to building self-trust as your own golden repair. You are joining all the beautiful, broken pieces of yourself, creating something even more magnificent, even more radiant. You are rejoining them to make this beautiful new woman – that is you – shine brighter than ever before.

So, with that, I invite you to take hold of your own inner kintsugi compass. Choose the direction *you* want to take, and start walking down that path, smelling the beautiful wildflowers along the way.

Choose the path that leads to the life that is truly, authentically yours.

A little side bar between us...

Let's pause here for a moment. I am wondering, are you feeling inspired, like your attitude is shifting and you're breathing easier with these new tools? Or are you feeling a little overwhelmed?

Whatever the feeling, please know it's not a sign of weakness. It's a sign that you're growing. You've taken on so much knowledge and broken down so many walls from within, and it's okay if the waters don't flow immediately.

Equally, I want you to know this is all within your reach, and at some stage soon you will be saying to yourself or a trusted friend, "It is so incredibly liberating to trust yourself, isn't it?" It's become one of my most prized possessions, I must confess. I can share with you now, without an ounce of shame, that for years, I didn't trust myself at all. And it was, truly, at the root of so much of my struggle.

But, as I was once taught, and as I now pass on to you, "Trust that the message is in the mess." The mess has answers. You just have to work out what the cost is in all the mess, how far out of line the mess is with your values, and whether how you show up in that mess is sincere or not. It sounds so simple, doesn't it? This, my friend, is a must-have life skill along this journey. But it takes practice, it takes courage, and most of all, it takes love. It takes a deep, unwavering trust in yourself. Trusting yourself is also loving yourself, yes? Can you see that?

> Give yourself permission to let these words settle in your heart at their own pace. There is no rush; there is only progress.

Your Light to Come Home

29. Your North Star

A New Perspective of Know-How
A Guide to Finding Your Way Home

My dear friend, as we bring this together, I wanted to offer you a short guide, a kind of roadmap, what I call "know how", to help you create a safe space as you journey along the path towards the life you truly desire. Think of this as your personal how-to manual, a way to integrate all the insights, the education, the awareness, and the connections you've made along the way.

> At its heart, and I want to share this with you from the deepest part of me, is this: You need to feel safe in order to do this work.

Embracing a new perspective to step out of those shadows, understanding and connecting with your own emotional blueprint so you can walk this healing path – it all begins with a foundation of safety.

I know it's tempting to look for shortcuts, to try to rush through it. But trust me, I've been there, and I've learned that true healing takes time and a willingness to face what's within. This isn't like a typical medical path for recovery from an illness with a six- to eight-week timeline. Trauma healing is different. It's not linear. It's a journey of rediscovering yourself.

Yes, sometimes medication plays a part, but it's not the whole story. This is about more than just dampening emotions. It's about truly feeling safe enough to make room for them, to delve into those old wounds, those trauma scars, and to finally resolve them. The skill is to learn to make room for your emotions to flow freely in and out of your life, without knocking you around, or having you reach for a bottle, chocolate bar, shopping cart, or numbing antidote.

I will say it one more time: this isn't a quick fix. There's no magic pill. This is a brave process of looking back, as the wise, mature woman you are now, and understanding what happened, how it happened, and why. It's about reframing those experiences in your mind, accepting the facts, and realising that someone else's actions don't define your worth. If you were neglected, invalidated, or abused, it doesn't mean you weren't worthy. You were a vulnerable child. And you are, and always have been, worthy of love, honour, protection, and being seen.

SO, THE MESSAGE HERE IS THIS: You can only do this when you feel safe and stabilised in your world. Having a safe space, and trusted people to support you, is vital. Only then can you begin to reprocess, to revisit the narratives you've held onto since those times when you didn't have that support, that validation, that gentle cradling of your wounds. That empathetic witness.

Here are three stages of healing that have helped me, along with many others, and I hope will guide you, too. **Think of this as your personal checklist** to help you navigate your own healing journey, in your own safe, expressive, and liberating way.

Let's Begin

 1. Safety: Creating Your Safe Space

You have the power to create your own safe space. It starts with:

- **Finding Stability:** Having a stable environment, whether it's your home, workplace, or community, is key. Feeling safe within your environment is also paramount. (You need to be free from threats to your emotional or physical mental health.)

- **Self-Regulation:** Create a space where you can learn to regulate your own emotions.

- **Trusting Yourself:** Begin to trust your inner voice and your own intuition.

- **Setting Boundaries:** Learn to set healthy boundaries to protect yourself.

- **Awareness of Triggers:** Be aware of your triggers so you can avoid them or choose a different path.

- **Kindness and Gentleness:** Be incredibly kind and tender with yourself.

- **Listening to Your Body:** Listen to the messages your body sends you and respond with compassion.

 2. Reframing Your Past Narrative: Seeing with New Eyes

Now, as an adult, you have the strength to reframe your memories and trauma narrative. Remember:

- **You Were Younger:** You were a child, an emotionally undeveloped and unconnected human, when these narratives were formed, without the tools or support you have now.

- **Acknowledge and Take Responsibility:** You now have knowledge, tools, and a support network. See your past with these adult eyes and a new perspective.

- **Create a Refreshed Narrative:** Resolve your past by creating a refreshed narrative, rooted in acceptance and facts.

- **Validate Your Younger Self:** Give your former self the validation she needed to hear then, which is also validating yourself today. Acknowledge that what happened was awful, without dismissing your experience. This is how you change core beliefs that no longer serve you. Remember your Inner Child exercise.

- **Identify Your Support Network:** Name three people who are your support network – people you can turn to for love, nurturing, or validation. This can help calm your nervous system.

- **Use Anchoring and Breathing:** If you feel unsafe or triggered, use the Dropping Anchor exercise, Name and Tame your emotions, and try the 4-7-8 Breathing exercise to steady yourself.

- **Return to Safety:** If you still feel unsafe, go back to your safety checklist and walk through it step by step.

3. Moving On: One Day at a Time

- **This Is a Day-by-Day Process.** There's no perfection here, and it's not a straight line.

- **Daily Safety:** Protecting your safety daily is your priority.

- **Trust Yourself:** Trust yourself always, in every moment. Live by your values.

- **Take One Step at a Time:** Just keep moving forward, one step at a time.

- **Expectations vs. Reality:** Recovery is a process, and your expectations might not always match reality. Be comfortable with things not going as planned. It's okay to still struggle.

- **Mistakes Are Friends:** You'll make mistakes as you learn new tools. Your mistakes are your friends, teaching you valuable lessons.

- **Acknowledge Progress:** Acknowledge every bit of progress you make. This will motivate you to continue to work on yourself and evolve.

- **Kindness and Compassion:** Continue to be kind and compassionate with yourself.

- **Healthy Attachments:** Seek healthy, secure attachments in your relationships.

- **Manage Triggers:** Learn to manage your triggers. Understand them, make peace with them, and recognise when they're coming so you can make an informed choice.

- **Practise Your Tools:** Practise your tools for regulating emotions. It takes time and practice, and that's okay.

- **Liberation Skills:** Practise your new liberation skills, over and over again.

- **Empowerment:** You are a woman with strength and insight. Make practical and healthy choices for your life.

- **Future Self:** Make conscious decisions to take care of her and lean on her as your guide if you feel unsure.

- **Journalling:** Journal to give form to your thoughts and daily experiences. Reflection is also a magnificent way to see how far you have come.

- **Joy:** Remind yourself of the simple things that bring joy to your life.

- **Peace:** Keep your commitment to finding and living in a place of peace.

Remember, this is *your* journey, no one else's. There's no right or wrong way, just your way. Be easy going with yourself, and trust that you are exactly where you need to be.

> I really hope this helps you to feel empowered, to feel ready, and to take that brave step forward.

...

30.
Your Beautiful Unfolding

A New Perspective on Your Emotions
Your Final Reflection Questions

Gosh, you've done well. Look at you, you've stuck with this, maintaining your focus, and now you're almost at the end of a massive amount of transformational work. I am so proud of you. Seriously, this is not to be sniffed at. What you've accomplished so far is monumental, and I absolutely hope you can see that for yourself.

So, now, I'm going to ask you to make one more big effort to look within. Perhaps this time, you will begin to perceive things differently. You might even find yourself feeling how the work you've already done has started to create real shifts in your emotional make-up. Why do I think you'll notice a difference? Well, think about it for a moment: You've journeyed through incredibly challenging terrain. You've faced your triggers head-on. You've understood what they are. You've started to appreciate and hear the powerful messages your emotions have been sending you. After that, you simply can't be the same. Changes will definitely be happening.

Now, with these last twelve questions, we are going to acknowledge and celebrate that considerable journey. This exercise will help you solidify your emotional mastery, allowing you to take another confident step forward, and walk on from here with more colours in your awareness of how change is manifesting in your life. This is the path you are now walking along to find that happy place within. Because sister, I am here to tell you, that happy place where peace, and joy, and not chaos, will become your lived reality.

Don't look at this reflection as a test, either please; it's a mirror. It's designed to connect all this wonderful new knowledge you are embracing to the physical sensations that come with turning up the volume on your message centre, your inner voice. These questions are only for you; they are your gift of progress, if you allow them to be, and it's your own responsibility to work through them. It is truly all up to you now.

Continue, as always, to read each question aloud, write your honest response, and then read your answer aloud once more.

> I know this process is making a huge difference in your thinking now.

Let's Begin

1. When a wave of emotion begins to rise, how do you now warmly guide yourself back to a place of calm?

   Thinking about what specific steps do you take? How has the tone of your inner voice shifted in these moments? What new observations are you making about the powerful message it holds for you? And what compassionate allowances are you now giving yourself to truly understand your Inner Child's needs?

2. Imagine your younger self, still carrying the echoes of past pain. What heartfelt words of empathy and deep understanding do you now offer her, as if she were right here, sitting beside you?

   Think about as you connect with her, describe the physical and emotional sensations that arise within you.

3. Think back to a time you perhaps brushed aside or dismissed your own feelings. How can you now lovingly validate those feelings, truly acknowledging their truth and importance?

   Think about what does it feel like in your body to give yourself this momentous validation, and how does your voice reflect this beautiful shift?

4. When the world throws an overwhelming trigger your way, what are your trusted, go-to grounding techniques to lovingly bring yourself back to the present moment, before you react?

   Think about the process and how it genuinely transforms your reactions and behaviours afterwards. What has been the most significant quick fix you've wholeheartedly done away with now?

5. What is the one recurring pattern (be it a trigger, behaviour, or consequence) that you are now able to recognise with such clarity and kindness?

Can you see how it will play out differently now that you can warmly catch yourself? What will truly be different for you going forward?

6. What core values are you now leaning on to help you gracefully manage the reactions to your triggers?

    Think about how does this beautiful alignment manifest in your daily life, and what has truly changed for you now, from the way you might have approached these scenarios in the past?

7. When you make a mistake (because we all do!), how do now allow yourself to find the reason for the mistake. How good are you now at allowing these mishaps to be graceful teachers in your life?

    Think about that internal dialogue and how that self-love is genuinely starting to become a beautiful reality for you.

8. In moments of struggle, how do you become your own tender, empathetic witness, acknowledging your challenges and embracing your newfound resilience?

    Think about the process of being the empathetic witness of your own experience.

9. Looking back, how has your beautiful ability to emotionally regulate yourself genuinely transformed your life?

    Think about how have those five steps to emotional regulation truly helped you to "calm the farm" when you feel triggered? After you've done an Inner Child exercise to soothe parts of your past, can you describe the feeling – can you feel more flexibility with your emotions now?

10. After you've done an Inner Child Exercise, can you describe how your nervous system feels, or, to put it another way, how does the peace within your body now feel?

Think about what specific sensations, images, or thoughts subtly arise when you connect with this feeling?

11. Getting in touch with acts of kindness towards yourself, when you experience joy, how do you now allow yourself to fully embrace it, without holding back?

    Think about what it feels like to wholeheartedly let go of fear and hesitation, and how does this beautiful release reflect in your voice?

12. Describe your beautiful new happy place in detail. Is it a physical place, a deep feeling, like a knowing, or a new state of being?

    Think about what makes it feel so safe and comforting, and how does your voice lovingly reflect this peace?

    ...

After the Questions

As you gracefully close this reflection session with yourself, remember that truly befriending your emotions, mastering your own regulation, and soothing the wild, unseen heart of your past isn't some finish line you cross. Oh no, my friend, it's a magnificent, continuous unfolding. Every breath, every sunrise, every little challenge offers yet another opportunity to practice the powerful skills you've so bravely, so beautifully, leaned into.

Like I talked about at the very start, I've met countless women crowned "resilient" simply because they've weathered a storm or ten. But to me, that's not resilience, that's just good old-fashioned surviving. True resilience, my friend, is when you take full, fabulous accountability for every single glorious facet of who you are – your actions, your beliefs, your dazzling light, and even your mysterious shadows – and you keep showing up, keep at it, with a sparkle in your eye.

> You've done the work, and you are no longer bound by mere survival, are you? Right?

So, embrace this exhilarating newfound emotional freedom. Trust yourself fiercely. Have empathy for your former self, accept her, flaws and all – because that is where you unearth your feminine power and your unbreakable resilience, my friend. And then, keep walking forward, strut if you wish, but this time, my friend, add a little extra swagger, would you?!

This isn't the grand finale of your story, but rather a powerful, exhilarating new beginning. In Book Three: *Liberated Connection*, prepare to dive even deeper into the work of harnessing your feminine energy with fresh eyes, an even lighter heart, and perhaps, just a touch more mischief.

> The best is absolutely, undeniably, yet to come.

31.
Bye For Now

The Journey Continues
Towards a Life You Love

Right, my friend, seriously, big, booming drum roll please. You've arrived at the end of these pages, and what a cracking job you've done. Nice work, lady! So, time for a short break, and then your incredible Change Experience journey is absolutely carrying on from here.

What you've done is truly enormous – the kind of "big-girl-pants-life-achievement" stuff so many people spend their whole lives avoiding. But not you! You're now joining the ranks of the lucky ones, those brilliant women taking the reins on the life they were born to live. Soon, I truly believe you'll wake up and realise there's something rather beautiful blossoming inside of you.

> Please feel proud of yourself.

Okay, let's just take a moment to appreciate what you have done here. You've transformed. The illusion of control you found in avoidance – be it through food, drinking, hot-mess-temporary-highs, or just outright denying your feelings – has been beautifully replaced by the real control that comes from facing your emotions with courage and a good dose of love, real love for yourself. You now grasp that those quick-fix avoidance patterns aren't about chasing some elusive state of constant happiness. Instead, you've got a much clearer picture of what peace looks like, and how to genuinely experience happiness from within.

You've dived deep into your emotional world, shining a light on the patterns and triggers that once held you captive. You've bravely faced the shadows of past invalidations, unearthing those unmet childhood needs and the lasting imprints from challenging times. You've cottoned on to something truly vital: the validation you once desperately sought from others, you can now wholeheartedly give yourself, finally breaking that tiresome cycle of emotional upheaval. You recognise those old messages from your past, that nagging, repetitive compulsion that kept leading you back to familiar pain. And, now, you have the means to rewire those old narratives, to more loving, more accepting, factual, new ones.

You're now acutely aware of what triggers are, how to spot your own, and how to meticulously lay out each trigger, behaviour, and consequence. You've learned to recognise the insidious nature of gaslighting, equipping yourself with the awareness and language to protect your own precious truth. And you've truly mastered the tenderness you need and the ability to be your own empathetic witness – oh, wow, as I've said, this really is your ultimate key to liberation.

And guess what? You've learned to interrupt those trigger cycles with powerful tools: grounding techniques, self-validation, and becoming your own empathetic witness. You've become comfortably aware that your emotions aren't enemies to be suppressed; you're now their loudest cheerleader, sticking around to truly understand what they're trying to tell you. You've learned to listen to your own language, catch your own signals, and love yourself enough to take action.

Think of all those new skills you've gained for a moment – grounding, strategies, step-by-step guidance, and those wonderfully liberating Inner Child exercises. You've learned how to unhook yourself from those narratives you spin about the past, present, and future, with all their rigid rules and reasons. Honestly, my friend, that's hundreds of hours of therapy right there in those strategies I've shared.

Sister, all of this, yes, a massive amount of work I know, is precisely so you can step up, reclaim your power, and stride into the life you truly desire. As you move forward, remember that this journey isn't about perfection, but a lot of imperfection arising in the fabulous progress of change. Embrace the ongoing process of self-discovery, celebrate your victories with a little shimmy, and extend genuine kindness to yourself when you inevitably stumble. You are the magnificent architect of your life, and by embracing this fresh perspective on your emotions, you now hold the power to create a life brimming with awareness, inner peace, and simplistic joy.

Honestly, do not underestimate the impact this will have on your life. Doors will now open where before there were only walls.

> And trust me, my friend, you'll be knocking them down with a cheeky grin.

What Comes Next ...

Now, take a few weeks, my friend, to let all this settle within you. Allow the insights, the reflections, and the questions to quietly percolate in your heart. Feel the shifts that are already beginning to happen. And when you feel that quiet nudge, that gentle pull towards the next step in your Change Experience journey, I'll be right here waiting with Book Three: *Liberated Connection*.

This next one? It's like sunshine after the rain – lighter, yes, but also incredibly powerful. We'll be gathering all these pieces together, wrapping up this chapter with a bow, and stepping into a space of pure inspiration. We'll delve into getting exactly what you want out of life, learning to harness your energy, setting those clear, loving boundaries that protect your spirit, and raising your vibration so you can step fully into the woman you are meant to be. We're going to nurture your Future Self, the one who deserves all the joy, peace, and fulfilment you're working towards. So, rest, reflect, and know that this is just the beginning of something truly extraordinary. I can't wait to continue walking this path with you.

Sending warm, glowing energy your way.

Fleur Elizabeth

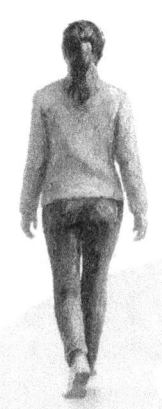

Appendix

I.
Must-Have Skills for Emotional Control

Grounding Techniques to Reclaim Your Inner Balance
Taking Back Your Emotional Power for Lasting Calm

Before diving into the heart of this book, I want to equip you with some valuable tools. Think of them as resources you can easily access as you explore these pages. I introduced these approaches in Book One, *Project Clarity*. Here, I'll offer a deeper understanding of why they are so effective and important. These techniques will empower you to ground yourself if any challenging thoughts or feelings arise.

> **Why are we revisiting these skills:** I want to give you a massive high five if you read Book One: *Project Clarity* and put these tools into practice. Honestly, if you even did them just once, I'm applauding you. And if you simply read them and moved on? That's completely fine, too.
>
> Taking on new skills takes time. Sometimes, you have to hit a brick wall, have a proper meltdown, or lie awake at night stressing about a difficult situation before that little voice in your head says, "Ah, maybe I should try that thing". It's totally human.

> Think of it like this: new skills need time to properly sink into your brain. So, please do yourself a favour and read through these tools again. I promise you'll pick up things you missed the first time, and it will help these ideas become more familiar and natural for you.

My hope is that these tools will allow you to navigate this material with confidence and support, ultimately leading to the best possible experience.

Why Do We Need These Tools?

Oh, my friend, emotional storms. We all know them, don't we? They're as much a part of being human as sunshine and rain. Emotions rise and fall, surge and recede, just like the weather. And, honestly, trying to stuff them down or pretend they're not there is like trying to hold back a tidal wave. It just ... doesn't work. In fact, it often makes them even stronger.

That's where grounding techniques come in. Think of them as your safe harbour in the storm. Or for those nights when you can't sleep, and thoughts are flying around your head, that you can't seem to stop. They're a way to navigate those turbulent feelings without getting completely swept away. It's not about making the emotions disappear – we're not trying to do that. It's about changing how we relate to them. It's about allowing them to pass through us, like clouds across the sky, without taking over our whole world.

We all have emotions that can really hook us, don't we? Guilt, shame, fear that freezes us in our tracks, furious rage, deep sadness and grief, and that constant, unsettling ripple of anxiety. When we're not aware of what triggers us, it can feel like these emotions attack out of nowhere. Something in the present moment acts as a trigger, a reminder of the past, and suddenly we're caught in that old, painful cycle.

> **SO, THE MESSAGE HERE IS THIS:** I want to say this loud and clear: It's okay. It's completely normal to struggle with these intense emotions and to sometimes slip into old, unhelpful patterns, especially if you've experienced trauma.

> I've been in that exact same spot, and it feels incredibly lonely, even when it isn't.

Let's Stop Losing Control

The beauty of grounding is that it helps us break that cycle of reacting automatically. When you feel yourself starting to get overwhelmed, simple things can make a world of difference. Focusing on your senses – what you can see, hear, touch, taste, and smell, can bring you right back to the present moment. It's like hitting a reset button. This shift in focus helps you step away from the spiralling thoughts and feelings that fuel anxiety and panic. And the more you practise these techniques, the more you'll start to notice those early warning signs, that little flicker before the storm hits, and you can take action before it escalates.

There's a physical side to this too. When we're stressed or anxious, our bodies release cortisol (your stress hormone), and our heart rate goes up. Grounding techniques can reverse that. They activate the rest and digest part of our nervous system, which slows down our heart rate, lowers cortisol levels, and brings a sense of calm. By learning to ground yourself, you're giving yourself a powerful tool to manage both your emotional and physical health. You're building resilience and finding inner peace, even when life throws its inevitable curveballs.

I want to share three simple techniques that my coach taught me. They were so helpful and transformative for me. They were another part of the reason I went on to study the psychology modality of Acceptance and Commitment Therapy. So that I could teach others and pay it forward.

- **Name and Tame:** This is a wonderful way to quiet those ruminating, recurring thoughts that cause so much discomfort. When you give the thought a name or speak about it out loud, it disrupts the repetitive pattern. As wise folks often say, "It dies with breath!"

- **Dropping Anchor:** Imagine finding a solid anchor in the midst of an emotional storm. This exercise helps you acknowledge your thoughts and feelings, connect with your body, and centre yourself, so you can gently return to whatever you were doing.

🔗 **4-7-8 Breathing:** A soothing technique for anxiety. Deep breathing helps redirect your focus. Because here's the thing: when you're focused on your breath, your brain simply can't hold onto whatever was upsetting you. It's a beautiful way to find calm.

Out of all the tools and skills I have learned over the years, these are my favourite, the three that got me through my toughest times. When I was triggered and my heart rate was 210/125 and I thought I was having a heart attack because my anxiety was so intense, they saved me. Originally, I had to take beta blockers to calm my heart down; otherwise, I could have had a stroke. But when I started using these three techniques, I could calm myself before I got to this dire level of heart palpitations.

! **WHAT IS A BETA BLOCKER, YOU MAY ASK?** Imagine your body's fight or flight response is like a car engine. When you're stressed or anxious, your body releases hormones like adrenaline, which hit the accelerator, making your heart race and your blood pressure surge. A beta-blocker is like a foot on the brake. It doesn't stop the engine, but it steps in to block those accelerator hormones, keeping your heart rate and blood pressure from going into overdrive.

> I will only ever recommend what I have personally experienced, seen the benefit from, and tried myself, so you know there is "know-how" and experience in all of these words!

Technique One: Name and Tame
Giving a Name to Your Thoughts and Taking Back Control

Let's talk about those swirling, overwhelming thoughts that sometimes feel like they're pushing you around. You know the ones, right? The ones that just won't quit, the constant rumination that can leave you feeling completely drained. The ones that keep you awake at night. Well, I have a technique for you that has been a true game-changer for me.

It's called Name and Tame. The idea is simple: you recognise the emotion you're feeling, give the recurring thought connected to it a name, thank your brain, and let it know you're okay. By noticing your thoughts, giving them a name, and then even thanking your brain (yes, you read that right!), you can break that endless loop. Gosh, it sounds so simple, doesn't it? Trust me, it works.

The aim of Name and Tame (or Naming and Taming) is to slow down those repetitive, negative thoughts. It's like shining a light on them, making them more visible and, in turn, less scary and more manageable.

You might be wondering why these thoughts keep coming back. Well, believe it or not, your brain is trying to help you. It's a throwback to our ancient, caveman brains, which were wired to constantly alert us to danger. Back then, it was about tigers and bears. Now, it's more about those imagined threats – the recurring thoughts that feel so real.

Here's the cool part: by giving a thought a name, you're giving it a form. You're accepting the thought and the message your brain is sending you. You're acknowledging the emotion and the thoughts around it, recognising that you aren't in any immediate danger. In doing so, you take away its power.

You calm the farm, so to speak!

When your brain keeps sending those thoughts, it's because it's identified something that caused you pain, grief, or discomfort. It sees it as a potential threat and repeats the thought to keep you vigilant. But when you accept the thought and name it, you signal to your brain that you're okay, so it can stand down. It realises there's no real danger, and those repetitive thoughts start to fade. You've changed how your brain sees that thought or event, and the swirling stops. Bye-bye, uncontrollable cycle!

This technique? It's my personal favourite. I've used it countless times when I've been stuck in that mental merry-go-round with a thought that just won't let go. And you know what? When these thoughts used to push me around, I would react in ways that weren't so healthy and just created more chaos in my life – like heading straight for the fridge, bottle, online shopping, or being a people-pleaser. Gosh, those nights when I couldn't sleep because a thought was controlling my mind were very costly to my mind, body, and budget! But then I realised, there was always a pattern, a behaviour that followed those overwhelming thoughts – that is when things changed for me. Naming and taming my emotions and thoughts has given me peace, better sleep, and helped me step out of that washing machine of negative thoughts that I know so many of you have experienced too.

When your past experiences get you hooked into the repetitive loop of unwanted thoughts, and you're going around and around again, stop, take a pause, use this technique, and give yourself a break.

> "When you notice a recurrent theme, story or thinking process, acknowledge it is happening and silently name it. Say to yourself: 'There's my "not good enough" story.'"
> – **Russ Harris, Acceptance & Commitment Therapy**

You will be amazed at how effective it is, and how fast!

The Technique

Here's how you can practise Name and Tame:

Step One: Notice the Thought and Feeling

- When you feel a thought swirling around, just notice it. Simply acknowledge it. "Ah, there's that thought about xyz." With no judgement, just awareness.

    For example: When you're feeling anxious, you might say, "Okay, I can sense a bunch of anxious thoughts bubbling up right now".

Step Two: Give It a Name

- Now, give that thought or feeling a name that makes sense to you. It doesn't have to be fancy. Ideally, it should be non-judgemental, but you can also be playful! I sometimes come up with funny names for things I find challenging.

    My example: "There's that thought about the Sultan of Silliness" (my ex-boyfriend who hurt me). And, yes, sometimes I use more colourful language!

For you, starting out, you might say:

- "Ah, there's that thought about 'Supreme Ruler of Lost Socks and Forgotten Promises'" (referring to your situation with your partner, Robert, who always let you down).

- Or "Gosh, there's that annoying thought about 'Grand Poohbah of the 3rd Floor'" (referring to your boss, Gordon who's been difficult).

- Or "Oh dear, there's that 'Illustrious Inventor of Unnecessary Drama' coming up again" (for your friend Barbara, crossing boundaries and creating chaos).

> **NOTE:** Play with it! Don't be afraid to give it a name that makes you smile. Naming them, especially with something humorous, takes the edge off what you perceive as horrible or stressful.

Step Three: Validate the Thought

This is key. The thought is real, it's yours, and it's normal.

- So, go ahead and validate it. Say it's okay to have this thought. It's perfectly natural. Tell yourself it's alright to have these thoughts. That's the validation part.
- You can even say, "At some point, this thought will probably come back to say hello, and that's okay".
- This process takes the power out of those destructive thoughts. It diffuses them and removes their hold on you.

Step Four: Thank Your Brain

Believe it or not, as I said, your brain is trying to help you. It's not that you're irrational or weird. Your brain is trying to look out for you, to keep you safe. It's like a tap, tap, tap saying, "Hey, there's something that needs your attention!" It's trying to save you from something that might go wrong or be unpleasant.

- So, your role after you have been through the previous steps is to say, "Thank you, brain". When you thank your brain, it gets the message that the job is done. It stops sending those warning thoughts.
- Then smile. It's like an affirming FULL STOP in your emotional process.

> This might seem strange at first, and it might take a little time to get used to, but please try it. Practise it and see what happens. You might just be surprised!

Technique Two: Dropping Anchor
Finding Your Centre in the Storm

Here is the third technique I'd love to share with you. It's your safe harbour during emotional storms.

Oh, my, when you get triggered, those emotional storms can be so overwhelming, can't they? It feels like you're being tossed around, completely at the mercy of the waves. That's where "Dropping Anchor" comes in. Think of it as your lifeline, your way of finding stability and balance when things feel like they're spinning out of control. It's about bringing yourself back to the present moment, back to your body, and back to your centre.

If anything in this material brings up difficult emotions for you, I want you to know that it's okay. You're not alone, and you have tools to help you navigate those feelings. This Dropping Anchor technique is one of them, and it can make a world of difference. It's not about making the pain disappear – we're not trying to pretend it's not there. It's about creating a space where you can feel those emotions without being completely swept away by them.

> **"To lose our connection with the body is to become spiritually homeless. Without an anchor, we float aimlessly, battered by the winds and waves of life."**
> – Anodea Judith

What Exactly Is an Anchor?

An anchor is anything in the present moment that's not part of the emotional storm. It's something solid, something real, that you can connect with right here and now. It's about expanding your awareness, staying grounded, and connecting with what's happening around you. It's also about taking conscious control of your physical actions – your breathing, your posture, even the way you move your body. Let's find your anchors together.

The Technique

Here's how to drop your anchor:

Find a place where you feel comfortable. It could be your favourite chair, a quiet corner, or even just lying down on the floor. You can do this for two minutes, five minutes, ten minutes – whatever feels right for you. It depends on how intense the emotional storm is.

Step One: Acknowledge What's Happening with Compassion

- Start by simply acknowledging what's going on inside you.

- What thoughts and feelings are showing up?

- Observe them without judgement, as if you were watching clouds drift by.

- Ask yourself: "What's happening for me right now? Am I replaying something painful in my mind? Am I still feeling shaken from a recent experience?"

- Whatever it is, connect with it. Give it space. Acknowledge it. Let your inner voice say, "Okay, this is what's happening." Try to observe it like you're an outsider looking in.

- Then, name the emotion you're feeling. Is it sadness? Guilt? Rage? Anxiety? Just say it to yourself: "I feel sad." "I feel guilty." "I feel anxious."

Step Two: Connect with Your Body

- If you're sitting, push your feet firmly onto the floor.

- Feel the connection between your feet and the ground.

- Feel every part of your body touching the chair.

Try these actions:

- Press your fingers together and notice the sensation.
- Feel your breath. Notice your lungs as you inhale and exhale.
- Sit up straight and feel your back and spine align. Roll your shoulders back three times, then forward three times, and feel the movement in your muscles.
- Can you feel the painful thoughts and emotions, and at the same time, feel your body around that pain?
- Be aware of your body – that you can move it, control it, connect with it.
- Place your hands on your legs and feel the contact.
- Wiggle your toes.
- Press your tongue against the roof of your mouth.
- Softly touch your face and notice how it feels.

Step Three: Notice Your Surroundings

- What can you see in the room or space where you are? Look around and name five things you see: a lamp, a bookshelf, a painting, a window, a plant.
- What can you hear? Listen for three distinct sounds and name them.
- Acknowledge that there are difficult thoughts, feelings, and perhaps memories present.
- Notice the weather outside. Describe it to yourself: "It's sunny and bright", "It's cloudy and overcast" or "It's cold and wet".

Step Four: Check in with Yourself

- Now, how are you feeling?
- Do you notice anything different?
- How is your breath? Is it calmer?
- How does the space around you feel? Has the emotional storm calmed down?
- Do you feel more in control of your actions?
- Do you feel like you can choose what to do next?
- Do you feel comfortable soothing yourself in a healthy, compassionate way?

The Result: Grounding Yourself

When you feel grounded, you're more likely to make conscious choices for yourself rather than reacting on autopilot. You're more likely to act in alignment with your values.

You can use this technique anytime you feel overwhelmed by your emotions. You can do this anywhere: in your office, your bedroom, your garden, sitting in a chair, lying on the floor – wherever you feel comfortable. For me, it often works best when I'm sitting in a chair, but I've also found it helpful lying in bed. Find what works best for you. Just try to give them all a go and try them on for size. I'd like to think you will thank me for them one day.

> **"Use 'ACE' if you can't remember: 'A' can be 'acknowledge your thoughts and feelings,' 'C' can be 'come back into your body,' and 'E' can be 'engage in current activity.'"**
>
> – Dr. Russ Harris, Psychologist for Acceptance & Commitment Therapy

Technique Three: 4-7-8 Breathing
Your Instant Calm Button

Oh, my friend, when those triggers hit and that familiar rush of panic or anger washes over you, the 4-7-8 Breathing method can be like a soft, loving hand reaching out, pulling you back to earth, back into yourself. It's not a magic wand, no, but it is a way to remind your body, "We're okay. We're here. We're safe". You know how it is, in those moments, your breath often becomes shallow and frantic. But by intentionally slowing it down, by inhaling deeply for 4, holding for 7, and exhaling slowly for 8, you're sending a direct, calming message to your nervous system. You're telling it to quiet down, to let go of that frantic energy. It's like rocking a frightened child, soothing them with a rhythmic lullaby. And in that quiet space, you can find a tiny sliver of peace, a moment to remember that you are so much more than the trigger, you are so much more than the storm.

Whilst this is an excellent technique to soothe yourself when you're being triggered, or to quell anxiety, I highly recommend you try it anytime you feel even a little flutter of emotion bubbling beneath the surface and see how it brings you back to a calm, balanced centre.

It's such a beautiful exercise because you simply cannot think about your stressors or overwhelming emotions simultaneously while doing this breathing technique. It's a natural, beautiful tool for your healing process.

The Technique

Find a place that is comfortable, quiet, and just yours. It can be your favourite chair, a cosy corner, or even an internal space you create by just closing your eyes wherever you are. Sit, close your eyes (if you like), and let's begin. You really can do this anywhere!

Step One

- Breathe in through your nose for a nice, slow count of 4.

Step Two

- Then hold your breath for a slow count of 7.

Step Three

- Then, exhale through your mouth for a smooth, slow count of 8. You can make a gentle "whoosh" sound while you do this – sometimes that helps release tension.

Repeat this cycle three to four times.

P.S. This is a technique that's also good for falling asleep!

A great habit to get into is doing this before you go to sleep at night. After doing this for a few days, you'll likely start to feel that you're getting strength back into your lungs and diaphragm. You'll also probably begin to notice that you sleep better. And more than likely, you'll experience some beautiful shifts in your anxiety, from anxious to a more relaxed state of mind.

REMEMBER: Deep breathing helps redirect your focus right back to the present moment. Because guess what? When you're focused on your breath, your brain simply can't hold onto whatever it was that was upsetting you. It's like giving your mind a little vacation!

Personally, in the last few years, this technique has gotten me out of an anxious, emotional, mind-overloaded bind, countless times. I used to suffer from uncontrollable anxiety. As I have told you before, my heart rate would skyrocket, way up there at 220/125, giving me the sign, I could be heading for a stroke. I would pop beta-blocker heart medication to slow my heart down and then a diazepam (Valium) to calm my nervous system down. Now, when I feel overwhelmed, I use this technique. It has changed my life for the better. I don't need drugs anymore. I don't need to call emergency services, and I'm nowhere near the risk zone of a stroke. It's truly been life-changing for me, and I so hope it can help you too.

My Hot Tip for Better Sleep

While you're going through this book, for the whole book series in fact, I highly recommend doing these breathing exercises thirty minutes before you go to sleep every night. And repeat them again every morning when you wake up.

I've found the 4-7-8 Breathing technique to be such a beautiful routine to get into, and it has helped promote a wonderfully peaceful process of drifting off to sleep.

> Be brave – try it! See how it feels. It's a great skill to keep in your toolbox to use at any time! Now, let's carry on, shall we?

II.
Your Emotional Compass

Skill Building: Your Practical Guide
Steering Through Life's Journey

This appendix serves as a practical guide to understanding and working with your emotions, drawing inspiration from the metaphor of emotions as a "friendly inner compass". As we discussed in the early pages on emotional regulation, emotions are not random occurrences but vital signals that propel us into action, help us communicate with others, and guide our self-understanding. We often fear or suppress them, viewing them as disruptive, but I encourage you to shift your perspective. I suggest that by leaning into your emotions, you can build a relationship with them and learn to interpret their messages rather than being controlled by them. This appendix will explore the three essential roles of emotions – motivators, communicators, and guides to self – and will offer tools and techniques to help you harness their power effectively. Just as a compass points us towards our desired direction, our emotions – when understood – can lead us towards greater self-awareness, healthier relationships, and a more fulfilling life.

Think of Your Emotions as Your Friendly Inner Compass

The best way to lose your fear of emotions is to lean into them, get to know them, and see what they are all about. Think of this like you would a new relationship; you are just getting to know each other. Nothing scary there, right?!

Emotions aren't random sparks; they're vital signals with powerful purposes. Think of them as an internal compass, guiding us through life. They serve three essential roles:

🔍 **Emotions as Motivation:** Emotions propel us into action. They're the first step in the cycle of how we respond to the world. For instance, if you receive a critical email (that's the trigger), you might feel anger and fear (those are your emotions). This could lead to a defensive response (that's your action). Then, your boss might react, and you might feel even more stressed (and that's the consequence). But here's the thing: by recognising those initial emotions of anger and fear, you have the power to change your reaction. You could choose to take a breath and respond calmly instead. It's about recognising that you always have a choice.

🔍 **Emotions as Communication with Others:** Our faces, our body language, and the tone of our voices – these all carry emotional messages. If someone has a tight jaw and avoids eye contact, they might be feeling angry or uncomfortable, even if they say everything is fine. Tuning into these cues helps us connect with others and build stronger relationships. It's like learning a secret language of understanding.

🔍 **Emotions as Communication with Ourselves:** Emotions are also how we talk to ourselves. That gut feeling when something feels off? That's your inner voice, your intuition, alerting you to something important. It could be a warning or a nudge in a different direction. When we listen to these internal signals, we honour our inner

> **"The best and most beautiful things in the world cannot be seen or even touched – they must be felt with the heart."**
>
> – Helen Keller

wisdom. Ignoring them might mean missing out on opportunities or even putting ourselves at risk. It's about trusting that inner knowledge.

The Wonderful World of Our Emotions

I'm sure a lot of this might seem familiar, maybe even a little like things you already know. And you probably do! But it's so easy to lose touch with something when we're constantly pushing it away. Our emotions are like that. If we never let them speak, we forget their language, their importance. So, I encourage you to take a moment to really listen.

Let's take a little journey back to school together, shall we? I want to share why our emotions are so incredibly important. They play vital roles in our thoughts, actions, and overall mental health. Let's dive in:

1. Our Built-in Survival Kit

Emotions like fear, anger, and even disgust? They're ancient, my friend. They're wired into us from way back when. They're like little alarms, telling us when something might be dangerous, triggering that fight-or-flight response to keep us safe.

2. Fuelling Our Passions

Think about joy and excitement. They nudge us towards things that make us feel good, things that help us grow.

And those not-so-good feelings, like sadness or frustration? They're signals too. They tell us when something needs to change, or when we might need a little extra support.

3. Connecting with Our Tribe

Emotions are the language of relationships. They help us understand each other, share what we need, and navigate our social world.

A smile, a furrowed brow, a gentle tone – they all speak volumes, helping us connect and work together.

4. Learning as We Go
Every emotion gives us feedback, little lessons from our experiences. They help us learn, grow, and make better choices.

That pang of regret? It teaches us to avoid repeating mistakes. And that swell of pride? It reinforces the good stuff.

 5 . Getting to Know Ourselves
Our emotions are like little windows into our souls. They reveal what we truly value, what we need, what we believe. When we listen to them, we learn more about ourselves and where we can grow.

Maybe anxiety points to a hidden insecurity, or joy highlights a passion we didn't realise was there.

 6. Unleashing Our Inner Artist
Emotions are a creative spark! Artists, musicians, writers they all tap into their feelings to create things that touch our hearts.

 7. Finding Meaning in the Bigger Picture
Emotions connect us to something larger than ourselves. Love and compassion, for instance, can inspire us to help others, to make a real difference in the world.

At the end of the day, emotions are such a vital part of being human. They guide us, connect us, and help us live richer, more fulfilling lives.

What We Might Be Missing

Let's understand the core emotions and their function. This may be simple, but it's a great reminder. So, please, do take a moment to look at the core emotions we all experience. I'll share a little about each one, its purpose, and what it often inspires us to do.

Love
Ah, love. It sounds simple, but it can be a tricky one, can't it?

- **The Function:** Love draws us closer to those we care about. It adds so much to our lives and the lives of those around us. It's the heart of relationships, families, and communities.
- **The Action:** Showing warmth, generosity, wanting to connect, and spending quality time with the people we love.

Fear
Deep down, fear is about survival. It's that instinct that kept our ancestors safe.

- **The Function:** Fear alerts us to danger, to anything that might threaten our world.
- **The Action:** Fear activates us to protect ourselves, to run, to escape.

Happiness
Oh, that elusive feeling we all chase. It's important to remember that happiness isn't a constant state; it's a wonderful, temporary feeling.

- **The Function:** To feel good about our experiences, even the simple things. To experience alone or bring people together to share joy.
- **The Action:** Sharing that joy, sparking happiness in yourself and others.

Anger
Anger arises from how we perceive things. It's triggered by things that feel like a threat, a frustration, a loss of control.

- **The Function:** To signal that something important is being blocked, a boundary crossed, trust broken, or that someone we care about is in direct danger or has been hurt.
- **The Action:** To stand up for what's right, to act when something feels unjust.

Guilt

Guilt is about what we've *done*, not who we *are*.

- **The Function:** To let us know when our actions go against our values.
- **The Action:** To make amends, to fix things, to learn and grow.

Shame

Shame is different; it's about who we believe we are. It's a heavy emotion, one that many of us struggle with.

- **The Function:** To warn us that we might face rejection from those we care about.
- **The Action:** To withdraw, to hide, to isolate ourselves.

Sadness

If expressing sadness wasn't encouraged where you grew up, it can be hard to do so now. It can be hard to ask for help when you need it.

- **The Function:** To grieve, to mourn, to feel the pain of loss, and to let others know we're hurting.
- **The Action:** To acknowledge that things aren't as we hoped or expected.

Disgust

That wrinkled nose, that "ewww" feeling – it's your body's way of protecting you.

- **The Function:** To alert us to something unclean, unpleasant, or potentially harmful.
- **The Action:** To steer clear of something that could be dangerous.

Envy and Jealousy

Envy is when we want what someone else has. Jealousy is when we fear losing something important to us.

- **The Function of Envy:** To show us what we desire or need.
- **The Action:** Sometimes, it can lead to negative feelings, but it can also inspire us to pursue our own goals.
- **The Function of Jealousy:** To signal that a valued relationship or goal is at risk.
- **The Action:** To seek reassurance, to be overly possessive, expecting the worst, and engaging in self-sabotaging behaviour.

It's easy to get caught up in an emotional whirlwind and struggle to name what we're feeling. I hope this little guide helps you understand what might be going on inside when those strong emotions arise.

> Did any of these emotions feel scary and unapproachable to you? If so, write them down, so you can work on them as we progress.

The Feelings Wheel

Throughout our journey together, we've talked about the importance of being able to **label** your emotions and **understand** what they're trying to tell you. We've explored healing strategies like **Mindful Self-Compassion, "Just-in-Time" Journaling,** and **the "Emotional Thermometer" Technique** – all of which require a clear awareness of what you're feeling.

The Feelings Wheel is a powerful, simple tool to help you with this. It provides a map for your emotional world, starting with broad categories and guiding you toward more specific, nuanced feelings. As you begin to use it, you'll find it easier to move beyond saying, "I just feel bad" and instead, connect with the exact emotion, whether it's disappointment, frustration, or vulnerability. This is a foundational step toward emotional literacy and building a deeper, more compassionate relationship with yourself.

The Feelings Wheel

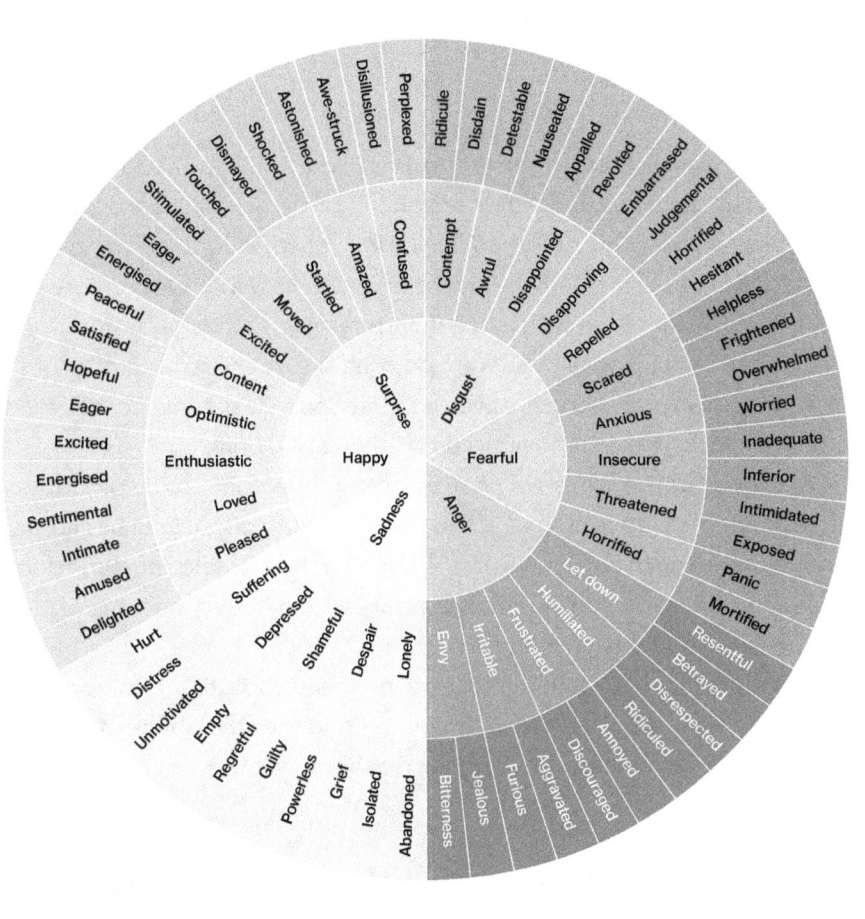

III.
Reflecting on Your Triggers

Let's take a wee moment together to explore what might be nudging or triggering you right now. We'll walk through this softly, hand in hand, okay? I'm right here with you. This is all about tuning into those patterns and emotional triggers that sometimes feel like they take the wheel. When we can carefully acknowledge these, we start to see them peeking around the corner, giving us the chance to choose a different path. It's like opening a secret door to making small, loving changes towards the life you truly dream of, and feeling freer from those tricky behaviours around food and drink.

Think about the whispers of stress in your life right now – perhaps a little friction in a relationship, a shift at work, a worry about your health, the beautiful journey of pregnancy, or the tender ache of losing someone dear. These can stir up big feelings and responses like a fluttery heart, a wish to hide away, or a delicate sadness.

Now, let's turn our attention to those moments that stir things up within us. We're simply going to notice the trigger and the little dance of behaviour that follows, with kindness and curiosity, okay?

❓ Questions for Reflection: Identifying Your Triggers

Remember: As you write, say your answers aloud to yourself. Allow your voice to be heard by your heart and your head. This process ensures that what is truly important to you will fully sink in and settle deeply within your being.

Let's Begin

Your Tribe of Support

Let's begin by picturing your tribe – those beautiful souls who walk alongside you, offering their welcomed guidance and support on this journey. Who are the people who bring a spark of joy to your day, whose company feels like a warm, comforting hug? You're dealing with some big feelings right now. Choosing your companions with care is like wrapping yourself in the softest, most comforting blanket. Think of the people who truly see you, who understand your journey. These could be friends who share your adventures, or those who have walked a few more miles and offer insights from their own path.

1. Who are the people in your life whose presence feels good, lifting your spirits and making your heart sing?

2. Who is that trusted friend, that wise person, you can always turn to when you need a listening ear, a safe space to share your inner thoughts?

3. Who are the kind, caring people who will hold space for you with love as you journey through these changes, offering you encouragement and understanding?

Mental and Personal Health

1. Recall a time when something triggered you deeply, and your mental health felt like it took a real beating. What was that inner dialogue you had with yourself in that moment? What words were swirling in your mind?

2. Looking back now, with the know-how you've gained, what do you think truly made that situation feel so overwhelming? How did you react to it in that moment?

3. Can you quietly observe any patterns you might have had with using food and drink to self-soothe or numb those feelings then? No judgement, just gentle observation.

4. What are the words your Inner Child needs to hear from you now? What loving message would help her rewrite that story connected to that trigger and feel truly safe and loved?

5. What would be a kinder, warmer way you could respond to yourself and the situation in the future, honouring your feelings and needs with compassion?

Relationships

1. Can you recall a moment in your relationships when you were triggered by something, and you reacted in a way that didn't feel quite right? You knew, deep down, that the person you reacted to wasn't truly to blame for your emotional response – you knew it was something from your past that had been stirred up, but perhaps you ignored it at the time. Describe that scene to yourself as if you're sharing it with a dear, trusted friend.

2. In that moment, what was your inner critics first response? What was the negative self-talk you engaged in – that inner dialogue of not feeling worthy, not enough, not good enough, or insignificant?

3. When do you think was the very first time you experienced that feeling in your life? Can you picture where that took place, and what happened for you in that moment, perhaps without an empathetic witness to truly understand?

4. How did your former self react in that situation? Do you feel, as the wise adult you are now, that you could gently change the narrative of that scenario? Could you create a new story, one

filled with self-love and compassion for your inner and former self, from an adult, supportive, and loving new perspective?

5. Do you notice any patterns with reaching for food or drink in response to that feeling? Just be open to observation, no judgement at all.

6. If you could whisper a wish to your heart, with deep acceptance and self-love, trusting yourself completely, what would you have loved to do differently in that moment?

Working Life (Career, Volunteering, Motherhood, etc.)

1. Think of a time in your work, your volunteering, your journey as a mother, or anything you pour your heart into, when a little cloud of stress appeared, and you felt like you were failing, even though you were doing your absolute best. Can you paint a picture of that moment for yourself?

2. What was the inner dialogue you had with yourself in that moment? And now, as the wise adult you are, with self-love and trust, can you ask yourself if that inner dialogue was factually true?

3. f you could factually talk to yourself about your talents, your real capacity with the tools and resources you had at the time, how might that scenario have played out differently?

4. When you have beaten yourself up for feeling like a failure or not good enough, what did you notice about your choices with food and drink in response?

5. With your hand on your heart, what kind words can you say to yourself now to forgive yourself for those actions? And what would you like to do differently from this moment forward?

Family Life and Relationships

1. Can you think of a moment within your family or close relationships when a scenario played out in which you felt unheard, invalidated, or unseen, and you reacted strongly, perhaps even flared up? What was that like for you, deep down?

2. How did you find yourself reacting in that moment? What emotions can you identify and label? Can you say them out loud to yourself with kindness?

3. Is there a go-to pattern for you when it comes to your family and numbing pain? Is there a particular thing you like to do with food and drink in these moments?

4. What shift do you need to make in your internal narrative with your Inner Child to carefully reform these patterns of behaviour with yourself? And how can you revalidate yourself as being enough, and more than good enough?

5. What might you wish to do differently in a similar situation next time, with empathy, self-trust, and a deep knowing that you are worthy of being heard and seen?

Moving Forward

1. What is the main trouble, emotional stressor, or challenge you feel you are possibly avoiding at the moment?

2. What emotions are wrapped up in that scenario? Can you label them and say them out loud to yourself with compassion and acceptance?

3. What messages do you think are hidden within that one issue – messages that you could learn from, grow from, and find more peace within?

4. What little words of validation does your former self need to hear from you now, in a warm, connected embrace?

5. What brave first step might you take towards facing this situation, in a bid to quietly resolve it and bring yourself more peace?

6. Who can you lean on for support if the process feels a little shaky?

7. Once you've taken that step, how can you invite more moments of growth and self-discovery into these situations? Perhaps choose just one more challenge to work on and see how you go, with kindness and patience.

8. Where can you work on inviting more acceptance into your life, to create more of a sense of ease, allowing life to flow more like an alluring, peaceful river?

· · ·

IV.
Deeper Self-Connection

This is the last little bonus I have for you, my friend! First, can I just say, "WOW – you've come so far!" Delving into your triggers, behaviours, and patterns, this is truly amazing work you have done here. Now, if you are willing, come with me and let's take it a step further, shall we? This is where we move from understanding to truly embodying self-connection. Think of this as a playground for your soul, a space where you can explore the depths of your inner world with curiosity and kindness.

❓ Diving Deeper: Questions for Insightful Reflection

As I like to say, these aren't just questions; they're invitations. Invitations to listen to that quiet voice within, the one that knows your truth better than anyone. As you ponder these, let that voice guide you. There's no rush, no right or wrong answers – just your authentic self, emerging into the light.

Let's Begin

1. **If your heart could speak freely, what would it tell you right now?** Close your eyes for a moment. Breathe deeply. And then, listen. What truths does your heart need to share?

2. **What are you truly hungry for, beyond physical needs?** Is it connection? Is it purpose? Is it peace? Dig beneath the surface. What is the thing you are craving in your core? (Perhaps, that you've been trying to fill with avoidance tactics or food or drink?)

3. **What stories are you telling yourself about who you are and what you deserve?** Are these stories lifting you up, or are they holding you back? Are they based on truth, or on old wounds and limiting beliefs?

4. **Where in your life are you abandoning yourself?** This might sting a little, but it's important. Are you ignoring your needs? Are you silencing your voice? Are you betraying your values? Be kind, but honest.

5. **If you were to treat yourself with the same compassion you would offer a dear friend, what would that look like?** Imagine your best friend is going through what you're going through. What would you say to them? How would you care for them? Now, turn that compassion inward.

6. **What small act of self-love can you commit to today?** It doesn't have to be grand. It can be as simple as taking a walk in nature, reading a book, or saying "no" to something that drains you. What will nourish your soul today?

7. **What are you grateful for in this very moment?** Even amidst challenges, there are always glimmers of light. What are you noticing right now that brings you a sense of peace, joy, or gratitude?

8. **What does it truly mean to you to live authentically?** What does that look like, feel like, sound like? Paint a picture of your most genuine self. What changes do you need to make to live that way?

9. **What are you afraid of?** Naming our fears is the first step to releasing their power. What are you truly afraid of losing? Of facing? Of becoming?

10. **What is one thing you can forgive yourself for today?** We all make mistakes. We all have regrets. What is one burden you can set down, one act of self-forgiveness you can offer yourself right now?

A Small Reminder

This journey of self-connection is not a destination, but a dance. Some days, you'll feel deeply connected; other days, you might feel lost. That's okay. Be patient with yourself. *Be kind.* And remember that every moment is an opportunity to return to your centre, to listen to your inner voice, and to choose love – for yourself, and for the beautiful, messy, miraculous human being that you are.

> Remember, I said: life is never a straight line. And that is okay!

•••

V. Six Considerations When Making Change

At the start of Book One, *Project Clarity*, I shared some questions to help you reflect on why change was so important to you, how you would approach it, and how confident you felt.

After all the questions we've explored, you might need a soft reminder to help you assess what truly feels right. As you embark on this next stage of your Change Experience, I encourage you to hold these questions close.

[?] What fuels your deepest desire for this change?

[?] How might you effectively invite this change into your life? What would it feel like for this change to become a part of your daily life and a new habit?

[?] How confident do you feel in making this happen? On a scale of 0 to 10, how sustainable does this change feel for you right now?

[?] Do you have the resources and time to nurture this change?

[?] What are your barriers to change? Who and what might get in your way or distract you?

❓ How will you celebrate and acknowledge your progress, the peace, and the balance you create along the way?

These questions are part of the skill-building you need to keep the door to change open – liberated and free from the emotional storms and triggers that keep you stuck. They are designed to help you become more consciously aware of your choices, ensuring this is a change you deeply desire for your real and raw self, and one you can live by your values.

> And don't forget – Rewarding yourself as you go is a powerful tool. It's how we tell our brain life is getting better.

VI.
References

General Research

Fletcher, T. (n.d.). *Trauma Series*. YouTube.

UK Trauma Council. (n.d.). *What happens when relationships go wrong?* [Blog post].

Mate, G. (n.d.). [Online resources]. [Website].

Whitaker, L. (n.d.). *How does Thinking Positive Thoughts Affect Neuroplasticity?*

Goleman, D. (2013). *Focus: The hidden driver of excellence*. Harper Collins Publishers.

Marien, P. A. (2015). *The linguistic cerebellum*. Academic Press.

Reynolds, S. (2011, August 2). Happy brain, happy life. *Psychology Today*. Retrieved September 15, 2017.

Fraser Stillpoint, L. (2018, July 26). *Empathetic Witnessing*. [Blog post].

Adverse Childhood Experiences (A.C.E.)

Harris, N. B. (2014, September). *How childhood trauma affects health across a lifetime*. [Ted Talk].

Harvard University. Centre on the Developing Child. (2018, August 3). *ACEs and Toxic Stress: Frequently Asked Questions*. [Resource articles].

Emerging Minds. (n.d.). *ACEs and their health impacts* (downloadable document) [Blog article]. *Adverse Childhood Experiences (ACEs): Summary of evidence and impacts*. [Online Resources]. (emergingminds.com.au) Australia.

CDC. (n.d.). *About the CDC-Kaiser ACE Study. The CDC-Kaiser Permanente adverse childhood experiences (ACE) study is one of the largest investigations of childhood abuse and neglect and household challenges and later-life health and wellbeing*. [Online Resources].

CDC. (n.d.). *What are adverse childhood experiences?* [Article]. [Online Resources].

Gaslighting

Gordon, S. (2024, September 10). Is Someone Gaslighting You? Look Out For These Red Flags. *The Very Well Mind Blog Post*.

Medical News Today. (n.d.). Examples and signs of gaslighting and how to respond. [*Blog Post*].

Mandeville, R. (2020, October 25). 5 Critical Things to Know About Family Scapegoating Abuse (FSA). [*Blog post*].

www.ingramcontent.com/pod-product-compliance
Lightning Source LLC
Chambersburg PA
CBHW071952070526
44583CB00015B/1168